WOMEN OF THE STREET

Women of the Street

How the Criminal Justice–Social Services Alliance
Fails Women in Prostitution

Susan Dewey and Tonia St. Germain

NEW YORK UNIVERSITY PRESS

New York

NEW YORK UNIVERSITY PRESS
New York
www.nyupress.org

References to Internet websites (URLs) were accurate at the time of writing. Neither the author nor New York University Press is responsible for URLs that may have expired or changed since the manuscript was prepared.

ISBN: 978-1-4798-5449-3 (hardback)
ISBN: 978-1-4798-4194-3 (paperback)

For Library of Congress Cataloging-in-Publication data, please contact the Library of Congress.

New York University Press books are printed on acid-free paper, and their binding materials are chosen for strength and durability. We strive to use environmentally responsible suppliers and materials to the greatest extent possible in publishing our books.

Manufactured in the United States of America

10 9 8 7 6 5 4 3 2 1

Also available as an ebook

CONTENTS

ACKNOWLEDGMENTS

On a freezing afternoon several years ago, Susan, this project's ethnographer, sat quietly on a motel room floor as she listened to a woman recount the series of events that led her to Denver's East Colfax Avenue, where many of the women in this book engage in street-based sex trading and other criminalized hustles while struggling with addiction, homelessness, and various forms of criminal justice system involvement. This encounter unfolded much like hundreds of others preceding and subsequent to it, except for the urgency and seriousness of the woman's parting words as she stood in the doorway, pointing at Susan and narrowing her eyes for emphasis. "Listen, sister," she intoned, her voice breaking slightly with emotion, "now you better get out there and do somethin' with what I just told you, because I was one hundred percent fuckin' straight with you today about life out here, and I didn't have to be." Her words remained an ever-present admonishment in Susan's mind whenever her commitment to this project wavered, and it is to her, and the many others who bravely shared their stories, that we dedicate this book.

After six years' ethnographic and intellectual immersion in the lives of street-involved women and the social services and criminal justice system professionals with whom they regularly interact, we continue to be humbled by the candor, trust, and genuine human kindness participants in this project showed us. Most need to remain anonymous precisely because they disclosed profound uncertainties and other sensitive information about their quotidian income-generation activities that could have legal ramifications or negative professional repercussions. We remain extremely grateful to them for this trust, their time, and the honesty with which they spoke.

We are extraordinarily fortunate that this book benefited from NYU Press editor Jennifer Hammer's acumen, faith in the project, and near-instant responses to our queries. Her vision, coupled with stellar insightful and constructively critical comments from five anonymous peer reviewers, shaped aspects of this book in ways that reflect abilities far greater than our own. We are likewise grateful to the University of Wyoming, which provided financial support for transcription, travel, and other research costs, and hosted Tonia for a year of incredibly precious in-person time for collaboration as part of the Gender & Women's Studies Program. University of Wyoming students and colleagues assisted tremendously with this project through transcription, coding, conversation, street outreach, and other generous gestures of support. We thank Mara Chopping, Kyria Brown, Rachel Surratt, Austin Morgan, Misty Heil, Josh Kronberg-Rasner, and Rhett Epler, as well as University of Wyoming Gender & Women's Studies colleagues Cathy Connolly, Bonnie Zare, Barbara Ellen Logan, Colleen Denney, and Wendy Perkins. Anthropologist Treena Orchard, with whom Susan worked closely on a U.S.-Canada comparative project that took place in conjunction with research for this book, provided insights that dramatically enriched Susan's thinking about the issues street-involved women face throughout North America.

Anthropologists and legal scholars rarely work together (or even interact), and our many years of successful collaboration have continued to push our thinking in ever more interdisciplinary and productive directions. Susan will never be able to find words that adequately express her overwhelming gratitude to Tonia for her friendship, mentoring, and patience in spending countless hours explaining complex legal concepts and other facets of the criminal justice system that Susan previously regarded as mysterious, arcane, and beyond her grasp. Tonia is most grateful for the opportunity to augment Susan's painstaking research, inspired writing, and overarching vision on this research project. Using her knowledge of the law to underscore Susan's ethnographic process opened new ways of listening to women and analyzing the sociolegal problems and solutions that touch their lives. Our work together has fostered an experience of disciplined learning, independent thinking, and a beautiful friendship—a rare combination in academic undertakings.

This project's long-term and immersive nature presented some difficult emotional challenges for Susan, particularly as she took on an increasingly intensive professional role within the criminal justice–social services alliance. Her support network of family and friends made this possible by emphasizing the importance of self-care in addition to empathic research and, later in this project, services provision. Susan's husband, Rob, is an unfailing source of empathy and compassion, even though this work frequently receives more of her time, love, and emotional investment than he does. Her dearest friends, Barbara Ellen Logan and Ruth Bjorkenwall, unfailingly provided encouragement and insights in addition to saving Susan's life on a regular basis by letting her stay with them when icy or otherwise treacherous mountain roads made travel home from work unsafe. Throughout the writing of this book, Susan's retired police officer father, who spent a good portion of his career working undercover, patiently answered hundreds of her questions about police procedure. There are many, many others who helped this project along, and although they are too numerous to thank here, Susan hopes that they know how much their insights inform this book.

Introduction

Through the thin polyester curtains shading the window of the dimly lit motel room, the red and blue flashing squad car lights illuminate the faces of NeNe and James in violent color.[1] They stare at each other, frozen in the light, listening to the static hiss of male voices on the police radio outside, whispering the standard list of questions frenetically among themselves, their voices tense and accusatory as they anticipate the officer's knock on the door. Is there dope in the room? Does anyone have a gun? Is the officer coming to arrest NeNe? Is he here for James? They each consider the answers and their implications in their own minds, collectively exhaling as the squad car pulls out of the motel parking lot. James, who is thirty-five and has spent the last seventeen years of his life in a Colorado prison following a drug deal gone very wrong, lies back on the bed and covers his face, still and quiet.

Outside, Officer Berman checks the time. He is exhausted, with only an hour left on his shift, and feels relieved not to have to make another arrest tonight. The ten-block stretch that comprises what police term a "known prostitution area" emptied as soon as he entered and found a woman with seven outstanding arrest warrants sitting at a bus stop, waiting for clients. She is now handcuffed in the back of his squad car, refusing to speak. He knows that out here she goes by Peaches, although the name on her lengthy criminal record is plain Mary Washington. Officer Berman is responsible for two of her twenty-six arrests on prostitution and drug paraphernalia charges. Tears glisten on her cheeks, her wig slightly askew, and Officer Berman feels sorry for her as he thinks about his daughter, who is about the same age and attending community college with plans to become a nurse.

"Mary, you gotta get it together, maybe think about gettin' into a treatment program or somethin'," Officer Berman says as he makes eye contact with her in the rear view mirror. "You can't live like this forever." Her silence as she nods in response does not indicate agreement with the officer; she knows that a camera in the squad car is recording their interactions and she does not want to provide evidence that may later be used against her in court. As the squad car pulls onto East Colfax Avenue, she is relieved that she dropped her two young children off at her aunt's place before leaving the motel room where she is currently residing, and wonders which of her neighbors and other acquaintances she will see in Denver County Jail tonight.

NeNe, James, Mary, and Officer Berman live and work on opposite sides of a gendered, classed, and racialized battle fought daily in neighborhoods with high levels of outdoor illicit drug and prostitution activity throughout the United States. As with all people caught in wars not of their own making, they do their best to care for themselves and their loved ones while making a living by following rules and engaging in behaviors that they do not always agree with or feel good about. By telling their stories, this book paints an ethnographic portrait of how they relate to one another within the context of fraught cultural and legal systems that both restrict their work activities and profoundly shape their lives.

This is a book about two groups of people: those who earn an income by engaging in street-based prostitution and those involved in criminal justice and social services efforts to curtail that prostitution through their work as police patrol officers, detectives, public defenders, judges, probation officers, and court-mandated therapeutic treatment providers. In Denver, Colorado, as in many U.S. cities, street-based prostitution's criminalized status, ties to the illicit drug economy, and public visibility result in frequent interactions among criminal justice professionals, social services providers, and women involved in activities that Colorado state law classifies as prostitution. Coauthored by an anthropologist and a legal scholar, this book explores these interactions and the cultural context in which they take place by drawing on six years of ethnographic research with street-involved[2] women and the criminal justice and social services professionals who regularly interact with them.

Systemic Intimacy: Street-Involved Women and the Criminal Justice–Social Services Alliance

Street-involved women exchange sex for cash or drugs as one of their strategies to navigate homelessness, addiction, compromised mental and physical health, and criminal justice system involvement. They face criminalization and stigmatization that isolate them from available legal, health, and social services, which generally regard sex trading and illicit drug use as pathological behaviors. Some services providers require that women agree to stop trading sex and using illicit drugs prior to receiving sustained assistance with obtaining housing, nonemergency medical care, and other necessary things. Hustling, as many women call street-based prostitution and the other activities (both legal and not) in which they regularly engage in order to get by, involves no such restrictive demands, and this stark reality explains why so many women choose working the streets over the vast criminal justice and social services apparatus designed to extricate them from the trade.

We term this apparatus "the criminal justice–social services alliance," a punitive-therapeutic confederation of federal, state, and municipal law enforcement agencies and state, municipal, or independent nonprofit social services entities. Despite their various individual and occupation-specific orientations, all alliance professionals must, as a condition of their jobs, implement a cultural ethos characterized by three primary beliefs described below regarding street-involved women's needs. Alliance professionals may mobilize this ethos in different ways throughout the course of their interactions with street-involved women during arrests, court hearings, and meetings with social services providers or other court-appointed officials, yet they nonetheless form a constant undercurrent that shapes street-involved women's lives in powerful ways.

First, the alliance ethos regards street-based sex trading and illicit drug use as the inherently harmful results of women's experiences with violent, grief-generating, or otherwise traumatic events. The second core aspect of this ethos maintains that street-involved women require sociolegal intervention through arrest, incarceration, court-mandated treatment, or, in some cases, all three, in order to stop these behaviors, irrespective of the women's own wishes or economic situation. Third, alliance professionals believe that women can only demonstrate progress toward ending their involvement in prostitution and illicit drug use by evincing readiness to change, expressing accountability for their individual actions, and complying with restrictions determined by alliance professionals. Taken together, these three core elements of the alliance ethos situate the individual woman and her decision making as the problem, rather than the constrained socioeconomic contexts in which she must often make very difficult choices.

Individual alliance professionals' personal beliefs and job descriptions indisputably differ, yet the ethos underlying their work is sharply distinguished from rights-based approaches that support women irrespective of whether they decide to continue sex trading or find another means of making a living. Alliance professionals tasked with street-involved women's regulatory oversight accordingly cannot endorse, or engage in, harm reduction or other peer-to-peer approaches that include the women as equal partners. This virtually ensures that street-involved women have little influence over outcomes related to their arrest, incarceration, court-mandated therapeutic treatment, probation or parole, and child custody determinations. Such an approach also demands women's ideological conformity, or at least a convincing performance of it, to the alliance ethos in order to achieve freedom from correctional control. The alliance ethos requires physical as well as ideological conformity: a woman who fails to convincingly demonstrate her commitment to finding a legal means of self-support while staying sober faces legal sanctions, including incarceration, if she tests positive, during court-mandated random screenings, for controlled substances or sexually transmitted infections.

We use the shorthand term "the alliance" to refer to the coalescence of punitive-therapeutic forces that work together to police or otherwise regulate street-involved women through arrest, incarceration, and court-mandated drug or other therapeutic treatment. Such policing and regulation, which enjoys significant public and political support on the federal, state, and municipal levels, relies on an interventionist discourse that narrowly positions women's sex trading as the result of traumatic life experiences rather than of the broader gendered socioeconomic realities that frame their lives. The alliance converges around the notion that street-involved women require intervention and supervised rehabilitation in order to address the trauma thought to motivate their involvement in criminalized and stigmatized ways of earning a living.

As part of a mutually reinforcing process, the alliance ethos interprets women's entrenchment in the criminalized economy that dominates the economically disadvantaged neighborhoods in which they live as evidence of their pathological individual and community traits. Alliance professionals accordingly have high levels of legally and socially endorsed discretionary latitude in policing or otherwise intervening in the "bad neighborhoods" where women engage in street-based sex trading. Such latitude results directly from dominant cultural perceptions that such communities are home to people with no respect for the law and whose activities threaten the prevailing social order. The alliance ethos accordingly ignores the reality that street-involved women as a social group face exclusion from equal opportunities and full participation in the legal economy.

These factors combine to make alliance professionals an easy target for academics, activists, and liberal media criticism because they, as a condition of their work, must enforce the alliance ethos even though they may well understand the fallacies that underpin it when applied to the daily business of living for street-involved women. Just as broader sexist, classist, and racist forces shape the lives of women who solicit publicly, alliance professionals' job requirements mandate that they tacitly enforce these inequalities in order to keep or advance within their respective professions. The ease with which alliance professionals do so depends on their individual moral and political orientations, such that those who prefer clear-cut punitive problem-solving approaches are less likely to critically examine their role in reinforcing inequalities than those who acknowledge the nuanced complexities that inform individual decision making.

Encounters between street-involved women and alliance professionals are ultimately exchanges that take place between individuals in the context of the abstract social forces that shape their respective understandings of the social world and their places within it. Street-involved women's descriptions of such encounters accordingly emphasize individual alliance professionals' abilities to invoke powerful sociolegal forces, rather than the political climate that undergirds such discretionary authority. Individual members of both groups utilize their discretion in conjunction with the prevailing beliefs they acquire from their peers in the setting where they earn an income, such that alliance professionals' workplace success depends on their ability to rapidly assess individual street-involved women's intentions, motivations, and inner states as a means to make potentially life-altering decisions about their access to services and freedom from correctional control. Street-involved

women likewise cultivate ways of interacting with alliance professionals, including (but certainly not limited to) evoking sympathy and trust
in ways that produce particular desired results, such as avoiding arrest.
Despite discretion's role in mitigating the alliance ethos, many alliance
professionals and street-involved women describe their frustration with
political and sociolegal forces that ultimately demand adherence to a
status quo that promotes class, race, and gender inequality, along with
self-serving assumptions that characterize street-involved women as in
need of interventions that only the alliance can provide.

Alliance professionals' use of discretion involves their obtaining public and personal information about street-involved women in settings
populated by a regular cast of characters who often recognize one another from previous interactions. Street-involved women, particularly
those who have engaged in the life for an extended period of time, often
have reputations among alliance professionals tasked with their policing
or other forms of regulation. For women whose family members also
engage in transactional sex, these reputations may span generations and
include an extensive history of criminal justice system involvement. Alliance professionals use the knowledge they acquire about the women
to characterize them as part of a continuum ranging from victims of
abuse to dangerous agents who spread disease or commit violent crimes.
Street-involved women likewise engage in information-gathering processes that allow them to characterize alliance professionals on a continuum ranging from empathic to sadistic. Officer Berman has a street
reputation as caring because he treats the women he encounters and
arrests with empathy, whereas another officer may inspire intimidation
and resentment due to her use of rough physical treatment or demeaning language.

We theorize the cultural dynamics that inform these encounters as
systemic intimacy, which refers to the interpersonal means by which individuals assess one another, and the broader institutional structures and
social forces of which they are a part, as they go about earning a living.
Cast in an adversarial relationship by the sociolegal norms that govern
their respective income-generation strategies, street-involved women
and alliance professionals both describe their interactions as fraught and
emotionally charged. We accordingly use the word "intimacy" to convey
three prevailing characteristics of the relationship between the women

and those tasked with their legal oversight: the need to make claims to expert knowledge about each other's motivations and inner states, the individual cultivation of fragile intergroup trust bonds as a means to obtain specialized in-group knowledge, and the personalization of broader social forces that inform inter- and intragroup encounters. This intimacy is "systemic" because it is legally and socially sanctioned, occurs as part of a social process by which individuals reconcile contradictions between their lived experiences and the legislative and policy frameworks governing them, and operates via powerful forces endorsed by prevailing social norms.

Systemic intimacy first and foremost demands reification of each group by the other such that these oppositional forces co-create individuals' ways of working with and responding to one another. Such reification involves the presumption of a generalized worldview and inner state to the extent that it enables an individual to predict or explain, with reasonable confidence, actions taken by a member of the oppositional group by drawing on previous experiences, collective knowledge imparted by other group members, or additional specialized forms of expertise. Hence an alliance professional might say with confidence, in support of programming or policies that restrict women's movements and autonomy, "for these women, instability is the norm due to the trauma they have experienced. We need to provide them with stability." In the explanatory model that accompanies such a worldview, a woman's unsanctioned departure from a drug treatment program or failure to report to probation becomes further evidence of her inability to adhere to structure without alliance professionals' guidance and associated punitive sanctions.

Street-involved women also claim such expertise, as when they characterize as a "cop mentality" binary worldviews that disregard the complex realities that may result in a woman's inability to report to probation or remain in a drug treatment program as a result of her childcare obligations or health problems. Alliance professionals and the women both need to accurately gauge one another's inner states in order to make rapid decisions regarding their conduct during encounters with one another, yet their failure to do so obviously results in very different consequences. A street-involved woman faces arrest and loss of liberty if she is unable to quickly identify and avoid an undercover police officer posing as a potential client, whereas the undercover officer may risk job loss or reassignment to less desirable work if he consistently fails to arrest women on prostitution-related charges.

Alliance professionals face indisputable challenges as they attempt to implement the ethos that informs their everyday work, yet the women under their purview face far more serious pressures to acquire the specialized knowledge necessary to manage alliance encounters. Encounters between street-involved women and alliance professionals take place in the context of the systemic socio-institutional failure to provide women with sustainable alternatives to sex trading, which consequently remains their primary solution to the immediate problems of homelessness and addiction. The women accordingly tend to individualize positive alliance experiences by describing specific professionals—rather than organizations, facilities, or the system more generally—as providing them with much-needed services, psycho-social support, or other benefits. For instance, women will praise the individual social worker who helps them to facilitate an open adoption, or the trusted police officer who warns them to avoid a particular city block due to the potential for an impending drug raid to turn violent. This practice underscores the women's prevailing view that while particular alliance professionals may perform acts of kindness, the punitive ethos to which they remain beholden reinforces the marginalizing forces that compel women to exchange sex for cash or drugs.

The individual cultivation of tenuous and often fragile trust bonds between alliance professionals and the women serves as a means for members of both groups to obtain specialized knowledge that they can mobilize to achieve particular goals. These bonds are often temporary and fraught with suspicion because of the inequalities that frame their cultivation and maintenance, and street-involved women remain ever cognizant of alliance professionals' disproportionate power and authority relative to them. Nevertheless, such short-term bonds can produce results that the women regard as desirable in at least some respects, as in the case of a detective who negotiates a suspended sentence for a woman who provides the information necessary to build a criminal case. The repercussions that ensue from such an exchange, of course, vary according to the circumstances in which it takes place and the individuals involved. Most street-involved individuals will positively regard a woman who identifies a serial rapist in a police lineup, whereas a woman who provides information to police about a neighborhood purveyor of controlled substances may have good cause to fear for her life.

Longer-term trust bonds, such as those between the women and their probation officers, diversion court workers, and social services providers, are difficult, if not impossible, to sustain in mutually beneficial ways. The powers that criminal justice professionals wield in the women's lives considerably limit the amount of information the women will openly share with them; most women aspire to be free of correctional control as soon as possible, and accordingly do their best to self-present in accordance with the alliance ethos while withholding potentially damaging information about their activities. Women may feel somewhat safer, and accordingly be more forthcoming, with social services providers than they do with criminal justice professionals, yet these providers face strong pressure from private, municipal, state, or federal funders that require them to demonstrate "success," which is often measured by the number of women who stop sex trading and illicit drug use as a result of receiving their services. Such demonstration of success involves a high-stakes proposition for many services providers, whose restricted budgets and overburdened, emotionally exhausted staff often struggle to meet women's basic needs in ways that make it difficult to establish strong trust bonds.

Social services providers are well aware that many of their street-involved clients will ultimately opt for the relative freedom of the street when faced with untenable services provision conditions. This reality sometimes results in women's relationships with services providers that are as tenuous and fragile as those among women and the criminal justice professionals who seek them out as informants. Providers are well aware of the women's significant socioeconomic constraints and accordingly must reconcile their desires to see each client's personal transformation become a success story that attests to the program's strengths with the knowledge that powerful socioeconomic forces constrain the women in ways that are far beyond the scope of their agency or organization. In this context, it is rather unsurprising that a services provider may decide to provide a particular woman, whom she sees as more capable of meeting benchmarks for agency success, with additional benefits or support. Yet many street-involved women could understandably experience this discretion as favoritism, or outright discrimination, rather than as the application of valid agency objectives as a means to meet funder or board expectations.

Systemic intimacy between alliance professionals and street-involved women also manifests in the personalization of both inter- and intragroup encounters and the broader social forces that inform them. Women, Latina/os, African Americans,[3] and working-class people more generally dominate in alliance occupations that involve the greatest amount of everyday contact with street-involved women. They accordingly face the challenging task of policing or otherwise exercising control over individuals who resemble them in gender, phenotype, and at least some elements of shared culture and experiences, all while reporting to White male supervisors and colleagues who may not be sensitive to the confluence of gender, class, and ethno-racial identity. Such a situation places these alliance professionals in a position where they face accusations of "taking sides" or, worse still, inadequately performing if they draw colleagues' or supervisors' attention to these issues.

Street-involved women are acutely aware of the ways in which sexism, classism, and racism collide for the women, African American, and Latina/o alliance professionals tasked with their policing or other forms of oversight in a work environment managed largely by White men. Street-involved women, rather than the alliance professionals, routinely and explicitly brought to our attention the complex ways in which gender, class, and ethno-racial identity intersect in their encounters with alliance professionals. They frequently dismissed female criminal justice professionals as having "somethin' to prove" in their male-dominated work environment and, much more generously, characterized working-class White male police patrol officers as "just doing a job" in enforcing laws they had no role in creating. Time and again, African American street-involved women conveyed some version of what Ms. Ella, who has many years of street experience, advised a younger African American colleague: "When you get arrested, you don't want a lady cop, and you better pray you don't get a Black lady cop, 'cause you out there embarassin' her."

Alliance professionals, following dominant U.S. social norms in professional settings staffed by men and women from different ethno-racial and class backgrounds, rarely have frank conversations about ethnicity, race, gender, or class, even when these issues may be central to the topic under discussion. Instead, alliance professionals follow prevailing U.S. cultural norms by obliquely conveying their attitudes and beliefs about these sensitive subjects through tone, word choice, and other subtle behaviors. This obliqueness may involve personalization, in which alliance professionals claim in-group knowledge to advance a particular point of view, which can consequently silence alliance professionals who do not belong to the same group. For instance, at a social workers' meeting about coordinating services for street-involved women, Susan watched a feminist Latina colleague bristle with visible frustration when a much older African American man stated, "This is an ongoing problem in the Black community: our women need guidance because they lack a father figure in their lives." In making unequivocal claims to in-group knowledge without attending to gendered socioeconomic realities, he effectively reinforced these inequalities while silencing others who could not make similar in-group knowledge claims.

In another instance that Susan observed, the only African American woman present at a correctional facility staff meeting defended an incarcerated African American woman's actions and received a rather dismissive response from her White and Latina/o colleagues. After she reasoned that the incarcerated woman's angry reaction to a White peer's racist remark was warranted under the circumstances in which they took place, her Latino colleague bluntly and rhetorically asked, "What does history have to do with why she's in jail? She made bad choices, and here she is. We need to move on." In this and numerous other instances, the nuances involved in such personalization—and colleagues' responses to it—actively discourage solidarity between alliance professionals and street-involved women based on shared membership in deprivileged groups.

The systemic character of the intimacy that pervades relationships between street-involved women and alliance professionals is evidenced by the pervasive and totalizing forms it takes, including official sanction, negotiations between contradictory individual experiences and official expectations, and the significantly negative impact it has on both street-involved women's and alliance professionals' lives and overall well-being. The first and most obvious way that this intimacy manifests in systemic form is through its codification in law and policy, which provides individual alliance professionals with powerful interpretive tools to guide and ascertain the limits of their discretionary decision making. Yet occupation-specific cultural and linguistic norms also inform alliance professionals' work in ways that do not always correspond to codified law and policy. For instance, an addictions-treatment-program staff member may inform her colleagues that a client is "not a good fit," thereby conveying a vast amount of information without needing to explicitly state her concerns about the client's mental health, personality, relationships with current program clients, or other issues that concern her. Likewise, police patrol officers may decide to intensify prostitution-related arrests or policing in response to citizen complaints from neighborhood business owners, rather than impoverished local residents, since the former enjoy considerably more political clout. Such decisions remain within the boundaries of codified law and policy, but sometimes only just, and always take place in a context characterized by the uneasy coexistence of alliance cultural norms with those that govern street life.

Recognizing and reconciling the often-considerable contradictions between alliance and street cultural norms is a quotidian element of work life for those alliance professionals who must build rapport with street-involved women in order to conduct criminal investigations, engage in undercover work, or perform street outreach. For example, a therapeutic-treatment-facility worker who calls weekly from her office to report her clients' drug test results to probation officers will fully expect to encounter these same women during street outreach and spend time with them while they are experiencing the effects of illicit drug use. Likewise, an advocate at a homeless shelter may advise a client who wants to receive in-patient mental health treatment to explicitly tell police officers that she intends to commit suicide, because the advocate knows that making this statement will legally obligate the officers to transport the woman to a hospital or psychiatric facility that will admit her. Individuals on both sides of this sociolegal apparatus reconcile these contradictions while simultaneously being affected by at least some aspects of one another's lives. Alliance professionals experience high levels of work-related stress and stigma by association that may result in the same types of substance abuse, intimate partner violence, and stress-related mental and physical health problems they are tasked with policing, treating, or otherwise regulating among the women. Police officers routinely witness extreme forms of violence and human suffering, while social workers support their clients through relapse, child custody loss, incarceration, and other grief-generating events. Street-involved women readily acknowledge that the emotional toll wrought by these experiences can seriously compromise alliance professionals' abilities to treat them with respect and empathy.

The concept of systemic intimacy captures the reality that alliance professionals and street-involved women share a relationship that features both shared physical spaces, including neighborhoods, correctional facilities, or agency offices, and sometimes-extensive knowledge of each other's normative cultural practices. Yet the alliance also disproportionately concedes power to the criminal justice system because social services agencies that derive financial resources from, or cooperate with, law enforcement organizations must conform to the correctional model of control. Social services providers coopted into the alliance under the guise of providing therapeutic treatment ultimately remain accountable to the correctional model of intervention, control, and rehabilitation on terms developed in the absence of any meaningful consultation with those most affected by illicit drug use, street prostitution, or related social issues. In many ways, then, the analysis presented here builds on an extensive body of social science literature that identifies and critiques the ways in which well-intentioned individuals find themselves promoting policy and law that they know to be ineffective at best and harmful at worst.

At core, this book argues that the criminal justice system's financial and ideological predominance within the criminal justice–social services alliance results in an amalgamation that highly individualizes women's sex trading and illicit drug use activities as pathological choices they make due to the cognitive distortions believed to result from abusive or otherwise traumatic life experiences. This approach advocates therapeutic treatment interventions, some of which are court monitored, for street-involved women while effectively ignoring the gendered socioeconomic circumstances that inform their decision making. Such incomplete (or even false) presumptions about street-involved women's experiences with illicit drug use, violence, homelessness, and sex trading accordingly engender counterproductive results reliant upon dominant U.S. cultural norms that support individualism and deny structural inequality.

Conceptualizing Bureaucratic Power and Control

Our analysis unites four primary theoretical-conceptual areas: street-level bureaucracy, the reproduction of violence through law and policy, therapeutic governance, and the disproportionate exercise of these social forces on individuals living in neighborhoods least able to contest state intrusion. We hope that systemic intimacy, our small theoretical contribution to this rich body of existing work, will help academics and practitioners to more fully analyze the complex means by which individuals negotiate the adversarial systems of which they are a part, whether willingly or otherwise. A thorough understanding of the means by which individuals create, negotiate, and protest these conflicting frameworks is essential to the development of evidence-based law and policy that enhances gender, race, and class equality.

Street-Level Bureaucracy

In his germinal *Street-Level Bureaucracy: Dilemmas of the Individual in Public Services* (2010 [1980]), political scientist Michael Lipsky documents the significant challenges facing public sector workers, whom he broadly defined as including police officers, social workers, teachers, and others tasked with the front-line implementation of law and policy. Members of the criminal justice–social services alliance fall squarely into this front-line category. Lipsky argues that public encounters with street-level bureaucrats constitute the "places where citizens experience directly the government they have implicitly constructed" (Lipsky, 2010 [1980], p. xi). These experiences are rarely positive, he contends, due to chronically inadequate resources, restricted capacities, ambiguous or conflicting agency goals, difficulties measuring success, and the reality that most street-level bureaucrats' clients are involuntary. While this characterization applies to the alliance workers as a whole, those in the social services describe greater difficulties in these areas, particularly with respect to the ambiguities and resource shortages that characterize their work.

Street-level bureaucrats in the alliance, as in Lipsky's conceptualization, contend with this significant gap between the ideals of public service and the often significantly constrained realities of its practice by exercising discretionary authority and establishing routinized means of dealing with clients. Lipsky notes that street-level bureaucrats employ these coping mechanisms in ways that, due to time and resource constraints, result in simplified client typologies and scripted modes of interaction. The pressures and realities of their jobs leave no alternatives for the alliance's street-level bureaucrats, who become interpreters of law and policy through the exercise of discretion. Yet Lipsky also argues that street-level bureaucrats deny their own discretionary authority as a means to limit their personal responsibility; in other words, by simply stating, "it's the law" or "that's how it is," a street-level bureaucrat is able to effectively evade a client's requests for exceptions to the rules or other special favors (Lipsky, 2010 [1980]).

As quintessential street-level bureaucrats, alliance professionals' discretion remains limited by the will of their political masters, who create the legislation and budget allocations that determine and direct the course of alliance action. The result is a self-referencing body of ostensibly well-intentioned law and policy that remains tautologically and hermetically sealed firmly within the alliance ethos, as in the example of the federal Victims of Trafficking and Violence Prevention Act's definition of anyone who trades sex while under the age of eighteen as a victim of trafficking entitled to assistance measures due to their inability to consent (U.S. Congress, 2000). The practical result of this legislation is that on a young woman's eighteenth birthday, alliance professionals have statutory tools at their disposal to prosecute her as a criminal perpetrator for engaging in prostitution rather than providing services to her.[4]

Reproduction of Violence through Law and Public Policy

The sharp age-based legal division between receiving services and facing criminal prosecution is just one example of the ways in which street-involved women, as well as some of the alliance professionals who work with them, experience the reproduction of violence through law and public policy that focuses on particular personal aspects (such as age) while ignoring or neglecting race, class, and gender. Our analysis is deeply informed by the work of political scientists Kristin Bumiller and Naomi Murakawa, whose research explores how the implementation of laws and policies designed to provide assistance to those in need may reproduce sexism, racism, and other forms of structural violence. Bumiller and Murakawa both provide examples of how federal and state government efforts to stem enduring inequalities can unintentionally reinforce the very exclusionary forces they sought to prevent. The application of the law's blunt force to complex and nuanced social issues likewise creates paradoxical or unintended results in encounters between street-involved women and alliance professionals.

Bumiller, who interviewed women seeking services at domestic violence shelters and studied media coverage of two widely publicized U.S. gang rape trials, argues that intensified state involvement in criminalizing and prosecuting violence against women resulted in the reification of women's vulnerability. Services provision and legal recourses available to women, Bumiller argues, take place on terms that mandate women's submission to authority, enforced dependency, and performance of the "good victim" role (Bumiller, 2008). Street-involved women in Denver likewise describe the alliance ethos' pressure for conformance as a means to obtain services and resources, particularly by eschewing street prostitution and foregoing illicit drug use in order to become what both street-involved women and alliance professionals gloss as "a productive member of society."

In her historical analysis of the U.S. criminal justice system's expansion, Murakawa documents the unintended consequences of law and policy designed to eliminate racism in the criminal justice system. She argues that civil rights activists and their political allies supported federal expansion as a result of their belief that further government oversight would reduce racial bias through a professionalization of the justice system. Instead, Murakawa contends that this resulted in a vastly expanded carceral state that continued to arrest and incarcerate African Americans at far higher rates than their peers of other ethno-racial backgrounds (Murakawa, 2014). Federal, state, and municipal efforts to create task forces designed to address street-based prostitution as a social issue in many U.S. cities, including Denver, have likewise resulted in disproportionately high rates of incarceration for poor women, many of whom are African American or women of color.[5]

Bumiller's work is particularly relevant in its detailed discussion regarding the extensive professional apparatus developed in response to the social problem of sexual and domestic violence against women. Bumiller describes attempts to prosecute abusers and provide assistance to their victims through a merger of the therapeutic-medical establishment and the criminal justice system. The result is a "highly rationalized form of social control" that neatly separates female victims of violence, who require therapeutic treatment and caseworker guidance, from male perpetrators who face criminal prosecution for their abusive or otherwise violent behavior (Bumiller, 2008, p. 14). Bumiller convincingly demonstrates how the discourse of trauma and victimization effectively demands that women seeking legal redress or social services submit to a highly feminized victim role through compliance with caseworker-mandated treatment protocols. Street-involved women who wish to receive alliance services must likewise self-identify as victims in order to fit the alliance ethos' understanding of their lives, often by emphasizing the formative impact that sexual or other forms of abuse had on them, irrespective of whether they actually regarded these events as victimizing.

Street-involved women routinely face the consequences of both the carceral state that Murakawa describes and the medicalization of trauma that Bumiller documents. As Krystal succinctly noted of her transition from working the street to court-mandated supervision, "My P[robation] O[fficer] is my new pimp; she makes sure she always tell me just how fucked up she thinks I am." Krystal's analogy emphasizes the manipulative power and control dynamic she regards as characteristic of her dealings with both probation officer, who uses the law to maintain authority, and pimp, who employs street-endorsed means of enforcing his will. Yet rather than acknowledging the reasons why street-involved women like Krystal regard these otherwise very different figures in similar ways, the alliance ethos employs trauma as a universal justification for various discretionary forms of intervention in street-involved women's lives. This positioning of street-involved women as inherently unstable victims who require intervention eclipses any analysis of the systemic exclusionary forces that limit women's options for making sustainable life changes, and thereby reinforces the alliance's power and control in what could be described as self-serving ways.

Therapeutic Governance

Therapeutic governance refers to state-endorsed intervention or other forms of oversight justified by the need to maintain order among individuals or groups deemed disorderly by sociolegal or other powerful cultural forces. First conceptualized in reference to persons displaced by war, therapeutic governance "makes a link between psychological well-being and security, and seeks to foster personalities able to cope with risk and insecurity" (Pupavac, 2005, pp. 161–62). This conceptual framework powerfully undergirds relationships between alliance professionals and street-involved women, with the former being tasked with policing such disorder among the latter. Prevailing state and cultural forces accordingly work in concert to advance therapeutic governance as the only viable solution to the various forms of internal disorder that the alliance ethos regards as destabilizing or otherwise compromising the women's abilities to change their lives.

Correctional facilities and other institutional sites of alliance control, in Denver as nationally, implement therapeutic governance in the form of addictions- and mental-health-treatment programs known as "therapeutic community." Such programs involve a totalizing group living environment in which women must enforce the alliance ethos by publicly holding one another accountable for the circumstances that resulted in state-endorsed intervention in their lives via incarceration or other court-mandated supervision (McCorkel, 2013). Accordingly, when women in therapeutic community groups tell one another to "fake it till you make it," they are also sometimes tacitly advising their peers' discursive adherence to the alliance ethos as a means to avoid being penalized with extended or intensified forms of correctional control. Women's successful adherence to these discourses and the ideologies of which they are a part result in considerable benefits, including the freedom from correctional control that accompanies the alliance's version of successful "rehabilitation" (Hackett, 2013; Pollack, 2010).

Therapeutic governance generally positions women's addictions and involvement in other criminalized activities as byproducts of their abusive relationships with men, low self-esteem, and traumatic life events. Yet, as Bumiller observed with respect to services available to women who have experienced violence, therapeutic governance often demands even more extreme conditions of submission to power and control than women have experienced in other areas of their lives. Clinical social work scholar Shoshanna Pollack argues that Canadian correctional facilities' attempts to implement therapeutic discourse in the form of self-esteem classes and related programming ignore the various forms of socioeconomic exclusion the women face (Pollack, 2007). Sociologists Susan Starr Sered and Maureen Norton-Hawk likewise contend that the twelve step ideology advocated by Alcoholics Anonymous, Narcotics Anonymous, and other addictions treatment groups, relies on a personal responsibility discourse that requires submission to a Higher Power in ways that reinforce criminalized women's marginalization while dis-acknowledging the already significant constraints on their freedom and decision making (Sered and Norton-Hawk, 2011). This occurs in sharp contrast to rights-based and harm-reduction approaches, often created and promoted by women of color and women who have traded sex, which advocate political education and agendas that hold society accountable for these enduring inequalities (Dewey and St. Germain, 2015).

Unequal Exercise of Bureaucratic Power and Control

Residential segregation into areas of concentrated poverty pushes individuals to engage in criminalized income-generation strategies as part of street cultural norms that sharply differ from, or even contradict, the ethos embraced by alliance professionals tasked with neighborhood policing. Despite the critical role gender plays in these complex social interactions, the majority of urban anthropological and sociological works addressing social relationships and everyday life in socioeconomically and ethno-racially segregated neighborhoods focus on men's experiences in ways that minimize or even erase women's roles in criminalized street life.[6] Their findings are nonetheless relevant to street-involved women's lives, in which neighborhood segregation, and street culture more generally, plays a powerful governing role in gendered divisions of sexual and other forms of illicit labor.

Segregation's deep socioeconomic roots are inseparable from the cultural norms that frame everyday life for street-involved women in communities created generations ago in the wake of deindustrialization's massive labor market reorganization, White suburbanization, and concomitant ghettoization of African Americans and Latina/os in urban neighborhoods with few legal opportunities to earn money. Sociologist William Julius Wilson argues that these conditions created an "underclass" effectively excluded from socioeconomic opportunities afforded to residents outside such neighborhoods (Wilson, 2012 [1987]). Wilson also contends, echoing findings by Canadian criminologists John Hagan and Bill McCarthy, that such exclusion encourages a process whereby individuals, sometimes from a very young age, socialize one another into available—and not always legal—ways of making a living (Hagan and McCarthy, 1997).

Sociologists Douglas Massey and Nancy Denton, building on Wilson's "underclass" theorization, concisely characterize segregation as "an institutional tool for isolating the by-products of racial oppression: crime, drugs, violence, illiteracy, poverty, despair, and their growing social and economic costs" (Massey and Denton, 1993, p. 217). Wilson, Massey and Denton, as well as many other social scientists, describe segregation as productive of a particular culture that sociologist Elijah Anderson (1999) neatly terms "the code of the street," in which respect and the individual responsibility to protect oneself are paramount. Despite the alliance ethos' positioning of street codes as inherently threatening to law and the social order, sociologists and anthropologists have clearly demonstrated that these codes effectively govern and self-regulate the illegal income-generation strategies available to residents of segregated neighborhoods (Venkatesh, 2009; Bourgois, 1995).

In this complex cultural context, our study design sought to capture the sometimes blatant and sometimes subtle means by which alliance professionals and street-involved women exercise, experience, negotiate, and resist these various forms of power and control. This considerable undertaking involved an equally intensive set of methodological and ethical considerations.

Methods and Ethics

Our unique collaboration between an anthropologist (Susan) and a legal scholar (Tonia) required an equally innovative division of labor for this book, which built on nearly a decade of interdisciplinary feminist work together.[7] Susan carried out the ethnographic fieldwork, interviews, and quantitative research, while Tonia offered sharp feminist legal insights that were instrumental in moving this long-term project forward over the course of six years. We worked hard in designing and carrying out this research to directly combat representations of the women with whom Susan directly worked, particularly by implementing a mixed methods approach that made her accountable to the potential implications of this research. This book is the product of our intellectual synergy and would not have been possible otherwise, but our division of labor presents challenges a bit outside the scope of conventional ethnographic writing. We solve this problem by switching between first person singular ("I," "me," and "my") to refer specifically to Susan's independent research interactions and first person plural ("we" and "our") to indicate our jointly defined arguments.

This project employed an iterative methodology, approved by the University of Wyoming's Institutional Review Board, that began when I received permission to live as an unpaid staff member at a Denver transitional housing facility for women leaving the sex trade. I spent approximately four days and three nights per week over the course of a year engaged in participant observation with the women and staff members; more specifically, this involved my attending house meetings, engaging in addictions and therapeutic groups, waiting at free medical clinics and social services offices, cooking and eating together in our shared kitchen, watching television, and interacting with women's loved ones and family members. Living together in this way resulted in the formation of close bonds between me and many of the women, with all the accompanying complexities and dysfunction that the term "family" implies.

I used my spare time in the evenings and early mornings at the transitional housing facility to enter data from paper-based client files into an electronic spreadsheet for use by staff members, who fully supported publication of the results. Staff members had assembled these client files from services provision encounters with 131 women who sought to leave the street over the course of a decade.[8] Such files constitute significant knowledge-production instruments because they are physical manifestations of the ways in which alliance professionals create and reinforce the rationale for specific programs and services by emphasizing particular aspects of women's lives. These files contain a wealth of information on women's general demographic characteristics (age, race/ethnicity, relationship status, children), experiences with employment and the criminal justice system (previously held legal jobs, arrests, charges, convictions), substance abuse and health (drug of choice, duration of use, mental health issues, family histories), and summaries of formative life events (referral processes, government benefits, reasons for help seeking).

My gradual integration into street prostitution's cultural and spatial world through the intimacies of shared living space allowed me, in the second and third years of this project, to conduct and audio-record one hundred semistructured interviews with women actively working the street or residing in the transitional housing facility. These interviews took place in the midst of my extensive participant observation in the East Colfax Avenue neighborhood where the women engage in transactional sex and where I was initially questioned by police officers and potential clients. While I did not trade sex for money or illicit drugs on the street, the experience of being closely watched by law enforcement officers and men seeking transactional sexual encounters provided me with at least some sense of what women experience working the streets. This participant observation would not have been possible in the same way without Leelee, whom I lived with in the transitional housing facility and who had years of East Colfax Avenue experience. An astute cultural broker who appeared to move effortlessly between street and alliance cultural contexts, Leelee offered insights that were instrumental in shaping the research for this book and the arguments presented here.

I designed the participant observation aspects of the research to resemble women's interactions with the alliance as closely as possible without myself getting arrested, being incarcerated, or engaging in street-based trading and illicit drug use. I regularly traveled, often with other street-involved women but sometimes alone, from motel rooms where women were using various controlled substances after "getting a lick," as they call earning money in a variety of illicit ways, to a police station, correctional facility, or addictions-treatment-oriented transitional housing facility. Moving from site to site conducting participant observation, as well as semistructured interviews when the women's time and energy allowed, was the closest approximation I could safely and legally take to the pathways street-involved women follow on a daily basis.

Although I regularly smoked cigarettes and drank alcohol with the women, I chose not to participate in street-based sex trading, illicit drug use, or other criminalized activities with the women because I do not believe that my doing so would approximate the experiences of women who engage in these behaviors on a long-term basis. My positionality as a stably housed White woman able to afford an attorney probably would have resulted in my having extremely different encounters with the criminal justice system, which would have rendered such engagement unproductive. Nevertheless, a number of street-involved women cautioned me that this research would always be incomplete without my experiencing the pleasures associated with smoking, injecting, or otherwise ingesting their respective drugs of choice, or the adrenaline rush that accompanies the various hustles they engage in to make a living. A few women also used this argument when they offered to work the street with me, most often through a mutually beneficial arrangement that would involve me sharing a portion of my earnings in exchange for their screening my prospective clients.

Despite my decision not to directly engage in these criminalized activities, I was constantly surrounded by them. I often had to make quick ethical decisions, such as when I opted to openly discuss my research on several occasions with justifiably puzzled neighborhood police patrol officers who questioned me regarding my reasons for being in what criminal justice professionals term a "known prostitution area." Women regularly used or were under the influence of illicit substances while we spent time together, and they often told me about illegal activities they had witnessed or engaged in themselves. I followed anthropological norms in nonjudgmentally observing these activities within their cultural context and attempted to implement this policy as much as possible with alliance professionals by treating them with the same empathy and suspension of judgment as I did the women. While these experiences and practices created sometimes intractable ethical challenges, they were formative in shaping my understanding of the everyday issues that street-involved women and alliance professionals face.

One of the foremost ethical challenges I struggled with in speaking to individual members of these oppositional groups, a number of whom knew one another from previous professional encounters, stemmed from my acquisition of specialized in-group knowledge. Particularly in meetings and interviews with criminal justice professionals, I tried to remain cognizant of the potential to unintentionally reveal information about specific individuals or trade-related knowledge that police might use to arrest the women. I likewise had to withhold from the women information about police procedures that officers shared with me in strict confidence as context for their stories. Doing so proved especially difficult when I listened to women share partial or incorrect advice with one another about procedural norms in undercover and other police operations, and yet I could not ethically compromise one group's confidentiality to protect another's.

Criminal justice professionals, especially those with years of experience working vice or patrol, expressed surprise and, less frequently, suspicion regarding the rapport I enjoyed with the women, which meant that I often had to work very hard to demonstrate solidarity and alignment with their alliance perspectives. I generally did this by positioning myself as "one of the family," typically by casually mentioning my father's undercover police work in a New York State narcotics unit. I often used humor to lower male officers' initial resistance to meeting with me by telling those who worked undercover, "My Dad bought a lotta dope in the '80s." Yet this rapport with criminal justice professionals sometimes made me uncomfortable in that I felt these friendly relationships betrayed the women to some extent. I often left interviews with criminal justice professionals, many of whom I genuinely liked, feeling deeply conflicted by what the alliance demands of its workers, particularly as I juxtaposed their perspectives with those of the women. These sentiments were further complicated as I watched officers with years on the force get emotional, or even cry, about the difficulties and risks of their work. Their courage in sharing this vulnerability with me deeply enriched this project by humanizing individuals whom it otherwise might have been easy for me to demonize due to their role as agents in a system that so dehumanizes the women.

An ancillary ethical dilemma that arose with criminal justice professionals involved my initial difficulties in building rapport as a means to elicit something beyond the kind of official occupation-specific rhetoric they might espouse with a journalist. Criminal justice professionals, like the street-involved women they arrest or supervise, must retain a degree of skeptical cynicism about outsiders' sincerity and motives in order to do their jobs effectively. My long-term involvement with the transitional housing facility played a pivotal role in providing me with entrée into the otherwise relatively closed criminal justice community. I was able to introduce myself as a staff member at a facility that regularly receives referrals from the Federal Bureau of Investigation as well as from Colorado public defenders, detectives, and other criminal justice professionals, which allowed me to make claims to at least some insider status with the alliance.

I consciously bolstered this status by telling criminal justice professionals about male members of my family who, like many of the men I spent time with in the research, worked in law enforcement after serving in the U.S. military. Officers who expressed reticence about doing an interview with me frequently opted to speak very candidly when I added something at the end of an e-mail or phone conversation along the lines of, "I know you're busy, but maybe you could think of this as a favor to a cop's daughter?" Claiming insider, or even quasi-familial status, worked to minimize the concerns raised by some alliance professionals' stereotypes about professors' leftist—and even anti-police—leanings. As my father succinctly put it when I bemoaned my initial failed attempts to build the kind of research relationships I wanted to have with criminal justice professionals, "Suze, they're just afraid you're gonna write a book that goes all liberal on 'em."

Once I succeeded in befriending a few detectives, I began to receive referrals to their younger colleagues, who I sometimes worried might feel coerced into speaking with me since they typically involved e-mails from superiors that read something like, "I sincerely hope you will consider talking to Susan." The few criminal justice professionals who generously allowed me to spend extended periods of time with them did so on strict conditions of confidentiality. As they began to share information more openly with me over time, I understood their initial reticence and the potential for misinterpretation regarding their accounts of encounters that rapidly turned negative during an arrest or of colleagues who had engaged in professional misconduct. Accounts of negative police encounters, which were very much the exception rather than the rule in my conversations with officers, were the subject of extensive news media coverage throughout the later stages of this project, which further complicated my efforts to build trust.

Even the few officers with whom I enjoyed a strong rapport worried that I might take an anti-police perspective in subsequent publications derived from this research. They would specifically state, particularly when we were engaged in lengthy unrecorded conversations, that I did not have permission to publish particular information they shared with me. There is much ethnographic material that, out of my respect for this boundary, consequently must remain unpublished although it definitely informs arguments presented in this book. So while I was very privileged to receive some insights into criminal justice professionals' relatively closed world, my membership in it was always partial at best, in sharp contrast to the extended periods of time that I was able to spend with the women and social services providers after they had sufficient opportunities to observe me and make assessments about my intentions.

In the fourth year of this research, I received permission to sit in on an otherwise closed Denver-area prostitution diversion courtroom, which I complemented with regular visits to criminal courts that are open to the public. These observations were particularly meaningful since my long-term engagement in this work meant that I knew a number of the street-involved women facing criminal charges or diversion court scrutiny. Sometimes women would sit next to me on a courtroom bench and engage in whispered running commentary regarding court activities; their perspectives dramatically informed my understandings of how women experience the criminal justice system. My presence in prostitution diversion court became such a regular feature in conjunction with my interviews with court staff that, during one particularly memorable instance, the presiding judge began court by smiling and asking, "So, Professor, how's life on the streets these days?" "Can't complain, your honor," I awkwardly responded while sinking lower on the bench as the other women laughed at me.

As a woman in my midthirties, I fit the demographic profile of many Denver street-involved women and consequently received similar treatment by social services providers, criminal justice professionals, and men seeking transactional sexual encounters. These interactions, which always occurred when I was in street-involved women's company, provided me with rich ethnographic insights into the everyday experiences that inform women's lives and worldviews as they engage with the alliance. One particularly powerful example of the complexities involved in services provision took place as I waited in the lobby of a drop-in center that provides counseling and therapeutic oversight for two Denver-area prostitution diversion courts, both of which offer weekly meetings with a judicial team and mandatory drug testing as an alternative to incarceration.

The drop-in center employs formerly street-involved women at the reception desk, and its case workers, one of whom I was waiting to interview, dress as casually as their clients and strive to create a welcoming atmosphere. Knowing this, I settled into a waiting room chair that morning wearing secondhand jeans, a tank top, and sandals, nondescript attire that did not visually identify me as a public defender, social worker from a state office, or other alliance professional. I had just begun casually conversing with a few women in the waiting room about a mutual acquaintance when one of the receptionists tapped her purple acrylic nails on the counter and exclaimed to her colleague, "What in the actual hell? Some people think they don't got to follow rules around here." She then turned to me. "What is your name?"

"Susan, ma'am," I respectfully replied.

She laughed derisively and affected an artificially sweet tone that a person might use in communicating with someone who lacks maturity or a basic knowledge of etiquette. "Well, Susan, you think you don't have to sign in like everybody else?"

"No, ma'am," I said, and stood up to write my name on the list of women waiting to see counselors, often as a condition of their probation.

Nodding her head toward the reception desk's large fishbowl filled with hundreds of multicolored condoms, she instructed me, "Now take you some condoms while you up here."

"Thank you, ma'am," I said.

I shoved several condoms in my pocket as the case worker entered the waiting room with her characteristic enthusiasm, shouting out her habitual teasing usage of my professional title, "Professor Susan!"

The other women shifted their collective gaze to the receptionist, who looked away as the oldest woman in the waiting room smirked and said, loud enough for everyone to hear, "Well, well, looks like Ms. Snooty High Booty just got *told*." The receptionist abruptly left the room and, judging by the peals of laughter among the waiting room women, this was a small victory against disrespect meted out by a formerly street-involved woman to those who remain in the life.

This ethnographic vignette demonstrates how the stigma related to street-based sex trading and illicit drug use pervaded all aspects of the research and necessitated the development of specialized research methods that accounted for these ethical complexities. A fundamental ethical challenge apparent in the services provision context emerged from the reality that formerly street-involved women, such as the woman at the drop-in center's reception desk, can appear judgmental due to their desire to distance themselves from stigmatized activities. In the street context, however, women with experience in the life have a powerful set of dual credentials as self-made women who have conquered addiction and use their street experiences to help others. My concerns about these ethical issues inspired a research design in which, in the street context, I cointerviewed with a research partner who had extensive sex trading experience, Leelee, while at the transitional housing facility I interviewed women alone.

Leelee and I cointerviewed women on numerous occasions from a motel room in the East Colfax Avenue neighborhood where she formerly lived and traded sex while struggling with addiction to crack cocaine. I loosely structured these open-ended interviews, the first of which took place in the second year of the research, around the themes of women's everyday activities, needs, and harm-reduction strategies. The findings that emerged in these early interviews resulted in the focus on the criminal justice system and social services that shaped the rest of the research. The majority of the women knew Leelee, and those who did not readily identified her as an expert due to the ease with which she approached women working the street and explained the study to them. Simply put, this aspect of the work would not have been as productive (or perhaps even possible) without her expertise; as one woman told us, first addressing me and then Leelee in the motel room we used for interviews, "You're a very sweet woman, but I would not have come up in here if girlfriend hadn't been out here and done did it herself."

In these interviews, which featured between one and four participants as per the women's preferences, Leelee would frequently interject with points of agreement or disagreement, prompting critical reflection on the women's perspectives about their lives and income-generation strategies. Women could stay in the motel room with us for as long as they wanted, providing a welcome respite from the often exhausting outdoor search for money and drugs. For this as well as other reasons, a number of women completed their interviews by asking to stay with us in order to help reassure the next interview participant of our good intentions and to add to the interview as they ate snacks we provided and smoked cigarettes with us. Women consistently praised this approach, particularly as Leelee's and my mutual involvement with the transitional housing facility's program, of which Leelee was a graduate, allowed us to provide women with resources and information about our services as well as those of other Denver organizations.

Macey, an African American woman in her fifties with a long history of street involvement, nodded approvingly as she observed us interviewing two women, noting, "Y'all hit it just right, 'cause see, she [Leelee] been out here for a minute [a lengthy period of time], but you [Susan] know how to write it all down in a way folks'll understand. Your program knows what it's doin'." Using the highest form of praise, another woman, Ellie, captured the sentiment shared by many others with respect to Leelee's wealth of experience when she happily interjected midway through our interview, "Girl, I feel just like I am talking to my *own* sister right now." The atmosphere of camaraderie Leelee and I worked hard to create during these interviews resulted in incredibly rich and nuanced material in which the women displayed their sophisticated knowledge about services providers' income-generation strategies, which included their rather blasé recognition of the competitive business of nonprofit work. For instance, a number of women matter-of-factly expressed some version of "I'll help y'all, I know you got to do stuff like this to keep your grant," following our explanation of the research and our connection to the transitional housing facility.

It was particularly revelatory to listen to the women talk about the harm-reduction strategies they develop in response to what they perceive as their occupational risks. Women consistently spoke about themselves as tough, independent, and ready to inflict harsh treatment on their adversaries, yet they described other women as vulnerable to violence, arrest, and other harms due to their comparatively inferior street knowledge. It became clear, after multiple reviews of our interview transcripts, that many women may have actually been describing their own experiences when recounting details of other women's violent or negative encounters. While interviewees frequently talked about the victimization of women they characterized as friends, relatives, or colleagues, they almost never self-identified as having experienced such events in their own lives. It is of course impossible to know whether this is actually the case, but this consistency suggests that while our free-flowing and inclusive interviewing strategy succeeded in creating a warm and supportive atmosphere, it failed to allow the women to overcome the street prohibition on showing weakness or vulnerability in the presence of others.

Likewise, my efforts to create collaborative and mutually beneficial research relationships through the establishment of close ties with both the transitional housing facility and street-involved women initially presented a set of ethical challenges related to my conflicting loyalties to both the women and the facility. I consequently faced a learning curve during the first of the five years I spent living and working there. During this time I struggled considerably with my desire to support the women in what sometimes appeared to me as a punitive environment that constantly monitored their movements, bodies, and inner states in the name of helping them through the addiction-recovery process. I occupied a liminal position somewhere between a staff member with keys to the building and access to case files, a volunteer without obligations to report minor rule violations to staff, and a resident involved with the women's everyday activities.

As I drove women to and from appointments and became a friend and confidante to many of them, I often found myself in unexpected situations that socialized me into the complexities of women's lives while also making me privy to information that I chose not to share with facility staff when my own ethical compass determined that sharing this information might produce negative consequences. One day Kayla, a new resident, and I had spent several hours waiting for food stamps when she asked me to make an unexpected detour to meet a person she vaguely characterized as "a friend." Recently released from prison, Kayla talked frequently about what kind of crime she might commit in order to return to the facility where the woman she called her prison wife, whose name she had tattooed on her neck, was serving a life sentence.

Other residents told me that when Kayla was in prison, she exchanged sex with a corrections officer, who eventually lost his job, in return for him allowing her time alone with her partner and other special privileges. After we had spent a few minutes outside a large office building talking with an especially friendly security guard who Kayla said owed her money, she smiled at me and asked, "You know who that was, don't you?" showing me the forty dollars he had given her. We then went to a big box store known for low-cost prescriptions to try to get her prescribed antipsychotic medication, which turned out to be far more expensive than we had hoped. I held her in the parking lot as she cried and said, "I just want to go back to prison so I can get my meds." Following our return to the transitional housing facility, a staff member casually asked me, "How did it go with Kayla?" and I shrugged and said "okay," not wanting to reveal the layers of secrets she had shared with me, or my complicity in keeping them.

I struggled throughout the research as I resisted my strong urge to selectively apply my own conceptions of "help" to the women. I often wanted to invite women with whom I had a particularly strong rapport to stay with me in the isolated university town where I lived when I began the research. It was very painful to think about the women hustling outside in the dead of winter, and I struggled ethically and morally with knowing that I could invite at least a few of them to live with me. Yet I also considered the challenging realities of what it would mean to have illicit substances in my home, as the vast majority of the women were disinclined to give up drug use. I likewise struggled with what it would mean to offer a place to stay or other benefits to women for whom I had an affinity, versus those with whom I did not share such a bond.

These ethical challenges did not diminish as the research progressed and my relationships with the women and the transitional housing facility deepened. Instead, they morphed into new and more complex forms predicated on obligations I incurred to those who had been particularly helpful. One especially significant example of this occurred during the fifth year of the project as I continued my work at the transitional housing facility, which over time allowed me to interact with hundreds of people employed in the fields of criminal justice and social services who otherwise might not have spoken with me about their work. I engaged in two dozen semistructured interviews with alliance professionals, many of whom I knew through my work at the facility and our previous joint efforts to coordinate services for the women, often under extremely constrained circumstances that necessitated the development of trust bonds. These participants included public defenders, public interest lawyers, police patrol officers, vice detectives, diversion court staff, probation officers, and corrections officers, as well as court-mandated addictions- and other therapeutic-treatment program staff. My interviews would not have been nearly as rich or as detailed if I had not shared significant rapport developed through years of work with these participants, yet this was not without ethical ramifications. Years of working together as colleagues, after all, led these participants to believe that I fully supported the alliance and its ethos in ways that may have encouraged them to speak much more candidly than they would have with a researcher they did not know.

I chose to stop collecting data in the form of field notes, interviews, and quantitative case file data when, in the project's sixth year,[9] the transitional housing facility's executive director asked me to take on the unpaid position of admissions coordinator, making me the first point of contact for street-involved women who wished to enter the program. This professional role provided me with a meaningful way to translate research into practice and, by putting me into daily contact with federal, state, county, and city law enforcement officials as well as correctional facility staff and numerous social services professionals, also had the unexpected benefit of helping me to develop, confirm, and substantiate the arguments presented in this book. The many roles I played in this project, including confidante, prostitution suspect, and social worker, allowed for careful consideration of the multiple perspectives that surround this complex issue.

My current work as the transitional housing facility's admissions coordinator provides me with first-hand insights on a daily basis into how, for many street-involved women, the criminal justice–social services alliance comprises a maze that requires specialized personal knowledge or access to an advocate with that knowledge. As an alliance professional, albeit an unpaid one, it is difficult for me to dismiss the existing system as broken and without redeeming potential. It would be irresponsible to do so given the sheer number of alliance professionals I know who genuinely care about the women with whom they work, or the number of times incarcerated women struggling with addiction have told me some variation of "going to jail saved my life." The system does in fact have the potential to create what women regard as positive changes in their lives, and my work at the facility allows me to see women realize these possibilities once they have stable housing in a supportive environment, sometimes for the first time in their lives.

Nonetheless, I would be remiss if I failed to note that I have also seen the continuum of coercion alliance professionals tread in their everyday work as they make decisions that can alter women's lives in profoundly negative ways. I have keenly felt the sinking sense of being part of a failed and intensely bureaucratized system when refused entry to visit a potential client in jail because I did not have a particular signature on a certain form, even though the sergeant on duty previously permitted me entry without it. I know women who will spend many years in prison on charges they could have avoided if they had cooperated with police or followed other rules stipulated by alliance professionals, and I have had friends murdered by men who may have deliberately sought them out because of their social invisibility as criminalized, addicted women. I have likewise listened to women tell me that they preferred jail or prison to residence in the transitional housing facility; as one woman put it with respect to the differences between incarceration and therapeutic treatment, "Susan, I know how to do time. This doin' me, it's just too hard."

Spending so many years of my life deeply embedded in this system makes it very difficult to write a book that does justice, in the true sense of the word, to the sometimes contradictory, and always complex, impacts that the criminal justice–social services alliance has on all that it touches. Irrespective of the political perspectives a person may take on these fraught issues, it is important to acknowledge that all the people whose stories are featured here are gifted cultural brokers who had an investment in helping us, as authors, to create a vivid portrait of how they make a living. We do so while working within limitations imposed with respect to authorship, the ethical need to protect confidentiality, and the hope that this book appropriately acknowledges our participants' versatile strategies for being human.

Chapter Overview and Structure of the Book

Chapter 1, "Workin' It, Advocating, and Getting Things Done," argues that women's street involvement comprises a variety of criminalized income-generation and resource-acquisition strategies, including sex trading, that result in part from their cultural and spatial-environmental estrangement from legal work opportunities and social services. Situating the women's everyday hustles within this gendered and racialized sociolegal and economic context considerably complicates centuries-old debates about prostitution by elucidating how, for most street-involved women, sex trading constitutes the most expedient solution to their needs for money, drugs, and shelter. This chapter details how women differ considerably by age, other sources of income, and life experience in terms of how they approach sex trading, just as alliance professionals engage in their work differently depending on their personal and/or professional subscription to particular ideological frameworks.

Chapter 2, "Occupational Risks," argues that the criminal justice–social services alliance pathologizes women's street-based sex trading and illicit drug use as individual responses to traumatic events that result in flawed thought processes that encourage what alliance professionals often characterize as "high-risk behaviors." The criminal justice system's ideological and financial predominance within the alliance necessitates a focus on women's individual decision making as the product of their trauma-related impediments to full social functioning, and actively excludes consideration of the gendered neighborhood socioeconomic relations that inform these decisions. As described in this chapter, the risk discourse that accompanies prevailing alliance understandings of women's street involvement has serious implications for alliance encounters with the women as well as for alliance professionals' own work and personal lives.

Chapter 3, "Harm Reduction and Help Seeking," analyzes discordant parameters of "help" among street-involved women, who face immediate requirements for housing and other basic necessities, and alliance professionals, who aspire to assist women in achieving long-term self-sufficiency. Yet alliance professionals offer few sustainable means to help women find housing and a legal means of self-reliance that would allow them to meet other alliance benchmarks for success. Many alliance professionals, particularly those who work directly with street-involved women, readily acknowledge the limitations of restrictive services-provision conditions that often include lengthy waiting lists, mandatory self-disclosure, and abstaining from illicit drug use. This chapter describes some of the significant conflicts that emerge as alliance professionals struggle with the systemic constraints that position the women's collective struggles as individual problems.

Chapter 4, "Discretion," engages with the nuanced implementation of both personal judgment and the mandates or norms governing particular ways of earning a living. Discretion comprises a dynamic process that fundamentally emerges in interpersonal encounters rather than being completely defined by law, professional procedures, or workplace norms. Accordingly, prevailing cultural forces at work in both professional and street communities constrain individual discretionary authority in interactions between street-involved women and alliance professionals, many of whom regard the law as a blunt instrument ill equipped to address the myriad factors that surround and inform women's sex trading, addictions, and homelessness. This chapter discusses these interactions by focusing on the everyday contexts in which they take place, including policing, criminal and problem-solving courts, and probation or other forms of court-mandated oversight.

The conclusion questions the utility of a criminal justice–social services alliance dominated by punitive paradigms that focus on changing individual women's decision-making processes while punishing them for choices they make in very restricted circumstances. In practice, the vast majority of women who come under the alliance purview leave it by returning to the same socioeconomic conditions that impelled them to work the street in the first place. Street-based sex trading both originates from and takes place within the context of women's complex lives in neighborhoods struggling with multiple oppressions; any attempts to provide women with real and meaningful assistance measures must confront these realities.

1

Workin' It, Advocating, and Getting Things Done

Janeiece can tell it is morning because she can see the red and blue veins that line her eyelids, which she does not want to open. She hears a faraway pounding sound and imagines that she is at the bottom of the ocean listening to sailors hard at work on a ship far above her, long stalks of seaweed elegantly waving around her as sparkling little silver fish weave in and out of her clouds of mermaid hair. Eyes still closed, she realizes that the vibrating sensation on her chest is coming from her phone, which has fallen into the pretty blue lacy bra she stole from her sister. A sharp pain shoots through her skull as she lurches over the thin mattress and vomits on the floor, spitting to get the bitter taste out of her mouth.

As she tries to lift her head back onto the bed, Janeiece opens her eyes even though the bright light feels like a thousand little knives cutting into her. Through her long dark hair she can see the thin green bile spreading liquidly over the floor and realizes that she has not eaten anything for a long time. The floors are faded white linoleum, the little squares dirty and peeling at the edges. She sighs and lays her head back on the bed, realizing that she must be in a motel because floors at the county jails are much cleaner. The pounding continues, and now Janeiece realizes that the sound is in the room with her, accompanied by a woman's angry voice. "I ain't playin', Janeiece," the high-pitched voice says. "You need to open this fuckin' door!" While she does not recognize the voice, she figures that maybe this person can get her a ginger ale from the soda machine downstairs. "Get Enrique to help you," Janeiece responds, adding, in a raspy voice that takes all her energy, "and bring me a ginger ale. Please."

The voice outside says something Janeiece can't make out, followed by footsteps down the cement stairs, a short conversation outside the motel manager's door, and, in what seems like seconds, Enrique's keys opening her door. "Ugh!" Enrique exclaims as he covers his face and turns to leave, recoiling from the smell. "Janeiece, you clean that up or you're not staying here no more, *comprende*?" She is too sick and exhausted to feel embarrassed, or to consider where else she can stay if Enrique will no longer let her live at the motel. Her little sister, Noelle, makes no comment on the scene as she enters the room and begins loading heavy black duffel bags onto the bed, making Janeiece wince each time the bed shakes with their weight. "Look at all this shit!" Noelle gleefully whispers to her sister, her eyes bright with thoughts about how much money she is going to make from selling the stolen clothing and big boxes of condoms inside. Like many women in their family, Noelle is an accomplished shoplifter and well known in the neighborhood for selling nice things at prices residents can afford.

Noelle hastily wipes up her sister's vomit with a nicotine-stained towel from the bathroom and begins to set up shop in Janeiece's room, using her pre-paid cell phone to call potential customers who might be interested in buying the duffel bags' contents, carefully instructing them on how to unobtrusively enter the room. Enrique, like most neighborhood motel owners, forbids groups of people from congregating on the cement walkways outside his motel's rooms because police patrol officers will quickly arrive to ascertain the nature of the often-illegal activities transpiring inside. Noelle tells her prospective customers to wait in the nearby 7–Eleven parking lot if they see anyone outside her room, and then to approach the room using the stairs opposite Enrique's office. Although Noelle gave Enrique oral sex in his office that morning in exchange for letting her stay in Janeiece's room until five o'clock, she still has to be careful while selling the bags' contents as she cannot be certain that his improved mood will make him ignore people who arrive to buy her stolen goods.

Janeiece knows that the room is going to be busy for the rest of the day as Noelle bargains with neighborhood residents over prices, which she likes to keep at about twenty dollars per item. When the bags' contents are gone, Noelle will probably use the room to turn a few tricks before deciding what to do once five o'clock comes and she has made about five hundred dollars. Janeiece stumbles down the stairs and gets a ginger ale from the soda machine, sitting in its shadow on the pavement as she surveys the midmorning street scene. She decides that she can be selective today about which cars to get into since Noelle owes her for using the motel room and she worries that she may have outstanding warrants that will mean a lengthy jail sentence if she unwittingly gets into an undercover officer's car. Rinsing the lingering bile taste out of her mouth with the remaining ginger ale, Janeiece adjusts her cutoff jeans, pulls her messy hair into a ponytail, and begins a slow walk down the street.

Ten minutes pass before a man, who Janeiece guesses is from Mexico or a neighboring Central American country, pulls up beside her, making eye contact but leaving the engine running. She rapidly assesses his older pickup truck and limited fluency in English, and, after deciding that he is probably not an undercover officer, tells him to pull off the main street into a more secluded area. Janeiece, like many women who work in her neighborhood, selects her clients using ethno-racial stereotypes that, while problematic, help her to make quick decisions about how the transactional sexual encounter might proceed. As she walks toward the truck parked on a secluded side street, she speculates that this man may be undocumented and carrying a large amount of cash in his pockets rather than keeping it in the bank. Janeiece gets in the truck prepared to agree to forty dollars for vaginal sex in the hope that she can search his pockets for the cash while he is otherwise occupied. He smiles warmly at her when she tells him this information, which the electronic body transmitting device he is wearing under his shirt instantly relays to the police car waiting nearby. As a uniformed officer approaches the truck to arrest her, Janeiece opens the door to vomit again and wonders if Noelle will use some of the money she made in the motel room to post bond.

What Is (Street-Based Sex) Work? Definitions and Practices

The numerous criminalized activities Janeiece and other street-involved women undertake to meet their immediate needs for money and drugs indisputably involve exploiting others through theft, deception, and other activities that the women themselves regard as unsavory. Yet these activities are also the result of their cultural and spatial-environmental estrangement, as women with sometimes-extensive criminal records and severe drug addictions, from social services and legal work opportunities.[1] Their involvement in criminalized and stigmatized sex trading and illicit drug use isolates them in what anthropologist João Biehl, writing about Brazil, terms "zones of abandonment," ghettoized urban areas populated by those who are addicted, mentally ill, homeless, or otherwise socially excluded (Biehl, 2013). Spending the vast majority of their time in a neighborhood dominated by the illicit drug and sexual economies, pawn shops, payday loan providers, liquor stores, fast food chains, and used car lots, street-involved women inhabit a totalizing environment characterized by its residents' highly visible struggles with precarious housing, addictions, and negative police encounters.

Most neighborhood residents are African American, Latina/o, or poor and White like Janeiece and Noelle, and all regularly experience the sensory elements of neighborhood life: the wail of police and ambulance sirens and subsequent desertion of the streets at regular intervals, intoxicated residents who disrupt traffic as they wander blissfully about, and people pushing shopping carts containing all their worldly possessions. Poverty renders nearly all of the women eligible for healthcare through Medicaid, groceries via the Supplemental Nutrition Assistance Program ("food stamps"), and federally subsidized housing, as well as various other services. Many women either have participated in these programs in the past or hope to do so in the future, and all are aware of their existence.

Yet addiction, homelessness, and lack of transportation to social services providers' offices all severely compromise most women's abilities to seek out or maintain these benefits as part of what sociologist Beth Richie describes as the "impact of competing demands" (2001, p. 380). Restrictive requirements, such as the need to meet with case workers, undergo drug testing, as well as the exclusion of those with particular felony convictions from subsidized housing, all give women pause for thought before they seek out services. Many women consequently view such services as either untenable due to restrictive provision conditions, or insufficient to meet the often-high costs of their addictions, which can require several hundred dollars per day. Street-involved women speak to their prevailing understandings of such services in frequently describing Medicaid, food stamps, and related services as being "on" or "off"—meaning accessible or not—painting a vivid discursive portrait of a resource tap either flowing or completely empty depending on factors that appear (and sometimes are) quite arbitrary.

Trading sex for money, robbing clients and others, and selling marketable items such as prescription or illicit drugs, food stamps, and shoplifted clothing or electronics all constitute normalized forms of income generation in the neighborhood where the women live and work. The unpredictable and sporadic nature of these income-generation strategies necessitates that women actively search for other ways to obtain shelter, drugs, food, and other basic needs. Most often they do so in an ad hoc manner that mobilizes immediate resources that unexpectedly become available, such as a client willing to offer a ride across town or pay for food, drugs, or a night in a motel, a peer who offers a place to sleep or turn tricks, or a relative willing to make a cash loan. Women must remain constantly vigilant for such opportunities in ways that consume the vast majority of their time and energy, leaving little room for other pursuits.

None of the women I spent time with classified any of their income-generation activities as "work" despite the all-consuming nature of their relentless search for money. As Ms. Ella, an African American street-involved woman in her late fifties, put it after I made the mistake of using the term "sex work" to describe what she and the women generally refer to as "hustling," "Girl, we out here survivin', this ain't no damn job. As a matter of fact, I feel sorry for you if you think it is." Ms. Ella subsequently advised me that I needed to "get to know the Lord" to correct what she regarded as my skewed moral compass. As with Ms. Ella, all street-involved women I spoke with embraced broader U.S. cultural norms that define "work" as labor performed legally in exchange for money. This is particularly interesting given that characteristics inherent to hustling resemble many aspects of the service sector occupations most readily available to women who stop using illicit drugs and obtain stable housing. The vast majority of service sector work, especially in its most feminized forms of cleaning, preparing or serving food, and caregiving, features erratic hours that change with weekly schedules. Cast as "part-time" employees undeserving of healthcare or other benefits, service sector workers depend on supervisors' arbitrary goodwill to receive preferred work schedules and small pay increases.

Hustling, likewise, requires the ability to drop other responsibilities at a moment's notice to pursue an opportunity for money, drugs, a ride, or a place to stay, some of which emerge from another person's arbitrary kindness or goodwill. Yet hustling also differs from service sector work, and in this respect is far more desirable for street-involved women, because despite requiring far longer hours under conditions much more likely to result in arrest or assault, hustling can coexist with addiction in ways that service sector jobs cannot. Women who leave the life often continue to face significant barriers to finding legal employment due to criminal records and limited or sporadic work histories. Leelee, who finally abandoned her efforts to find full-time legal work five years after leaving the street, often wistfully commented on how engaging in what she termed "the work" of addiction recovery had not garnered her the opportunity to earn a living wage.

One evening as we strolled up and down East Colfax Avenue, watching women go about their hustles, Leelee observed, "Man, look at these women out here rippin' and runnin', tryin'a get their next lick. Bein' homeless, bein' a addict—it's a full-time job. I wish I had me a full-time job." The very constraining forces that compelled Leelee to work the streets continued to restrict her choices long after she opted to change her life, which caused her to constantly question her decision to end her street involvement despite praise from alliance professionals who touted her as a success story because she had found stable subsidized housing and received monthly state benefit checks as a result of her bipolar disorder diagnosis.

Simply put, sex trading and hustling more generally *are* the most readily available ways of making ends meet for many poor women struggling with addiction in neighborhoods isolated and alienated from opportunities for legal employment. Yet transactional sexual exchanges are just one aspect of the women's complex lives and hustles, albeit one that receives a particularly harsh spotlight from alliance professionals as well as popular culture more generally. The fact that the women publicly enact these struggles in highly policed neighborhoods makes them the target of scrutiny by the alliance and researchers alike. Many social scientists and public health researchers describe street-involved women as "survival sex workers" because their sex trading is a means to negotiate their everyday struggles with homelessness, addiction, and other mental health problems, as well as poverty more generally.[2]

We remained highly cognizant of this spotlight's bright glare as we conceived, carried out, and analyzed the results of this project. People whose lives involve prostitution, illicit drug use, incarceration, or homelessness as ordinary features rarely have the opportunity to decide for themselves how academic work, popular culture, or other fields will represent them. U.S. entertainment media is replete with caricatured representations of individuals involved in these activities or circumstances. The fact that popular cultural depictions of incarceration, street prostitution, illicit drug use, and policing generate billions of dollars for the entertainment industry gives pause for thought to those of us who work with people battered by these social conditions. Their embeddedness in a "hyper-represented field" (Wilson, 2004) forces us to consider what it means, both politically and morally, to work with and write about women who fit all of these categories and belong to historically oppressed ethno-racial and class groups.

Street-involved women face a different set of gendered and racialized vulnerabilities than their male peers struggling with addiction and homelessness: as women, they have an increased likelihood of engaging in transactional sex, which is more lucrative than other criminalized income-generation strategies, such as panhandling, readily available to them. Women and men both play roles in the illicit drug economy that suffuses street prostitution, yet, as in almost all other spheres of the U.S. economy, women routinely have less access to more lucrative activities and experience sexual and intimate partner violence more often than men.[3] Yet men's greater participation in criminalized activities that involve violence or larger-scale illicit drug sales means that many men who play important roles in the women's lives consequently face higher rates of arrest for felony offenses and generally receive longer sentences, often in prison rather than jail. Women and men alike live and make their money within gendered, classed, and racialized socioeconomic constraints framed, and sometimes violently enforced, by deeply entrenched inequalities.

These inequalities are especially evident with respect to the uncertain position street-involved women occupy in ongoing sex industry polemics among abolitionists, sex workers' rights advocates, and researchers who attempt to present full and complex portraits of their lives. The women's enmeshment in the criminal justice system, refusal to identify their sex trading activities as work, and historic race and class oppression all confound efforts to neatly characterize their experiences within the narrow parameters of existing debates, which tend to pivot on varying definitions of "choice." This is further compounded by the reality that street-involved women have little, if any, ability to control representations of themselves produced by individuals or groups with an interest in making a particular political point. Accurately representing the complexities of street-involved women's daily lives and their efforts to negotiate them presents numerous challenges to core values held by abolitionists, sex workers' rights advocates, and researchers.

Contemporary activists who support prostitution's criminalization often argue that violence, addiction, and other forms of abuse are conditions inherent to the exchange of sex for money. Many such activists, whose perspectives enjoy widespread political support, reference the nineteenth-century movement against the transatlantic traffic in enslaved persons from Africa by calling themselves "abolitionists" who wish to end "modern-day slavery" (U.S. Department of State, 2006). The explicit connection self-identified abolitionists draw between slavery and prostitution is typically devoid of any meaningful discussion about the role that racism plays in pushing African American women into the most highly policed and violent sex industry venues. Hence these self-identified abolitionists support criminalization despite the consistency with which the criminal justice system consequently forces street-involved African American women into the shackles of the criminal justice system for prostitution-related offenses at rates that surpass those of their White peers relative to population size (U.S. Department of Justice, 2012, p. 2).

In contrast to abolitionists, sex workers' rights advocates support prostitution's decriminalization or legalization on the grounds that doing so recognizes the provision of transactional sexual services as work. While street-involved women would certainly benefit from decreased rates of arrest, incarceration, and other forms of correctional control, this position does little to address the criminalization of addiction and disproportionate exercise of the alliance's bureaucratic power and control in disadvantaged neighborhoods. Sex trading is a means to an end for women who solicit clients on the street, not a vocation that fits neatly within the language of choice. Street-involved women have not played a significant role in U.S. sex workers' rights movements because of the everyday struggles they face as well as the reality that their lives are replete with the addiction, violence, and other forms of abuse that sex workers' rights activists seek to distance themselves from in positioning transactional sex as legitimate labor.

Researchers who attempt to balance these opposing views through particular types of engagement with street-involved women face challenges with respect to the consequences of foregrounding a particular aspect of women's lives, which risks casting a rather murky shadow over other aspects that individual women may regard as far more important. Focusing on sex trading, illicit drug use, incarceration, homelessness, or any of the other issues that significantly impact the women also risks reifying stereotypes about African American women, Latinas, and poor White women as hypersexualized or somehow uniquely afflicted by addiction, mental illness, or other social pathologies. Yet this work is absolutely essential because of the way in which the criminal justice system disproportionately targets women from these groups, in conjunction with the sex industry's replication of racist imagery and labor practices prevalent in other spheres of U.S. social life.[4]

The long-term immersion required by ethnography helped us to overcome some of these challenges by focusing on the minutiae of street-involved women's lives. Interacting with large numbers of women over an extended period of time revealed that street-based sex trading is not a static or monolithic category. Even within the narrow geographic scope of a single urban neighborhood, women who engage in it differ considerably by age, experience, characterizations of their activities, and other important factors. Most published research conducted with women involved in street prostitution presents their perspectives in a rather unitary voice, and we have been guilty of this offense in our own article-length writings.[5] We attempt to demonstrate key differences between women's particular orientations as a means to highlight street prostitution's place within their broader repertoire of income-generating activities. Yet these distinct orientations also encourage women, in conjunction with extreme socioeconomic constraints, policing, and stigma, to disassociate themselves from their street-involved peers who also trade sex; as thirty-year old Brandy clearly and succinctly explained to me, "There ain't no *we* out here."

Ain't No "We" Out Here: Different Ways of Workin' It

The ways in which women organize and engage in sex trading vary considerably according to their age, relationship status, drug use, and numerous other factors unique to each individual woman. Yet because street-involved women do not consistently use a shared set of clearly identifiable terms to talk about themselves and each other, we had to think carefully about how to describe the different ways in which women characterize their (and other women's) experiences with transactional sex. Detailed reviews of ethnographic field notes, interview transcripts, and other material collected as part of this project allowed us to elucidate six distinct types of sex trading among the women. The majority are emic terms that the women use to distinguish themselves from other street-involved women or, in the case of *bonded* and *intergenerational* women, to characterize situations and relationships to others that the women regularly discuss.

Women generally use the terms articulated here to describe particular behaviors or ways of being, as in "I'm not a *frequent flyer* at Denver County Jail like some of these other ladies," or "Macey's one a them *old school cougars* who been out here for a minute." Women also use these terms, or variations on them, to describe the circumstances that compel them to exchange sex for money or drugs. For instance, a *caretaker* with exclusive or significant financial responsibilities for small children or other loved ones might explain how she exchanges sex for money at the end of the month when she has no remaining food stamp benefits. Our use of these six descriptive categories is intended as a respectful decision to use emic language or concepts to describe a complex social world that requires a broad repertoire of knowledge and skills that women acquire, and put into practice, in very different ways.

Throughout the book, we will refer to women using these descriptive categories along with a pseudonym of their choice as an attempt to help the reader contextualize a particular interview excerpt or ethnographic anecdote within each of the women's complex life circumstances. Most importantly, however, delineating these different orientations to street-based sex trading underscores the unique and often rather individualized strategies the women devise in the context of difficult life circumstances. The contextualization of women's perspectives within their particular orientation to sex trading is intended to highlight the creativity that suffuses the women's strategies, rather than reinforcing well-entrenched stereotypes about street prostitution as the last resort of the unskilled and destitute.

This project involved hundreds of unique individual women with diverse experiences, which both dramatically enriched the findings presented here and made it difficult to generalize about their personal backgrounds, family histories, specific circumstances, and dreams. Introducing the women whose voices and narratives appear repeatedly, along with a description of their approach to sex trading, helps to situate their perspectives within the context in which I knew them throughout the research. Old school cougars, intergenerationals, caregivers, bonded women, frequent flyers, and women who work under the radar are all equally represented in accounts that inform subsequent chapters.

Old school cougars are women in their forties and fifties with more than ten years of street experience. Women who fit this descriptive category are predominantly African American, independently solicit clients without sharing their profits, and often comment negatively on what they regard as younger women's lack of street acumen. These women were an incredible resource throughout this project because of their historical knowledge regarding the street scene, as well as their abilities to critically reflect on how they developed their respective income-generation strategies over the years in response to particular life circumstances. Some old school cougars also have parents, children, or other family members who are involved in neighborhood sex trading, while others speak proudly about adult children who hold legal jobs and have attended college or trade school.

Macey, Shirley, Wanda, Ms. Ella, and Pearlie are all African American old school cougars who, like their White colleague Deb, have decades of street experience. All of these women are neighborhood personalities well known to both other street-involved figures and police, and during our motel room interviews as well as participant observation, I often saw inexperienced younger women seek them out for advice and assistance. Despite their collective wisdom, their relatively advanced age, combined with years of sex trading and illicit drug use, has taken an indisputable toll on their bodies. Pearlie, who is missing a leg from a hit-and-run accident that hospitalized her for several months and is legally blind, proudly told me that her lack of vision has not diminished her ability to avoid arrest, as evidenced when she opened a police car door under the mistaken impression that the driver, a young officer she has known for several years, was a prospective client. "Shit," she laughed as she recounted the events that followed. "I heard 'Pearlie, I'm the damn po-lice, get your blind ass home!' and I apologized up and down; see, that boy is my son's age, he ain't about to take me in." While Pearlie prides herself on avoiding arrest due to her age and perhaps her disabilities, other old school cougars, like Shirley and Ms. Ella, continue to rely on arrest-avoidance strategies derived from their years of street experience.

Women in the distinct *intergenerational* descriptive category have mothers, aunts, or other older female relatives who have engaged in street-based sex trading, or whose daughters or younger female relatives have also become involved in such exchanges. Some intergenerational women feel conflicted about their own or their younger family members' involvements in prostitution while others regard it as an economically shrewd use of female sexuality. As Kyra, an intergenerational, recalled her mother saying, "You're givin' it away for free anyway, might as well get somethin' for it." Women who regard themselves as the first in their family to engage in transactional sex often have strong opinions about intergenerational women, especially those who recruit or encourage younger female family members into the life. Brandy, for instance, felt very hurt when Jacie commented on the street debut of Brandy's daughter Kelliann by saying very loudly, in front of other women standing near a neighborhood motel, "Well, well, looks like this is the family business now."

African American women Kyra, Keanna, and Traci, as well as their White peers Brandy and her daughter Kelliann, and Noelle and her sister Janeiece, are all intergenerationals. Socialized in at least some respects into the cultural norms of street prostitution from a young age, these women tend to resemble old school cougars, irrespective of their age, in their knowledge about how to carry out various street hustles while avoiding arrest. Keanna, for instance, takes great pride in her ability to earn relatively large amounts of money by, as she puts it, "only trickin' with White guys from the suburbs who smoke crack," while Brandy occasionally profits from other, often younger, women's sexual labor by mentoring them into the trade. Yet this socialization process also isolates women and accordingly discourages them from leaving prostitution to pursue other options; as Traci put it as I sat with her in a Denver-area county jail where she was serving a year-long sentence, "This is all I know; I have no idea how to live a different kind of life."

Caregivers are women with significant economic responsibilities for others, including young children, extended family members, or intimate partners who are either unemployable as a result of criminal convictions (particularly felony offenses) or do not wish to work. These women all provide at least part of the money they earn to stably housed family members who are caring for children to whom the women have given birth. Other women do not have financial responsibilities for small children but support intimate partners who do not have an income. Sometimes these relationships appear exploitative to the women themselves, as well as their street-involved peers, because they conjure the racialized specter of the "pimp" due to gendered social norms that heavily stigmatize men who do not earn an income, irrespective of constraints on their ability to do so.

Caregivers Marie, NeNe, and Mary are African American, Dion and Eileen are White, Elena is Latina, and all share significant financial and familial responsibilities for other people. NeNe's intimate partner spent his entire adult life in state prison and cannot find legal work of any kind, while Eileen is involved with a disabled and much older man who is unable to work. Mary, Dion, and Elena all have children under the age of five, who, depending on the women's housing situation and other factors, shuffle between living with them, with relatives, or in foster care. None of these women can participate in residential addictions-treatment or other therapeutic programs because doing so would force them to terminate or otherwise restrict these relationships that constitute significant aspects of their lives and conceptions of themselves.

Bonded women are affiliated with gang members, or men who enjoy positions of prominence in the neighborhood drug economy, who collect part or all of the money they earn in transactional sexual encounters. These women tend to be young, generally ranging in age from their late teens to early twenties, and predominantly Latina and African American, although some are White. These women trade sex in highly controlled, coercive settings in which they often share complex loyalty ties with the individuals who direct their transactional sexual activities. Due to their involvement with men who play organizing roles in the illicit drug and sexual economies, bonded women are also likely to have experiences with more lucrative indoor sex-industry venues. Bonded women may leave these relationships as they age, seek increased economic and social independence, and develop increased familiarity with sex trading as an income-generation strategy.

Ximena, Marlee, Vanessa, and Florencia are Latina bonded women affiliated with male-dominated gangs that profit from their involvement in prostitution, as are African American women K'neisha, Ashanti, and Kenya, as well as Sam, who is White. All of these women are in their late teens or early twenties and feel a profound sense of loyalty to the men who organize, and profit from, their transactional sexual encounters. Some of these women, like K'neisha, Ximena, Florencia, and Kenya, are affiliated with street gang members engaged in drug trafficking and other criminalized activities, and their gendered role as women necessitates their involvement in prostitution. Some bonded women, like Vanessa, Marlee, Ashanti, and Sam, provide all or part of their earnings to just one man and regard their dealings with him as something between an intimate relationship and a business partnership.

Frequent flyers struggle with severe addictions that push them to trade sex more publicly, more often, and with greater numbers of clients than other neighborhood women. Often characterized as "out of control" or "clock-blockin'" due to the frequency with which they steal other women's clients by agreeing to very low prices for sexual acts (thereby wasting other women's time), these women find themselves isolated on the street in ways that compound the difficulties they face in accessing various forms of support. Police patrol officers regularly recognize frequent flyers by sight because they have been arrested and incarcerated so many times. As well-known figures both on the street and in the criminal justice system, frequent flyers often have lengthy arrest and conviction records that may include extensive time served in jail or, less frequently, prison.

Annette, Gianna, Layla, and Krystal, who are White, Latinas Mariah and Magdalena, and African American Joyce are all frequent flyers who have little support from family members, friends, or the street-involved people they interact with on a daily basis. A police patrol officer who stops one of them on the street to check if she has outstanding warrants may also consult with the NCIC (National Crime Information Center), which contains a complete list of all individuals' federal, state, county, and city criminal charges and convictions. In Denver, this information will also include a woman's HIV-positive status if she has previous prostitution arrests, and this health status alone is enough, when combined with an additional prostitution-related arrest and conviction, to result in a felony conviction and subsequent prison sentence.

"You gotta be a jack of all trades to make it out here," said Marisol, who is Latina and, like her peers working *under the radar*, uses street-based sex trading as an income-generation strategy that supplements her earnings from shoplifting, small-scale drug dealing, selling food stamps, and other criminalized activities, few if any of which involve violence. Such women are often coupled with an intimate partner who also struggles with addiction, and together they are always on the lookout for money-making opportunities, including sex trading. These women, despite their sometimes long-term engagement in transactional sex, rarely have a history of arrest or criminal justice system involvement, and often confine their sex-trading activities to a few neighborhood clients, some of whom pay them by providing illicit drugs. Women working under the radar often manage their illicit drug use in such a way that they are able to maintain stable housing and receive state or federal benefits to supplement their income, which, in turn, reduces their likelihood of arrest and other negative encounters because they are more able to effectively screen clients than women who are homeless and struggling with severe addictions.

"I have a lot of men I rely on out here, because it's tough bein' a woman," said Native American Kay, who grew up on a reservation in the Dakotas and, like many women working under the radar, couched her descriptions of transactional sexual encounters within heteronormative exchange practices that enjoy widespread cultural acceptance. Other women working under the radar, such as Carla, who is Latina, and Corinne, Lexi, and Julie, who are White, likewise described sex trading as something they do when money is tight. Lexi and Julie, for instance, both support their addictions via small-scale illicit drug sales and only turn tricks when this money proves insufficient. Carla, Kenya, and Corinne all described prostitution as a "last resort" they turn to when in need of immediate funds for shelter, drugs, food, or other basic needs.

Despite significant differences in their living situations, ways of engaging in illicit drug use and sex trading, and relationships with others, all street-involved women face the alliance's scrutiny. Alliance professionals draw on their own personal characteristics, values, and available resources, just as street-involved women do, in the course of their everyday work activities. Yet as they do so, they also subscribe to particular socio-ideological models and professional orientations that combine to dramatically impact their interactions with street-involved women.

Advocating and Getting Things Done: Alliance Professionals' Approaches to Work

Alliance professionals work in the context of five dominant socio-ideological models for addressing street-based prostitution as a social issue: state, quasi-state, faith-based, grassroots human rights organizing, and harm reduction. Each model features an approach derived from a particular dominant narrative or textual reference that advocates a unique set of responses to women's street involvement. These five dominant socio-ideological models are prevalent in all U.S. cities but feature very different levels of financial support and social endorsement dependent on the prevailing political and cultural climate. Global and national ideologies also inform these frameworks and their implementation, most significantly through "End Demand" initiatives first developed in Sweden (and often referred to internationally as the Nordic Model), which promote the arrest and incarceration of men who purchase sex, but not the women who sell or trade it.

The alliance ethos dominates in state and quasi-state models, which regard prostitution and illicit drug use as inherently harmful, such that women engaged in these behaviors require sociolegal intervention and subsequent correctional monitoring. The state and quasi-state models rely primarily on the Constitution and municipal, state, and federal legislation as textual frames of reference within a dominant narrative that emphasizes the importance of the rule of law. Public servants such as police and corrections officers, public defenders, judges, and court staff, as well as attorneys in private practice and others tasked with the law's interpretation and implementation, must adhere to the state model of arrest, incarceration, or court-monitored therapeutic treatment. The state model views women engaged in illegal prostitution and drug use as in violation of the law and hence unworthy of offering input on or consenting to criminal justice system intervention.

Federal or state grant recipients, especially those that work with the criminal justice system, follow the quasi-state model because their funding obligates them to terms that reflect the state-endorsed alliance ethos. Hence social workers and other therapeutic staff at addictions-treatment groups in correctional facilities, diversion courts, and transitional housing programs that receive federal or state funding must support arrest, incarceration, and court monitoring as appropriate and effective responses to women's street involvement. In so doing, staff must agree to report women's legal or programmatic violations to probation, parole, or other correctional entities that may use this information to justify further punitive sanctions against women. The quasi-state model provides street-involved women with some opportunity to consent to an intervention, such as court-monitored drug treatment or other forms of alternative sentencing, but the reality that incarceration is often women's only other choice considerably constrains the decision-making processes that inform such selections.

Alliance professionals beholden to state and quasi-state models often face the difficult task of attempting to locate safe temporary housing for women who have been apprehended but not charged in criminal cases, or who are being released from correctional facilities. In the former instance, the most common scenario involves women who agree to testify in state or federal court against more powerful street-involved figures, including men alleged to have forced them into prostitution. State and quasi-state models support incarceration as an appropriate response to law breaking but offer no assistance to women in finding long-term housing, legal work, or other basic necessities. Consequently, after being incarcerated, street-involved women often return to the very conditions that they left on arrest, and their post-arrest loss of belongings, disrupted social ties, and conviction-related stigma all virtually guarantee their continued involvement in criminalized activities, often on an intensified scale.

For instance, women released from the Denver Women's Correctional Facility, one of two Colorado women's prisons, receive a voucher valid for a week's stay in an East Colfax Avenue motel. While these motels certainly offer lower prices and a willingness to accept women directly from prison, they also feature high levels of illicit drug and prostitution activity. Frequent flyer Gianna sarcastically described this practice by noting, "Now isn't that just a recipe for success? I have been so consistently impressed by how DOC [Department of Corrections] works so hard to free us women from a life of crime." Women leaving jail have often served shorter sentences yet face many of the same obstacles; indeed, Leelee and several other women first engaged in street-based sex trading when, following their release from jail, they found themselves homeless and destitute.

State and quasi-state models' systemic failure to address the socio-economic factors that inform women's street involvement effectively outsources these necessary services on an ad hoc basis to nonprofit organizations. These organizations are often faith-based and employ a dominant narrative, guided by the Bible or other religious texts, that mandates service to the poor and proselytization. Faith-based groups range dramatically in size and orientation, from transitional housing facilities that provide shelter to small numbers of women leaving prostitution to large-scale and corporate board-governed organizations like the Salvation Army. Yet faith-based groups that provide direct services to street-involved women are often small-scale, and their existence is dependent on the goodwill of church donors and volunteers.[6]

Street-involved women consent to participation in the faith-based model, although some organizations often agree to receive criminal justice system referrals by cooperating with probation requirements, such as reporting women's violations of program rules or failure to pass mandatory random drug screenings. This is significant because, despite the glaring lack of well-funded social services for street-involved women, the powers wielded by the criminal justice system strongly enhance the possibility that a woman will remain in a program for an extended period of time given that (sometimes long-term) incarceration is her only alternative. For many small-scale nonprofits operating on the faith-based model, client retention is an important and necessary measure of program success, irrespective of the reasons why the women stay in the program. The result can render street-involved women's ability to consent to participation in such programs somewhat murky, particularly in instances where criminal justice system referrals of women who wish to avoid incarceration become the main means of retaining clients.

Grassroots human rights organizing and harm-reduction models generally enjoy far less support, funding, and widespread public approval in the United States in comparison with state, quasi-state, and faith-based models. The criminal justice system's overwhelming dominance in prevailing approaches to illicit drug use, prostitution, and homelessness leaves little room for human-rights and harm-reduction models that regard these as social issues that require compassionate responses. Espousing either a grassroots human-rights-organizing or harm-reduction model can exclude organizations from state or federal funding,[7] and both consequently depend on volunteer activist organizers and outreach workers directly engaging with people most affected by illicit drug use and sex trading in ways that may clash with the state model.

The grassroots human-rights-organizing model employs a dominant narrative that draws on social justice movements' efforts to actively involve individuals who disproportionately suffer the consequences of policing, criminalization, mass incarceration, and stigma in efforts to combat these issues. Prostitution is an ancillary issue in these organizing efforts, which are nonetheless more generally relevant to the experiences of street-involved women than sex workers' rights movements' predominant focus on decriminalizing and destigmatizing sexual labor. Both grassroots human-rights-organizing and harm-reduction models frequently cite recommendations from international bodies, such as the United Nations, the World Health Organization, and Amnesty International, that support decriminalizing both addiction and prostitution. In the United States these international bodies' recommendations contradict prevailing support for continued criminalization and policing of those involved in prostitution and illicit drug use.

The harm-reduction model relies on the core "do no harm" principles of the Hippocratic Oath while prioritizing the health and safety of individuals who do not wish to cease their involvement in illicit drug use, sex trading, or other stigmatized behaviors. Harm reduction emphasizes the need for services providers to work with street-involved women in developing measures and practices that can minimize the women's likelihood of facing violence, contracting sexually transmitted infections, overdosing, and experiencing other negative outcomes. This model's commitment to "meeting people where they are at" often results in harm-reduction advocates skirting the edges of the law in their efforts to protect individuals' health and safety through the provision of sterile syringes or crack pipes, condoms, and the opioid antagonist Naloxone, which reverses the effects of an overdose of heroin, morphine, or prescription opioids.

All five models produce particular types of conventional wisdom about women's street involvement that inform the experiences of individual street-involved women and alliance professionals as they go about their regular income-generation activities. Although state and quasi-state models dominate within the alliance and in U.S. society more generally, individual alliance professionals' personal beliefs may encourage them, in particular contexts and with specific women, to exercise discretionary authority in employing elements of each model. Physical sites where the alliance ethos predominates, such as courtrooms, court-monitored transitional-housing or addictions-treatment programs, correctional facilities, or street encounters in which police officers exercise disproportionate authority, ultimately rely on individual alliance professionals' discretion in terms of the best way to translate that ethos into practice.

Alliance professionals are individual people with their own personal struggles, some of which stem from the enormous stress of a job that requires them to make rapid (and sometimes regretted) decisions in adrenaline-charged crisis contexts that actively discourage self-care. A vice officer participating in a months-long undercover investigation into an international drug trafficking cartel, for instance, is constantly aware that he may face imminent execution on exposure of his true identity. A social worker following orders to take minor children from a motel room where addiction and related mental health problems impair their mother's decision making likewise faces the threat of violence as well as the wrenching emotions inherent in removing children from a familiar environment.

While both the officer and the social worker may genuinely believe that their jobs provide a necessary service to society, carrying out this work takes a heavy toll on their health, emotional state, and loved ones. The masculinized culture most criminal justice professionals work within values stoicism and control rather than the display of emotion, which may discourage an officer from seeking out available support services. A social services provider may likewise prioritize caring for others, sometimes to the extent of striving to assist clients in receiving the benefits those providers working at nonprofits often do not receive, such as health insurance and a living wage. It is perhaps unsurprising that these stressful work conditions encourage alliance professionals to develop different ways of working based on the models available to them within the parameters of their particular jobs and their personal characteristics, values, and available resources.

As with our descriptive categories that articulate street-involved women's different approaches to sex trading, review of interview transcripts, ethnographic field notes, and other materials elucidated the four distinct working styles generally adopted by alliance professionals. These distinctions in alliance professionals' approaches to their work also became clear through long-term involvement in their professional lives, which allowed insight into their personal backgrounds, histories, and goals. Individual alliance professionals work in specialized occupations that they may regard as a calling they feel honored to undertake, a sacrifice they make to earn a living, or, more commonly, something in between, and street-involved women frequently make observations about the sometimes dramatic impact that such orientations have on their interactions with these professionals. Likewise, participant observation on the street or in more obviously alliance-dominated settings such as courtrooms and correctional facilities confirmed the nuanced impact these orientations have on encounters between the alliance and street-involved women.

Spending more than a year in daily contact with other alliance professionals as the transitional housing facility's admissions coordinator played a critical role in allowing me to confirm the validity of the four primary alliance types: idealists, enforcers, transgressors, and bureaucrats. Each of these general approaches to work can change throughout an individual's career, and alliance professionals may shift between these different orientations depending on the context, the personalities involved, and the state of their personal lives. A police patrol officer whose wife tells him immediately before he leaves for the night shift that she plans to file for divorce if he refuses to seek treatment for alcoholism may be more aggressive in encounters with those he arrests that night even though he normally regards his work as a job with good healthcare and pension benefits. A young, idealist public defender or social services provider who stays late in the evening working tirelessly as an advocate despite considerable health, emotional, and interpersonal costs, only to

have her client fail to appear in court may likewise feel abused and manipulated in ways that impact her encounters the next day.

Idealists tend to be young and genuinely believe in their work's potential to have what they regard as positive impacts on people's lives, although this belief, like all four orientations, takes slightly different forms
specific to criminal justice professionals and social services providers
within the alliance. Idealist social services providers often work for nonprofit entities that provide direct assistance to street-involved women
and regard their services-provision activities as a moral calling and
meaningful manifestation of their personal ideological, political, or religious orientation. Idealist criminal justice professionals believe that they
play an essential role as advocates who protect from harm individuals,
neighborhoods, and the society of which they are a part. They have faith
that their efforts reinforce, or help to ensure, the constitutional principle
that all individuals should enjoy fair and equal treatment under the law.

Some alliance professionals can maintain an idealist orientation
throughout their careers, whereas others later shift orientations due to
exhaustion, disillusionment, or both. Alan, a White idealist detective,
spent decades meeting with street-involved women who provided evidence in criminal cases he investigated, and although he was frustrated
by his sometimes adversarial encounters with social services providers, he believed strongly in what he regarded as his critical community
role in potentially changing women's lives. César, a Latino prostitution
diversion court counselor, abruptly quit his job, which he previously
described to me as "a calling from God" and changed professions following the murder of a woman with whom he had worked for many
years. As with all professional orientations, personality combines with
work-related events to determine the trajectory an individual will take
with respect to his or her job.

Enforcers likewise strongly support the rule of law and the powers of
the Constitution but differ from idealists because they position arrest
and correctional control as the best responses to illegal drug use and
prostitution. Criminal justice professionals with an enforcer orientation take pride in their strict interpretation and implementation of the
law because they believe that existing correctional mechanisms are the
only means by which some street-involved women will stop engaging
in criminalized activities. Social services providers also adopt an en-

forcer orientation in reporting to probation or parole when clients do not adhere to addictions treatment paradigms that demand women take accountability for their actions. While services providers cannot invoke the law as readily as criminal justice professionals can, those with enforcer orientations tend to work for organizations that closely cooperate with law enforcement because they regard the system's coercive powers as the only effective means by which to mandate sobriety among women who do not wish to stop using illicit drugs.

Enforcers generally regard their work as serving an essential function by maintaining order, both in society and in street-involved women's lives. Steve, a White detective, echoed many enforcers in emphasizing that the powers of the law do not go far enough and, in some instances, he felt that legal and procedural practices inhibit or prevent him from working effectively. Janine, a Latina probation officer with a caseload devoted exclusively to women with prostitution charges and convictions, spoke at length about women's needs to cooperate with law enforcement for their own good, including by providing evidence against their intimate partners or others with whom they regularly interacted. This orientation requires a strong belief in a human need for regulatory oversight and order, in sharp contrast to other orientations that allow for greater flexibility in understanding street-involved women's needs.

Transgressors enjoy the seditious elements of cultural familiarity with, and peripheral involvement in, activities that law and popular culture alike position as dangerous and taboo. Such individuals often envision themselves as possessing special gifts, skills, or other abilities that exempt them from the rules and generally accepted practices of their respective professions. As insider-outsiders knowledgeable about street and alliance norms, transgressors believe that doing their job effectively requires them to push legal and procedural boundaries. Transgressors are more likely to be found in jobs that involve cultural brokering between street-involved women and alliance professionals who otherwise might never interact. Undercover officers and services providers who regularly conduct street outreach are particularly likely to adopt transgressor orientations because their jobs require implementing extensive cultural knowledge about members of both groups.

Transgressors must maintain a fine balance between procedural or legal limits on their behaviors and their respective work requirements to convincingly engage with street-involved women. Kara, a White social worker, provided services to street-involved women until she became romantically involved with one of her clients and, following their tumultuous breakup and subsequent reunification, addicted to prescription pain medication. Conversely, Kurt, a White senior vice detective, attributed his success in building large-scale narcotics and prostitution cases to his lifelong interest in many aspects of street life that his work allowed him to emulate and engage with, as well as the fundamental suspicion with which he regarded most people. Kara and Kurt, like many of their transgressor peers, regarded themselves as distinct from other alliance professionals in ways that made them very effective workers as well as quite susceptible to engaging in many of the same behaviors the alliance tasks them with policing or otherwise overseeing.

Bureaucrats generally regard their work as little more than a reliable income with healthcare and retirement benefits. Bureaucrats tend to be skilled at the dispassionate implementation of legal and policy minutiae and may respond to clients' or colleagues' protests against such a "one size fits all" approach by emphasizing the importance of following established rules. They are especially prevalent in state or federally funded positions that provide permanent work after the employee passes a probationary period and abides by particular rules. Rarely do individuals with a bureaucratic orientation work for nonprofits due to the low pay, lack of benefits, general instability, and level of emotional commitment demanded by such jobs. Bureaucrats tend to be older and focus less on direct contact with street-involved women through agency or organizational activities such as task forces, grant writing, and other desk responsibilities. In some cases, a bureaucratic orientation can be a byproduct of exhaustion in a profession that requires levels of emotional energy difficult to sustain over an extended period.

Sometimes alliance professionals with a bureaucratic orientation find their way into criminal justice or social services occupations via other fields or life experiences. Calvin, a White diversion court evaluator who was unable to find a coveted tenure-track academic position, used his research skills to assess various parameters associated with success at problem-solving courts throughout the country. Doris, an African American probation officer, had a world-weary air after nearly three decades of work in the criminal justice system following her husband's untimely death and her need to find a stable job with health insurance benefits while singlehandedly raising three children. A bureaucratic orientation, which regards work as little more than a means of making money and ensuring future stability, helps to protect those who subscribe to it from many of the negative emotional consequences faced by those with other orientations.

In their interactions with street-involved women, individual alliance professionals must engage on a daily basis with these work orientations, the dominant socio-ideological models informing them, and their own life circumstances. These encounters can take place on street corners and in motel rooms or in venues controlled or prone to surveillance by the alliance, such as services providers' offices, correctional facilities, and courtrooms. Regardless of where they take place, however, all these encounters are inexorably shaped by the cultural and legal frameworks that govern everyday life in a neighborhood characterized by police as a "known prostitution area."

Street Prostitution and Its Policing in Denver: Ethnographic and Legal Context

Ethnographic Context

Surrounded by the snow-capped peaks of the Rocky Mountains, Denver is the only major city for hundreds of miles in the vast expanse of the American West. This geographical space holds a privileged and romanticized status in the American popular cultural imagination as a place populated by tough, independent characters undeterred by adversity in their quest for a brighter future. Prostitution is part of that history, with frontier brothels and other sex industry forms trailing the expansion of the almost exclusively male-dominated resource-extraction industries that prompted conquest of the U.S. West (Butler, 1986; MacKell, 2009; MacKell, 2007). Tourist attractions throughout the U.S. West routinely feature photographs, or even life-size models, of curvaceous White women wearing what popular culture imagines as the frontier brothel's corseted, revealing garb. Often this stylized imagery appears alongside equally problematic images of a stoic Native American man in elaborate headdress, or a solitary, taciturn White cowboy. Such pervasive images engage in a historical erasure of genocide committed against Native

American peoples as well as the lack of class and gender privilege that drove many poor and working-class people of European and African descent to search for a better life in the rough but potentially transformative land out west. It is in this complex cultural-historical terrain that this ethnography is set.

Situated on Arapahoe and Cheyenne tribal land commandeered by White settlers in the mid-1850s, contemporary Denver, with its 2.9 million metropolitan area residents,[8] comprises over half of Colorado's total population (U.S. Census, 2012). Denver's economy remains dominated by the oil, gas, and mineral extractive industries that are the modern-day equivalent of gold-prospecting ventures that staked claims on tribal land. These lucrative industries, in conjunction with large-scale agricultural production and an extensive outdoor tourism industry oriented around the Rocky Mountain region's spectacular beauty, all result in Denver sustaining higher than national average economic growth rates for the past eight decades (Metro Denver Economic Development Corporation, 2015).

Denver enjoys a high degree of generalized economic stability relative to other metropolitan areas such that, unlike other U.S. cities of its size, it has no neighborhoods dominated by shuttered businesses, vacant lots, and abandoned buildings. The East Colfax neighborhood, where most of the women who participated in this study spend the majority of their time, has none of these characteristics, although it does experience higher than city average rates of violence, including physical altercations, public shouting matches, and the occasional shootout (Denver Police Department, 2015). The Denver Police Department classifies the neighborhoods surrounding both East and West Colfax Avenue as "high crime density," a designation indicating the city's greatest numbers of emergency calls to 911, police responses to citizen complaints, and other reports of criminalized activities.[9]

East Colfax is certainly not the only neighborhood where street prostitution takes place, as Denver, like other U.S. cities, is home to diverse sexual economies that vary tremendously in the cost of services provided, likelihood of arrest or other risks, and demographic characteristics of individuals involved in selling and buying sexual services. There are other Denver neighborhoods where women, men, and transgender individuals engage in street-based sex trading, as well as myriad online sex markets that transcend physical boundaries. Hence this ethnography is not intended as a comprehensive discussion of transactional sex in the United States or even of prostitution in Denver, but rather as a detailed portrait of encounters between street-involved women and the criminal justice and social services professionals tasked with their regulation.

East Colfax Avenue has a significant regional reputation for street prostitution to the extent that people who live elsewhere in Colorado and surrounding western states also recognize this neighborhood's name; high school students hundreds of miles away in rural Wyoming will admonish girls and young women whom they regard as provocatively dressed by saying, "you look like you belong on East Colfax," and many visitors to Denver take pains to avoid the area. Nonetheless, "the 'fax," as many of the street's residents refer to their neighborhood, enjoys some amount of popular cultural celebration as a bohemian space of transgression; in Jack Kerouac's *On the Road*, the author writes at length about the street's many bars and related establishments (Kerouac, 1957). Some of the street's bar and music venue proprietors manage Colfax.com, a website that advertises cultural events in conjunction with monthly midcentury-styled pin-up photographs of scantily clad women ("Miss Colfax," 2015).

East Colfax Avenue's notoriety stems from the massive post–World War II infrastructural changes that accompanied the construction of Interstate 70, the major cross-country highway that extends from Baltimore to Utah. This highway provided a much quicker and more efficient cross-country route than did U.S. 40, of which Colfax Avenue's twenty-six miles is a part. This prompted a significant change in clientele for the numerous motels that formerly catered to cross-country motorists passing through Denver, such that many of these motels are still in operation today as sites for prostitution and illicit drug activity. In one particular five-block stretch, more than ten such East Colfax Avenue motels, with grandiose names such as the Riviera, cluster closely together with western-themed establishments called the Sand and Sage, the Silver Spur, the Ahwahnee, and the Westerner.

These motels have changed little since midcentury, yet increased policing and gentrification of the downtown Denver area surrounding the gold-domed Capitol Building in the 1960s effectively dispersed illicit drug and related transactional sexual activities to Colfax Avenue's eastern and western extremities, where these motels served as a convenient place for the women to live and work (Wyckoff, 1992). Women generally avoid publicly soliciting clients past Yosemite Street, where Denver County ends and Jefferson County begins, because of what they regard as significantly different jurisdictional sentencing practices. As frequent flyer Layla, who is White, put it, "You don't cross over Yosemite unless you real desperate, 'cause you gonna do all your time in Jefferson County, whereas in Denver it'll be maybe sixty days."

Both street-involved women and the police patrol officers who arrest them regard the four-mile stretch along East Colfax Avenue, comprising sixty-one city blocks from York to Yosemite streets, as the city's major stroll. Denver, like northern Colorado more generally, has experienced a decades-old affordable housing shortage (Murray, 2002, p. 286), which has resulted in sustained encroachment into this area by condominiums, gyms offering yoga and Pilates, and restaurants catering to young professionals. The stroll's first seventeen blocks, from York Street to Colorado Boulevard, one of Denver's major thoroughfares, contain an eclectic mixture of artsy coffee shops, restaurants, stylish tattoo parlors, bookstores, and upscale salons catering to young White clients. The area west of York Street has been so gentrified via the introduction of such establishments that women no longer feel comfortable soliciting there.

In the seventeen blocks from York Street to Colorado Boulevard, establishments catering to those with disposable income also exist alongside less ostentatious businesses of interest to residents who have been in the neighborhood much longer. These include hair-braiding salons, discount electronics stores, nail salons, dive bars, run-down fast food establishments, and storefronts offering high-interest payday loans to those with poor credit scores. In the twenty-three blocks of East Colfax that span Colorado Boulevard to the Monaco Street Parkway, the next major city thoroughfare, the characteristics of neighborhood businesses shift considerably toward those providing car repair and auto parts, legal marijuana and electronic cigarettes, discount electronics and hardware, fast food, and inexpensive Ethiopian and Mexican restaurants run by recently arrived migrants.

Many street-involved women spend most of their time on the stroll's final twenty-one blocks, from the Monaco Street Parkway to Yosemite Street's border with Jefferson County. With the exception of a popular fitness franchise and a trendy salon catering to White clients, this neighborhood contains none of the gentrification readily identifiable on the western side of East Colfax Avenue. A reasonably streetwise visitor to the neighborhood could easily identify many opportunities to purchase illicit drugs or sexual services, with purveyors of both seated at bus stops, congregating outside fast food establishments, or lingering near the area's numerous motels. Prostitution and street drug sales are highly gendered activities, with women handling most of the former and men predominating in the latter. Women and men involved in these gendered activities routinely cooperate in their respective income-generation strategies, such that a woman who primarily trades sex will sometimes make a profit by reselling a client illicit drugs she has obtained from her regular supplier. Likewise, a man who generally sells illicit drugs can charge a man looking to purchase sexual services a fee in exchange for introducing him to a woman who will have sex with him for money.

The area stretching from the Monaco Street Parkway to Yosemite Street is bustling with economic activities of both licit and illicit varieties, although this area is visibly poorer than neighborhoods to the west. The used car lots, pre-paid cell phone vendors, barbershops, low-cost hair and nail salons, liquor stores, small grocery shops, and motels that dominate this area all engage in vibrant trade with local residents. Street prostitution and open-air illicit drug sales concentrate most prominently in the stroll's final five blocks with at least ten motels surrounding Yosemite Street's border with neighboring Jefferson County. These motels provide an essential service to individuals facing homelessness, although they do so on anything but charitable terms. Charging an average of sixty dollars per night, area motel owners profit handsomely from guests unlikely to complain about a room's general disrepair, noise, and limited amenities despite the relatively high price. As a point of comparison, a savvy online shopper could reasonably expect to find a discounted rate at a Denver-area Hilton or similar hotel for about one hundred dollars. This discrepancy stems from the activities neighborhood motel owners are willing to tolerate from their guests, as well as these motels' proximity to illicit drug sales and opportunities to trade sex for money or drugs. These motels are able to charge such high rates because they provide full-service venues for those involved in criminalized ventures that would probably receive increased police scrutiny or be otherwise more difficult to conduct elsewhere.

Most neighborhood motel rooms feature white-painted cinderblock walls and aging linoleum floors and are dominated by a metal-framed bed with a thin mattress covered by an almost transparent bleach-scented white sheet, a hard pillow, and a polyester bedspread. The bathroom contains a single thin towel, a very small bar of soap, a clear plastic shower curtain, and a sink marked with multiple cigarette burns. Some of the nicer rooms have a table and chair along with a small microwave and refrigerator, but overall the rooms are sparse and hence easier for hotel staff to maintain at a minimum level of cleanliness.

Rooms typically smell strongly of cigarette smoke, and residents leave their doors open whenever possible, irrespective of the weather conditions outside, to improve ventilation since the windows are generally very small and located near the ceiling. While illicit drug use and sex trading are common in these rooms, all motel residents are on the brink of homelessness regardless of how they earn a living. The Road Home Program, which is part of the Denver City Council's ten-year plan to end homelessness, estimates the number of Denver residents who have experienced homelessness over the past three years at between 8,315 and 6,204, with an additional 2,230 precariously housed (Metro Denver Homeless Initiative, 2014, pp. vii–viii). Those who can no longer afford motel shelter can often be seen in the neighborhood, passing the time until a friend will take them in for the night or a shelter opens. Some of these individuals carry visible signs of homelessness, such as a large bag or shopping cart, which can make them vulnerable to theft and assaults.

Women who live in the neighborhood and do not engage in sex trading, whether because they regard it as dangerous, morally repugnant, or otherwise undesirable, generally speak disdainfully about women who trade sex for money or drugs. During the warmer-weather phases of my participant observation and interviews, I often sat outside in my rented motel room's plastic chair smoking menthol cigarettes with a full pack in open view to encourage casual conversation with my neighbors who might enjoy smoking and passing the time talking about neighborhood life. Women who reside in these motel rooms or, for some of the more fortunate, rental housing, spoke to me at length about how frustrated and disrespected they felt when solicited by men or questioned by police while walking in their neighborhood. Several women stated their aversion to sex trading and explained that while they pitied women who worked the streets, they also resented how their activities rendered all neighborhood women suspect of prostitution by police and potential clients alike.

I also faced this reaction from a small number of neighborhood residents when I engaged in street outreach for the transitional housing facility, and on several occasions women and men alike told me that engaging with street-involved women was a waste of time. These residents regarded such women as instrumental in creating and sustaining the area's negative reputation and decreasing their overall quality of life. A few women went so far as to tell me that they called the police every time they saw a woman soliciting, partly because they felt frustrated that street-involved women would sometimes knock on their motel room doors and solicit their boyfriends or husbands. Although the frequency with which sex trading takes place makes it unlikely that such women actually do call the police every time they see women soliciting, such statements underscore how the criminalized context in which the women earn money occurs in a neighborhood where socioeconomic and other forms of stress result in limited empathy for street-involved women.

Legal Context

Street-involved women's likelihood of arrest on East Colfax Avenue, as in other similar neighborhoods throughout the United States, depends on citizen complaints, policing priorities, and visibility in an area where open-air drug and sexual transactions commonly occur. The Denver Police Department, like other police departments nationwide, does not disaggregate data on prostitution arrests by the diverse sex-industry venues in which such arrests occur. Hence it is unproductive to characterize street-involved women's experiences by discussing police arrest statistics, which include the arrests of escorts and other women who generally enjoy considerably greater economic and other privileges relative to their street-involved peers. Women's self-reports of their arrests and convictions are far more illuminating than police data because they clearly demonstrate the complex income-generation strategies women employ in an equally nuanced social context.

Analyzing a decade of street-involved women's case files from the transitional housing facility revealed that women face arrest and convictions for a variety of offenses, as depicted in figures 1.1–1.4. Eighty percent of the women report being arrested at least once, with 38 percent arrested multiple times, as depicted in figure 1.1. The majority of women have approximately equal arrest and conviction rates for both misdemeanor and felony offenses, including the misdemeanor offense of prostitution and the felony offense "Prostitution with Knowledge of AIDS" (25 percent), drug paraphernalia and possession (24 percent), property crimes (22 percent), violent crime against another person (13 percent), and probation violations or failure to appear in court (7 percent), as figures 1.2 and 1.3 demonstrate. Only 9 percent of women have been convicted solely of a prostitution-related offense, as most women have also been convicted of both prostitution *and* another criminal offense, including property crimes (37 percent), drug-related offenses (33 percent), probation violations or failure to appear in court (25 percent), and violent crime against another person (5 percent), as depicted in figures 1.3 and 1.4.

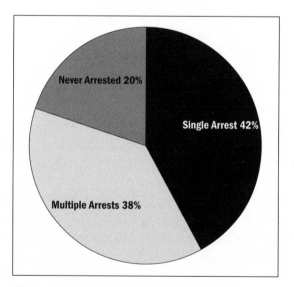

Figure 1.1: Arrests

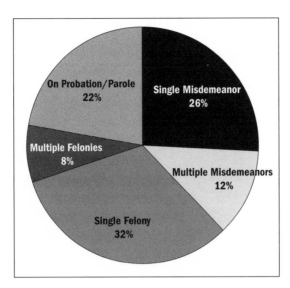

Figure 1.2: Convictions

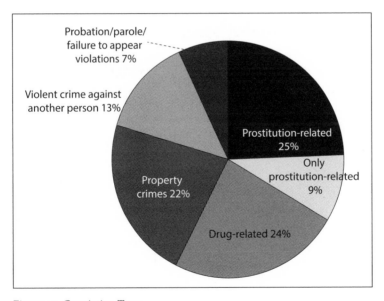

Figure 1.3: Conviction Type

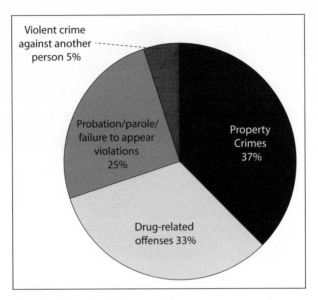

Figure 1.4: Co-convictions

Arrest, incarceration, and subsequent monitoring by probation officers, social services caseworkers, or both, are regular features of most street-involved women's lives. Legislation and the police procedures that enforce it play a central role in defining both street prostitution and the ways that women engage in it. For instance, street-involved women develop arrest-avoidance strategies that draw on their collective beliefs that police may indiscriminately arrest women with impunity in a neighborhood where sex trading and illicit drug use are commonplace (Dewey and St. Germain, 2014). Acknowledgment of these restrictive conditions shapes a set of three primary arrest-avoidance strategies that can be broadly defined as intuition, conspiracy, and subtlety, which women employ in tandem with one another while interacting with or attempting to avoid police officers in the course of their quotidian activities.

Intuition comprises the ability to identify undercover police officers through particular behavioral and contextual cues. The women are highly suspicious of a prospective client who has a rigid body posture or piercing gaze, or who wears a high-necked, long-sleeved shirt that may conceal a bulletproof vest or an electronic body transmitting device, colloquially known as "a wire," used to record verbal evidence. Women also attempt to avoid arrest by encouraging a potential client who they suspect may be working undercover to use illicit drugs, expose his genitalia, or engage in other conspiratorial behaviors they believe are forbidden to police officers. Practicing subtlety involves avoiding flagrant behaviors such as flagging down cars, wearing flamboyant clothing, conspicuously carrying drug paraphernalia, or engaging in violent or property crimes (Dewey and St. Germain, 2014). As Kenya, who is bonded, put it, "You don't wanna get a reputation as a thief, a liar, or a fighter—that's just gonna make 'em watch you more."

Even as women actively resist policing practices by consciously formulating their illegal income-generation strategies in response to them, open-air soliciting dramatically increases their risk of negative police encounters. Frequent flyer Layla concisely described this situation as one in which "you gonna get arrested; now the who, what, where, and how, that depends." Policing priorities, citizen complaints, and individual behavior all play critical determining roles in a woman's likelihood of facing arrest on a given day. Officers typically arrest a woman on prostitution-related charges[10] after witnessing behaviors associated with this legal offense, such as repeatedly entering cars or motel rooms with different men, hailing male passersby, or even extended periods loitering on the street. Women also face arrest in undercover operations, in which a plainclothes officer obtains sufficient evidence to make an arrest following a woman's statement of a particular sex act's price. After gathering evidence in one of these ways, the arresting officer informs the woman that she is under arrest on prostitution-related charges and reads her the Miranda warning, which informs her of the right to remain silent and of the criminal justice system's right to use her subsequent statements as evidence against her.

This encounter evolves very rapidly from a woman's agreement to, or engagement in, a sex act in exchange for money to a situation in which she faces incarceration for a month or more depending on her history of criminal convictions, outstanding warrants, and the jurisdiction in which the arrest occurs. Ensuing events will take multiple trajectories determined by her criminal history, which the arresting officer can quickly ascertain through records obtained electronically or via radio contact while the woman is handcuffed in the back of the squad car. While transporting the woman to a district station holding cell where she will stay until booked into county jail, the arresting officer may decide to question her regarding information she might have about what the officer regards as higher-stakes and larger-scale drug or gang-related activities. The officer makes this decision on the basis of details gleaned from her criminal record, previous contact with her, or even just an intuitive sense that she may have information of interest. She may also volunteer this information without the officer's prompting in the hope that it could help her to reduce or avoid charges against her.

Hence a woman can find herself quickly transformed from a person facing a potential criminal conviction to an informant in a criminal case against prominent figures in the illicit drug or sexual economies. Law enforcement may consider street-involved women ideal informants due to their connections to illicit drug markets both as consumers and as intimate partners to men who play active roles in producing, distributing, and enforcing the drug economy's order. Prostitution's relatively low status as a misdemeanor offense akin to loitering allows police considerable discretionary latitude in bringing charges against women; as one vice detective concisely stated, "I get my bad guy through what she tells me, and he's the one I really want." In instances where a police officer asks a woman to volunteer such information with the potential to avoid charges or receive a reduced sentence, she must rapidly weigh the consequences of her own incarceration versus her likelihood of facing retribution from a street-involved figure she may provide information about. The effects of controlled substances considerably mitigate the circumstances in which a woman makes these potentially life-changing choices, as do sleep deprivation and other factors that compromise her decision making.

Generally a woman arrested on prostitution-related charges will spend less than twelve hours in a holding cell, followed by her transfer to booking in the county jail, where she will be photographed and provided with a uniform while she awaits her court date, which typically takes place within two weeks. Women fortunate enough to have friends or family members with sufficient cash or personal property to post the bail or bond amount set by the arraigning judge may leave jail at this point, but most of the women's struggles with homelessness, addiction, and intergenerational poverty render them indigent and unable to mobilize such assistance. At the time of their court date, most women receive a public defender who reviews their case and meets them for the first time just minutes before they stand in front of the judge for sentencing.

A woman may choose to speak directly to the judge during the few minutes that precede her sentencing or opt instead to allow her public defender to communicate any extenuating circumstances that surrounded her arrest on prostitution-related charges. County courtrooms are busy, crowded places, and a woman uniformed and handcuffed on a bench before the judge hears her case may notice that the public defender's files are several inches thick and contain hundreds of cases in addition to hers. She may also notice the often-considerable difference in the amount of time and consideration a case receives before the judge when a defendant is able to hire an attorney. Many, if not most, cases in county court face adjudication within minutes before the judge moves on to call the next case. Everyone who has a case before the judge sits together in the courtroom, which grows gradually emptier throughout the day as those involved in adjudicated cases either leave the court on their own or follow deputies who transfer them to a correctional facility.

Sentencing for prostitution-related convictions varies according to the jurisdiction in which it occurs but generally ranges from five to ninety days in county jail. A number of factors inform judicial decision making in such cases, including consideration of a woman's struggles with addiction, her previous record of arrests and convictions, and her HIV status. A woman charged with a prostitution-related offense, or a public defender speaking on her behalf, may choose to inform the judge that she only engages in transactional sex as a result of her addiction to a controlled substance. The judge weighs this information in conjunction with her previous record of arrests and criminal convictions, and then imposes a sentence. A woman with no criminal record may receive only probation and a fine, whereas a woman with a lengthy list of convictions could spend a year in county jail, sometimes in a specialized addictions-treatment unit if she self-identifies as a person struggling with addiction. Women who have previously been arrested on prostitution charges and tested positive for HIV on completion of a court-mandated health order at Denver Health, the city's largest hospital, can face felony charges that will send them to prison if convicted.

At the hearing, the judge could also recommend a woman for participation in a problem-solving court, typically referred to as "diversion court" because of its intended purpose to support women in redirecting their lives away from illicit drug use and sex trading. Alliance professionals and street-involved women use various colloquial names in reference to diversion courts that derive from the specialized issues they address, including "drug court," "prostitution diversion court," "homeless court," or "wellness court." These courts require participants to appear weekly before a judge to report on their progress toward the goals of sobriety, obtaining stable housing and legal work, and other specialized criteria determined by the judicial team. Additionally, probation officers supervise diversion court participants through mandatory drug testing in conjunction with therapeutic support staff who provide mental health counseling to the women. Sometimes these courts mandate participants' residence in a shared living environment, where a social services case worker will report additional positive drug tests, unapproved absences, or other rule violations to probation officers, who have the authority to arrest and incarcerate the women on criminal charges.

Street-involved women encounter a number of alliance professionals as a result of their engagement in criminalized and stigmatized activities. These individuals include uniformed police patrol officers, undercover officers, vice detectives, public defenders (or, in rare instances, privately hired attorneys), diversion court staff, corrections officers, addictions- and other therapeutic-treatment program coordinators and staff, and social workers who make assessments about their mental health and suitability for child custody. Women involved in street-based sex trading and illicit drug use accordingly face a level of institutional scrutiny in their lives that systematically denies them full citizenship by questioning their abilities to determine their own best interests, care for their children, and remain free from correctional control.

The alliance ethos and the powerful sociolegal system that undergirds it explicitly endorse such fragmentation of citizenship rights by mandating arrest, incarceration, and other forms of correctional control over those who break the law. In this worldview, breaking the law comprises a violation of the social contract that effectively voids an individual's right to freedom as a means to protect the rest of society from further harm that the individual might cause. Encounters that arise from this seemingly straightforward perspective take extraordinarily complex human forms for alliance professionals who, irrespective of their individual work orientations, are sworn to uphold the law. Police officers in particular routinely perform their work in conditions that can rapidly change from quotidian, even boring, patrol and surveillance activities to adrenaline-charged encounters that result in death.

Going Undercover

"I was eighteen when I told the Army recruiter I wanted to become a police officer," Michael says after he lets me buy him coffee, but nothing else, at the small restaurant near his office. "So the recruiter suggested joining the infantry. I really enjoyed that part of the army, when I got to do marksmanship in infantry school. I went to sniper school twice, and I actually shot top gun, on the top sniper team." Michael sinks deeper into his chair as he summarizes his twenty-year journey to the undercover investigative work he now carries out in vice.

> I did a lot of sniper work with Special Forces, which I really enjoyed, and then when I got back from deployment I was ready to get out of the Army, so I started looking for places to become a cop. I drove all the way from Wisconsin to take the written test in Denver, because I really wanted to live out here. I was the first one in line, and after just getting out of the Army it was a breeze getting through the [Police] Academy because it's semi-militaristic.

It is difficult for me to picture Michael as a soldier, or even walking the beat as a police patrol officer. With hair that extends past his shoulders, a long beard, and vividly colored tattoos that extend from his wrist to his chin, he looks remarkably like some of the more successful purveyors of controlled substances the women have pointed out to me on East Colfax Avenue. I ask him if he sometimes feels like he never left the military since, in his own as well as many others' estimations, the police force features a similar hierarchical structure. Michael laughs, spreading his arms apart to show off the many tattoos that cover his muscular arms. "Look, if I was in SWAT, I definitely would—there'd still be the same kind of communication, planning, fortitude and integrity to complete the mission, but the way I look now, my tattoos, the way I walk, not shaving, it's totally the opposite of that, it's not a strict environment."

Perfectly on cue to emphasize his point, Michael retrieves a file folder from his bag and spreads dozens of eight-by-ten color photographs across the table. The most striking thing about the pictures, which feature large quantities of firearms and controlled substances seized in police operations he organized, is the absence of people. I am not accustomed to seeing illicit drugs or guns outside of a social context, and to my naïve eyes they look like artifacts on display when tagged and photographed as evidence used to build a case. He studies my face to gauge my reactions to each one of the photographs and takes pains to explain the quantities of cocaine, methamphetamine, and heroin contained in the large clear plastic bags, especially in instances where he is particularly proud of the amount seized directly as a result of his investigative undercover work.

Michael becomes more reflective about his police career as we look at the photographs together. "When I first started out on patrol" he continues,

> I started seeing a lot of these guys in plain clothes and unmarked cars, so I really started asking what they did. Those guys were with the street crimes team here, and I wanted the opportunity to get on that team. So I busted my butt on patrol, did proactive police work and then I started working plainclothes, training on how to work undercover.

Michael's undercover training involved conducting observations with other recruits on East Colfax Avenue, where a sharp division quickly began to emerge between him and his colleagues who were less suited to undercover work and the bodily practices that accompany it.

Undercover work requires officers to master the linguistic and bodily practices that allow them to convincingly self-present as trustworthy, competent individuals in both street and alliance contexts. "You have to learn how to be a chameleon," Michael explains. "I didn't grow up that way, a hustler on the streets selling dope, so I had to do everything I could to try to consciously change. Those new recruits, they walk with purpose, but the guys on Colfax, they got no place to go—they don't wear a watch, they're looking out for cops." I tell Michael how difficult

I find it to switch from hanging out in motels with the women to the world of campus, where I must carefully monitor my language, body posture, and ways of interacting with others so as not to appear impolite or aggressive. "Michael," I ask, "how do you turn it off?" He nods meaningfully. "You have to learn how to hustle, and it's really hard to turn that hustle off."

Michael describes some of the difficulties I have listened to anthropologists convey regarding their struggles in switching from one cultural world to another; unlike an anthropologist's, however, Michael's professional responsibilities demand that he maintain a firm boundary between the two worlds that his job requires him to simultaneously inhabit. "You have to have that conscious ability to turn it off," Michael says. "A lot of guys can't turn it off because we can drink on the job, and it's easy to start going down that bad road. Turning it off isn't easy, because you could be getting gas and a guy hits you up for something and you gotta get his number—you constantly have to be out there hustling."

"There's a lot of adrenaline," I say, thinking of how when I am out at night with women on East Colfax, I feel fully present and alive in ways that I never do in other spheres of my life.

"It's really exciting, but it's also really scary," Michael says, "and if you talk to a cop and he pretends he's not scared out there, he's lying out his ass." Michael leans in closer and tells me, "That's where guys get into trouble, because you're handling dope, money the [Police] Department has given you, an attractive female in close physical contact, clothes being taken off. All those things are in play." Michael's gaze is firmly fixed on the eight-by-ten photographs when he looks up and says, "I'm able to deal with this stuff because of the Army, being shot at, in hostage situations, jumping out of helicopters. This is nothing after that. But for some other guy, I could see how he might end up going down that dark path."

Michael feels called to his work, although he contrasts this sentiment with some of his colleagues' motivations for engaging in police work. "Some of these other cops," he says,

> it's a paycheck, they were bullied, and they got into law enforcement so now they're in charge. I don't know how a lot of those guys handle what they see and do on this job, because you will see the epitome of evil if

you're a good cop. Being religious, my mindset veers toward the good versus evil outlook, and it really helps me. A lot of cops commit suicide because they can't handle it.

I am unprepared to respond to Michael's assessment of his work, and fill the awkward silence by pointing to a photograph of a white substance in a sealed bag and wondering out loud whether it is cocaine or methamphetamine. Michael quickly clarifies that the bag contains methamphetamine and then continues.

He tells me about the first immediate-entry search warrant he executed following a citizen complaint about a man selling narcotics from a house near East Colfax Avenue. Michael describes the tense emotional cocktail of anxiety, fear, stress, and pride in his investigation that he felt as the SWAT team used a battering ram to force their way into the house in order to make arrests and seize the large cache of guns and narcotics. The story, as he tells it, has the flat tone of someone recounting a series of events that happened to someone else. "I saw SWAT going up the stairs," he says, his eyes devoid of emotion. "They throw the flash bangs [grenades] and I hear pop-pop-pop and then somebody yells 'we need a medic in here!' because they shot the suspects. They were all dead, and I was freaking out that they killed these guys."

The room feels smaller as Michael continues, and I realize that he is no longer monitoring my reactions. "Those guys that got killed on my first warrant," he says,

> I saw their brains coming out on the sidewalk in front of me. It had a real impact on me, but then I started to think about it and I saw it another way. They were poisoners of our streets, trafficking women. That's three less drug dealers, three less pimps out there. When I think about it that way, it makes me feel better about what I do.

We talk for another hour after Michael shares these events with me, my eyes diligently fixed on my notebook as I try to mimic Michael in not emotionally reacting to his account of the operation gone horribly wrong. Eventually he tells me that he needs to get ready for work, and I have a sinking feeling that our conversation has brought up some emotionally loaded issues for him. The stoicism and emotional control that his profession values so highly make it impossible for me to tell whether Michael feels that sharing his perspectives has been cathartic or upsetting. "I hope we can see each other again," I say to Michael as he gets up to leave. He leans over the table and looks intensely and silently into my eyes for a moment before adding, "Just make sure you do right by the police in this book, Susan. It's not easy for us out there."

2

Occupational Risks

Clustering around several small tables pushed to the center of the room, the five-person treatment team of alliance workers begins preparations for a two-hour meeting during which they will discuss incarcerated women's everyday activities in the addictions-treatment unit. We sit in the same hard plastic chairs the women use for classes on trauma, accountability, and other subjects that the alliance ethos regards as essential for them to overcome addiction and cease involvement in criminalized activities. The room has the unmistakable antiseptic smell of a correctional facility, and our conversation is punctuated by the sound of radio static as correctional officers communicate with one another. Sandra, the treatment team leader, has invited me to join them during one of my visits to meet with incarcerated women interested in entering the transitional housing program.

Sandra begins the meeting by asking Kendra, Maria, Orlando, Tina, and me to talk about our activities the previous weekend as we eat the packed lunches we brought from home. Kendra, who is in her late twenties, describes her disappointment at moving back to her mother's house since she is no longer able to afford to rent her own apartment. Maria and Tina both talk about the health problems their close relatives are having and exchange brief pieces of advice about specialists. Orlando shares his excitement about preparing to go camping in the mountains with his nephews the following weekend, and complains about the high cost of renting a campsite. I am impressed by the team's collegiality and warmth as I listen to them support one another in their struggles with stressful jobs that, while stable, clearly pay less than what the team members would like to earn.

Sandra uses the brief silence that follows to transition to the meeting's purpose, which involves decision making on sanctions or rewards, derived from team members' observations, for women in the addictions-treatment unit. Kendra begins by noting, "There was a serious issue this weekend with Macey after the women watched *Selma*, you know the one about the Civil Rights movement? After the movie was over, Brittany asked her, 'How'd that make you feel?' and Macey responded very inappropriately."

Sandra, who, like Kendra and Brittany, is White, crosses her arms as she sits back in her chair and asks, as if she knows what is coming, "Oh, no. What did she say this time?"

Kendra continues, "Well, she told Brittany, 'That movie made me feel like I want to spit on every White person I see.' Brittany was really taken aback."

"Well," Sandra says, "I can imagine she was!"

Maria, who is Latina, laughs derisively and adds, "That's Macey for you." I find myself trying hard to avoid speaking up and am certain that all the team members can tell I am upset. Just that morning Macey had talked to me for an hour about how she feels labeled as what she termed "a crazy angry Black woman" whenever she attempts to advocate for herself in the addictions-treatment unit, a situation she feels has led to numerous punitive sanctions that have considerably extended her incarceration.

Tina, who is in her early sixties and African American, briefly closes her eyes and slightly shakes her head, and the room's attention shifts to her. "I feel that was an inappropriate question for Brittany to ask."

Kendra and Sandra respond, almost in unison, "She didn't mean it like that!"

Tina leans her head to the side and speaks in a measured tone. "You would not, after watching one of those Holocaust movies, turn to a Jewish person and ask, 'Well, just *how* did that make you feel?' because there's no way for them to explain it, it's like an all-encompassing feeling. If somebody asked me a question like that, I'd probably just walk away." It remains unspoken that Macey, whose movements the correctional facility tightly regulates, cannot walk away, not even while watching a movie; she must first ask for and receive permission to leave.

Sandra, with a beleaguered expression, continues her line of argument that positions Macey as the problem. "Tina, you're a clinician, so you can see that. Brittany doesn't have that capability. She's a sweet girl." Kendra nods.

Orlando, who has been shaking his head as he eats his lunch, adds, "I don't care what your ancestors, or you, have been through, that's no excuse to be uncivil, especially in a treatment context. She needs a write-up to hold her accountable." A "write-up," which comprises a notation of troublesome behavior in a woman's file by a clinician or caseworker, is very serious and can extend a woman's time in a correctional facility by weeks or even months.

Tina appears to be working hard, like me, to reign in her acute disappointment with the treatment team's race-neutral approach, which engages in a historical erasure of the reasons for Macey's reaction. "Well, then," Tina sighs, "that is a serious point of disagreement between us. You know, I tell my grandchildren, 'I am the history book, I was there marching with dogs and guns pointed at me. Anything you want to know, you just ask me.'"

The treatment team remains unmoved by Tina's powerful imagery, and within seconds Orlando shakes his head again and says, "Macey needs a write-up. Now we need to talk about how else we're going to hold her accountable." After deciding that Macey needs to apologize to the women in the addictions-treatment unit for making this statement, the treatment team moves on to other business.

Later that afternoon Tina calls me into her office and tells me that she knows of three other women she would like me to meet before I leave that evening. I tell her that I do not want to disrupt her meetings with the women or upset the afternoon's schedule. "Oh, no, as long as you're here we're going to use you. These sisters in here need all the help they can get," referring to my presentation to the women earlier that day about the transitional housing facility. She holds my arm tightly as she leads me into an adjacent room where a group of eight young African American women are just finishing a group facilitated by a staff member. "This woman is going to help you," Tina states in a firm, authoritative voice as she pushes me forward into the room, and the women, who have noticeably straightened their posture on seeing Tina, respond loudly and clearly, "Yes, ma'am, yes, Ms. Ellis." Tina nods at me and then returns to her office; through the window she looks exhausted as she sits back down, diminutive behind the huge stacks of paper piled high on her desk.

Conceptualizing Risk

Risk, like work, is a highly subjective and context-dependent concept that nonetheless holds enormous cultural significance for practitioners, the general public, and academics. Public school teachers and administrators routinely refer to "at-risk students," public health researchers refer to "at-risk populations" or "risky sexual practices," and insurance agents conduct proprietorial risk assessments on a policyholder's likelihood of becoming a potential claimant. Sociologist Ulrich Beck's theoretical articulation of the "global risk society" helps to explain some of the reasons why "risk," a concept first articulated in the insurance industry, has acquired such cultural resonance in the United States and Western Europe. Beck argues that subscription to risk discourse ultimately positions an individual's likelihood of experiencing a particular undesirable outcome as the product of "systematic events that call for political regulation" (Beck, 2007, p. 26). In this vein, "at-risk" individuals require a more intensive level of criminal justice or other forms of social scrutiny to which others are not subjected because they are presumed not to face such risks.

Beliefs about risk dramatically inform interactions between street-involved women and the criminal justice and social services professionals they regularly encounter in a variety of contexts. Individual street-involved women and alliance professionals are by no means monolithic in their formulations of risk, yet each group's shared cultural norms contribute to general understandings regarding the challenges and consequences they face in their respective ways of earning a living. The alliance ethos that dominated the treatment team's discussion of Macey's reaction to the film effectively prohibited full consideration of the important points Tina raised regarding the team's refusal to discuss race at all, let alone in a meaningful manner. Yet, as Macey shared with me prior to the treatment team discussion, those same staff members' unspoken (and perhaps even unconscious) ethno-racial stereotypes may play a significant role in imposing additional sanctions that keep her behind bars.

Taking this dissonance as its analytical target, this chapter demonstrates how the alliance ethos pathologizes street-involved women's decisions to engage in sex trading and illicit drug use by characterizing these choices as individual responses to traumatic experiences and flawed thought processes. This ideological stance draws on prevailing U.S. cultural norms, as well as attendant structural forces, regarding personal responsibility and appropriate gendered sexual behavior. In so doing, the alliance ethos focuses on particular aspects of street involvement, specifically homelessness, substance abuse, criminal justice system involvement, and interpersonal violence, as the major issues facing street-involved women.

In so doing, the alliance ethos positions professionals tasked with its implementation as agents of intervention in the lives of women deemed essentially vulnerable subjects "at risk" for numerous forms of trauma, violence, and other harms. This ethos fails to acknowledge how these compound negative effects directly result from the cultural and structural forces, specifically criminalization and stigma, that create what most street-involved women regard as the greatest risks they face in their lives. Individual alliance professionals, especially those with whom the women have sustained direct contact or shared characteristics, recognize this disconnect and accordingly struggle with an attendant set of individual emotional and professional risks as they reconcile the sometimes significant gulf between ideology and reality. Hence we carefully distinguish the "alliance ethos," a static construction to which professionals like Tina must adhere as a condition of their jobs, from "alliance professionals," who are individual people with their own work orientations.

Individual street-involved women also have their own beliefs about possible negative consequences that may arise from their activities, and they routinely alter or otherwise amend these in response to particular contexts and needs. For instance, a woman who swears she will never solicit east of Yosemite Street because she knows she will receive a longer jail sentence if arrested in Jefferson, rather than Denver, County, will probably run the risk of arrest by crossing the county line if business is unusually slow. Yet taken together, the shared conditions in which the women live and make money produce a culture characterized by a constellation of occupational risks that generally center on two major concerns: policing and gendered socioeconomic relations in a neighborhood dominated by the illicit drug economy.

Alliance professionals who participated in this project also identify arrest and arrest-related outcomes as a major risk the women face, although their descriptions of these risks vary according to their work orientations. The alliance ethos positions arrest-related outcomes as playing a critical intervening role in mitigating women's substance abuse and addiction, homelessness or precarious housing, and trauma-related psychological consequences. Those with an enforcer orientation may regard the women as a risk, to both society and themselves, which arrest stems or helps to manage. Alliance professionals of all orientations may acknowledge the intersectional harms that emerge from a woman's age, ethno-racial background, gendered caretaking responsibilities, and homelessness. Nonetheless, all alliance professionals must adhere to the criminal justice method that prioritizes arrest and incarceration.

Even when accounting for differences in individual orientations and opinions, rather significant differences remain between the ways in which street-involved women and the alliance ethos conceptualize their own and each other's occupational risks. The vast majority of women who participated in this project characterize their own occupational risks as geographically limited in scope to the heavily policed neighborhood in which they live and work and the relationships that they cultivate and sustain within it. The alliance ethos also acknowledges these risks but additionally focuses on individual women's decision making in ways that position many of these relationships as harmful. In this respect, the alliance ethos that governs policing and other forms of regulation fails to account for the critical role that women's relationships play in helping them to negotiate their sometimes very difficult life circumstances.

All street-involved women regard their social relationships as integral aspects of their everyday lives, decision making, and understandings of themselves. Caregivers and bonded women especially envision sex trading as part of their obligations to children, intimate partners, or groups to which they feel a strong sense of affinity and loyalty. Intergenerationals and women working under the radar both position transactional sex as part of the relational bonds they share with others, whether with female family members who have sex trade experience, as with the former, or with an intimate partner struggling with addiction in the case of the latter. Old school cougars evince a more independent ethos but emphasize that their orientation to prostitution initially took one of the other forms. Even frequent flyers, who face social isolation from both family and peers as a result of their severe addictions and relative disregard for others, sometimes describe themselves using a discourse of lack that emphasizes their fractured bonds with children, family, and other loved ones. I have often heard women who fit this description express some version of "I got nobody out here," lamenting their absence of a support system.

In direct contrast to women's descriptions of their social bonds, the sociolegal intervention mandated by the alliance ethos through arrest, incarceration, court-mandated treatment, or, in some cases, all three, effectively positions the women's relationships as part of a systematic set of structural constraints that shapes their lives. This contradictory set of professional practices, in conjunction with the emotionally charged nature of their work, at least partially leads the majority of professionals I interacted with to characterize their own occupational risks, which stem from their role as interventionists, as feeling ineffective in struggling with the status quo, experiencing racism and sexism at work, and experiencing gendered discomfort with sexually charged issues.

A substantial body of research articulates the mutually reinforcing gendered and racialized harms that manifest in the social, structural, and interpersonal factors, including problematic substance abuse and violence, that surround street prostitution.[1] The theme of risk, a powerful cultural construction predicated on prevailing beliefs that particular sexual behaviors or types of drug use are inherently dangerous or harmful, saturates the interdisciplinary literature on women's street involvement. Indeed, much of the public health and social sciences literature on this subject focuses on the combination of structural and institutional forces that create these risks in the context of women's constrained individual choices.

For instance, medical anthropologist Nancy Romero-Daza's research with street-involved women in Hartford, Connecticut, found that traumatic events, substance abuse, and compromised health conditions such as HIV infection and mental illness, combine to create a totalizing set of factors that compromise women's safety and well-being (Romero-Daza, 2003; Romero-Daza, Weeks, and Singer, 2005). Similar findings emerged from work in San Francisco by anthropologists Philippe Bourgois, Bridget Prince, and Andrew Moss, who described how gendered socioeconomic vulnerabilities push young women struggling with addiction into relationships with older, and often abusive, men who control both their access to drugs and their knowledge about how to inject drugs or otherwise prepare them for ingestion. The result, the authors argue, is higher rates of hepatitis C infection among the women relative to their male peers (Bourgois, Prince, and Moss, 2004).

Research from the fields of criminology and public health also suggests that many of the risks culturally ascribed to street-based sex trading are the byproduct of the criminalization of prostitution and illicit drug use. Criminologist Gail Caputo's study of African American women living in socioeconomically deprived Philadelphia neighborhoods documented the women's use of sex trading and shoplifting as a means to generate money for basic needs, including the need to manage an addiction (Caputo, 2008). The women's engagement in criminalized and stigmatized income-generating activities in neighborhoods suffering from already high rates of violence and disenfranchisement actively works to render women targets of further harm. Homelessness only compounds these problems due to the likelihood that women will experience violent assault or other harms in the absence of a safe place to sleep (Jasinski, et al. 2010; Kushel, et al. 2003). Hence the set of structural and institutional forces that create risk enjoy impunity while street-involved women face social opprobrium for engaging in sexualized strategies that help them to navigate systems that often appear to actively exclude them.

Quantifying Occupational Risk

Thanks to staff and client consent, I was extremely privileged, throughout my work at the transitional housing facility, to review a decade of case files on a total of 131 women. These files provide a wealth of rich, nuanced information about the women's lives, particularly when juxtaposed with the participant observation and interview aspects of the research. While it is important to note that this information refers specifically to women who approached the transitional housing facility to receive services, there is a great deal of overlap between women actively working the street and those who seek services, and hence this is a generally representative quantitative sample.

Street prostitution is a low-status activity in the cultural milieu of the illicit drug economy and the neighborhoods in which it takes place.

It is also a low priority for law enforcement in the absence of citizen complaints, which is why, in turn, this activity remains confined to neighborhoods where residents may hesitate to contact police due to distrust, lack of confidence regarding the potential for a response, or their own involvement in criminalized activities. The intention in juxtaposing quantitative data about women's ages, ethno-racial identifications, affective relationships and kin bonds, and economic situations is to demonstrate that a variety of individual and social factors determine the definition of "risk." For instance, this quantitative material clearly demonstrates the overrepresentation of African American women and Latinas in street prostitution, the sex industry venue where they are most likely to face arrest and least likely to enjoy significant financial benefits or protection from violence and other harms.

We can interpret this reality as reflective of the structural racism that shapes their lives, but there is also the potential risk that this could be misconstrued to reinforce problematic stereotypes that hypersexualize and criminalize African American women and Latinas. Anthropologists typically do not have access to or collect large amounts of quantitative data, and hence I was fortunate to work with this material, which provides valuable insight into patterns that would not have emerged through the qualitative methods of participant observation or interviews alone. Yet this data also actively refutes prevailing popular cultural stereotypes about women in prostitution as social outcasts; instead, it clearly demonstrates the normative frequency with which street-involved women are mothers of young children or in long-term relationships. This helps to underscore how street-involved women are not culturally or otherwise distinct from other neighborhood women and how, in most cases, women's sex trade involvement stems from situations of extreme economic need.

Age and Ethno-Racial Identification

Data on age and ethno-racial identification presented in figures 2.1 and 2.2 clearly illustrate that street-based sex trading is by no means exclusively a young women's economic pursuit, and that women come from a variety of ethno-racial backgrounds. Some women may only periodically engage in this income-generation strategy throughout their lives,

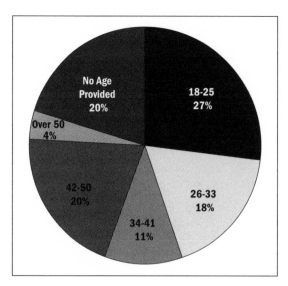

Figure 2.1: Age at Facility Entry

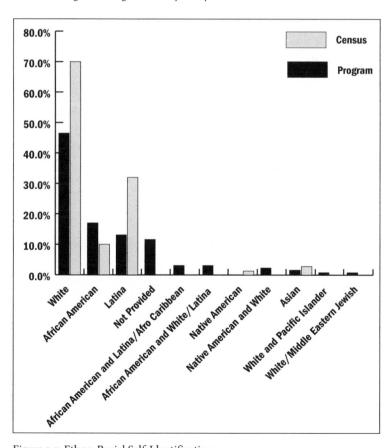

Figure 2.2: Ethno-Racial Self-Identification

while others regard it as an economic mainstay, and it is significant that the vast majority of women seeking services list "no income" on their intake form. Women's self-reported ethno-racial backgrounds reflect the gendered socioeconomic inequalities that frame their lives more generally; while there are women of all ethno-racial backgrounds working the street, just under half (46.5 percent) self-identify as White in a city where 70 percent of census respondents do so (U.S. Census, 2012). In contrast to street prostitution, young White women dominate in better-paid sex industry venues where they face limited or no risk of arrest, such as erotic dancing, pornography, escorting, or webcam modeling.

Affective and Kin Relationships

As depicted in figure 2.3, the majority of women (72 percent) are in intimate relationships with men and women who do not pay them for sex. The percentage (17 percent) of women who have never been married to a man resembles patterns among women of similar ages and class backgrounds who are not street involved. As in other spheres of life in the United States, intimate relationships vary tremendously, and it is unsurprising that some of the women are in relationships they describe as subscribing to the culturally valued ideal of monogamy. Yet serial monogamy is as common among the women who are street involved as it is among those who are not, and women leave or enter into intimate partnerships for equally complex reasons, including a new partner's kindness, sexual attractiveness, or access to money, housing, or drugs. A small number of women keep their transactional sexual activities secret from intimate partners, a difficult and potentially exhausting task given the public nature of this work.

Street-involved women have kin and social ties that shape their lives and decision-making processes in the context of severe economic constraints. Sixty-seven percent of the women seeking services have at least one child, and 58 percent of women have more than one child, almost none of whom reside with them due to the women's homelessness, addiction, and other mental health issues. These children, 87 percent of whom are under eighteen, generally reside in foster care or with women's relatives; as figure 2.4 demonstrates, 69 percent of the women reported child custody revocation by the state, whereas 31 percent of the children live

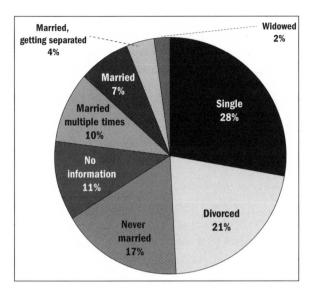

Figure 2.3: Relationship Status

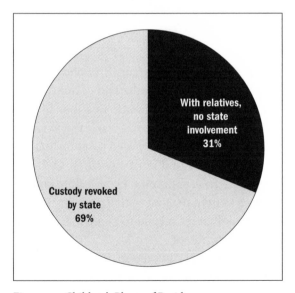

Figure 2.4: Children's Places of Residence

with women's relatives. This latter arrangement is far more common among women who self-identify as African American or Latina, and many women readily acknowledged this as a community strategy that actively resists the state surveillance that accompanies structural racism. As twenty-six-year-old African American intergenerational Keanna said regarding her pride that none of her family's children have ever been in foster care, "In my family, we don't let nobody go to the system."

Examining women's ages, ethno-racial identifications, and affective and kin relationships helps to demonstrate the means by which factors both structural and interpersonal function to inform women's perspectives on their occupational risks. The dangers women face in their daily pursuits cannot be neatly separated from the gendered and racialized socioeconomic realities that shape their lives, and, taken together, this data suggests that street-involved women face a wide array of challenges that stem from both economic need and complex relationships with loved ones, including children; their struggles with addiction and homelessness only compound these challenges.

Women's Perspectives on Their Occupational Risks

The women trade sex in a socioeconomic context characterized by a multitiered set of risks that fall into the two major thematic categories of policing and gendered socioeconomic relations in a neighborhood dominated by the illicit drug economy. Each thematic category comprises a number of distinct but interrelated components that combine to create what the women's cultural norms position as their occupational risks. Taken together, these components constitute cultural forces that shape women's lives as they struggle with a powerful set of exclusionary social and institutional forces related to gender, class, and race, as well as their own individual choices.

Policing-related risks entail three major components, the first of which involves the constant vigilance necessitated by the inevitability and frequency of arrest as well as women's fundamental uncertainty regarding police procedures, legal statutes, and specific criminal conviction-related sanctions. The second component comprises the disrespect and harassment the women associate with gender profiling in a "known prostitution area" where officers may suspect any woman in public space of attempting to solicit men. Third is the speed with which encounters leading to arrest and women's subsequent decision making unfold, such that women may face lifelong consequences as a result of events that transpire very quickly.

Women describe three risks related to gendered socioeconomic relations in the neighborhood, the first of which involves the constant economic pressures faced by street-involved women, some of whom support intimate partners and children while struggling with the knowledge that at any time their criminalized activities could result in serious consequences, including loss of child custody. Second, many women heavily restrict their street-based social networks to reduce their potential for encountering peers who may have opportunistic motives, steal clients, or exact retribution for personal slights. Client-related risks, a third component of gendered socioeconomic relations, span a continuum comprised of nuisance behaviors, theft (including posing as police officers), and violence.

These risks coexist and even overlap in the criminalized and economically precarious social context that informs women's decision making. Such relationships and "street identities" shift according to the actors involved, their relationship to one another, and the terms of the exchange that takes place between them. Sometimes these relationships are temporary and straightforward, as in the case of a street-involved woman who performs a quick sex act for a man she has never met and may never see again. Yet among individuals who co-reside in the neighborhood, these relationships are far from static, such that a woman's dope buddy, with whom she uses illicit drugs, may become a client by providing her with money or drugs in exchange for sex. Likewise, a regular client could become a woman's dope buddy by purchasing drugs or a night's stay in a motel in lieu of paying her for sex. Women's intimate partners who need money to support an addiction are similarly indistinct from those the law and popular culture might categorize as "pimps,"[2] as are other types of family and intimate relationships common among the women. Yet despite the complexity of these interpersonal dynamics, the fact that women tend to associate specific types of risks with particular actors and social forces justifies this analytical separation.

Policing

Women universally describe police surveillance and arrest as regular features in their lives as a result of the significant time they spend outdoors searching for clients, other money-making opportunities, or illicit drugs, or simply because they are homeless and have nowhere else to go. African American Wanda, an old school cougar, described the inevitability of arrest by noting that "it happens even to the veterans, you know, that's just part of it. I look at it as when we're out here doin' this we're not payin' taxes so when you gotta do time, that's payin' taxes." Corinne, who is White and trades sex under the radar, observed that women who spend a significant amount of their time soliciting in public face a dramatically increased likelihood of arrest and subsequent incarceration, such that "every time they turn around they're goin' to jail."

Yet the women's certainty regarding the inevitability of arrest exists in conjunction with their fundamental uncertainty about police procedure, including behaviors permissible for undercover officers, criteria for making an arrest, and the consequences of prostitution-related criminal convictions.[3] Like most U.S. cities, Denver and its suburbs have a range of municipal, state, and federal statutes related to prostitution, all with varying levels of evidence required for a prosecutor to obtain a conviction.[4] A Denver municipal statute, "Furthering the Act of Prostitution," for instance, criminalizes behaviors surrounding the transactional sexual exchange in ways that Italian American frequent flyer Gianna, like most of her colleagues, characterized as arbitrary and unfair:

> They can get you for furthering. If you're standing out there, let's say somebody pulls up and asks you if you're working, you say, "No, but can I get a ride?" and you get in that vehicle and get a ride to, say I just wanna go ten blocks, up there to the liquor store, they can get you for furthering. Or if you're stickin' your thumb out, tryin' to hitch a ride, they can get you for furthering. It's crazy! They can get you for furthering. Furthering what? What the hell is furthering? It's just another word for prostitution. They try to come up with new stuff all the time to try to keep you from gettin' in any vehicle, regardless. What if I was stabbed and I needed to go to the hospital, and I stuck my thumb out because I needed a ride to go to the hospital? Then they could get me for furthering.

Gianna's characterization of furthering as oblique enough to potentially result in her arrest following a violent assault underscores the fear and frustration women feel about the unknown parameters of their encounters with police. For instance, frequent flyer Annette, who is White, and Ximena, who is Latina and bonded, disputed what officers can and cannot do during an interview in which they debated the limits that police procedures impose on undercover officers. Both shared the belief that undercover officers can sexually touch women and use illicit drugs, but sharply differed in their assessment of whether or not an officer had a legal obligation to identify himself as such when explicitly asked:

> ANNETTE: They can touch you, they can smoke dope, they can do whatever. The only thing they cannot do is expose theirselves.
> XIMENA: I got hemmed up like that one time, and the cop actually put his hand down my shirt, and has me touch his stuff too. And he was a cop, and he drove about a block and a half from where he picked me up and there were cops everywhere. He was a police officer, he put his hand down my shirt, groped me, had me touch him, and he was a cop, all day long. But if you ask if he's a cop, he got to tell you.
> ANNETTE: Oh no, he don't, not like back in the day. Girl, please, when you been out here for a minute [an extended period of time] like I have, then come talk to me.

Annette's claim to expertise due to her extensive time working the street highlights both the knowledge she has accumulated through multiple criminal justice system encounters as well as her recognition that changes in police procedure do occur, sometimes in response to street-involved women's pervasive knowledge about them. African American caregiver NeNe alludes to these procedural changes in describing how women need to closely observe the man behind the wheel of a car, even if the vehicle looks familiar:

> You gotta really pay attention 'cause when you're out there on the streets you actually gotta *look* at the people behind the wheel of the vehicle, because you can see the same person drivin' by, tryin' to flag you down, wave you on, and then later on you'll see them in a different vehicle doin' the same thing, therefore you know it's a cop. Or they're just switchin' up

in the vehicles tryin' to get the girls who thought, "Okay, okay, this is the vehicle they're drivin' around in, they're not going to get me," then they switch up on vehicles and, "Aw, shit, they got me!" You know, you gotta really pay attention to faces and if you're too high or you're too tired, that's what'll get you busted a lotta times.

Despite their development of arrest avoidance strategies such as NeNe's, women universally express a sense of injustice at what they regard as misguided policing priorities whereby, as Dion, who is White and a caregiver, put it, officers are "more worried about bustin' a whore than a gang shooting a block away."

Women's presence in public is a necessary condition for street-based sex trading to take place, but this outdoor activity exposes the women to police scrutiny that often leads to arrest. Lexi, who is White and takes great pride in her ability to avoid arrest while working under the radar, described a formative experience that convinced her that officers who suspect women of engaging in street prostitution will go to great lengths to arrest her:

> I've been in a position where they have already set up this shit before and they might have thought I wasn't a hooker but they couldn't quite eyeball me. So I kinda felt like one day they had set me up with this one client in this one car. He kept eyeballin' me all day and honking, and driving by and waving and doin' all the shit that a John would do to get your attention if you were on the street. One day he pulled around the corner right when I was walking, 'cause he'd been circling me for quite a while. I'm not chasin' no one down the street. So he pulled up, I come walkin' by, and here comes a cop, right there, pulls right up on the corner right as I was about to walk toward the car. And that's when I knew, right then and there, it was a set-up, because he seen me walk that way, and he drove off in the direction of the cop, and that's how I knew right then and there it was a fuckin' sting, they were tryin' to get me. I'm sorry, but they were, they were tryin' to get me. They had their eye on me for a minute 'cause I'd been workin' Colfax for a minute and I'm sure all the cops seen me out there.

While Lexi acknowledges that she was involved in street-based sex trading prior to her arrest in the sting operation she describes, her account also underscores the challenges women face while soliciting in a neighborhood that police and city residents associate with street prostitution. Consider these descriptions of police encounters that African American Kyra, an intergenerational, and Ashanti, who is bonded, have had as they go about their everyday activities:

> KYRA: The police officers, they think that because you're a woman it's always about prostitution for some reason. And I had one officer say to me, "I'm about to arrest you for prostitution" because the guy in the car is giving me a ride to a motel, 'cause I was homeless. Now this wasn't about no sex or nothing, and he separated us when he pulled us over. And then the dude in the car said, "I was goin' to pay her for sex" and I said, "Bullshit, he ain't gonna get nothin' from me" and plus I already had my own money anyway. If I had two dollars in my pocket, I'm doin' better, you know what I'm sayin', ain't no man about to run me around.

> ASHANTI: The police, they had searched my backpack, I had four condoms in my backpack and they harassed me about it. I said, "What are you talkin' about? I just came from [a drop-in center], they give you free condoms. I just got off a bus!" One night I walked down here to get a Dr. Pepper and I had some ones [dollar bills] in my hand, ended up going to jail for forty-five days. They just pulled me over for nothing. Wasn't even doing nothin'. Walked in, bought a Snickers and a Dr. Pepper. Just took a bite of the Snickers and they were like, "Put it down!" and I'm like, "It's a Snickers [laughing]. It's a Snickers."

Both of these accounts highlight how quickly encounters that lead to arrest occur, often in situations that require women to very rapidly make decisions with potentially lifelong consequences in the form of a criminal record.

Street-involved women often have intimate knowledge about individuals and events of interest to police as a result of their intense involvement in ancillary illicit drug economy activities. A chain of events that begins with police contact, whether initiated by an officer or a street-involved woman who enlists police aid, can rapidly escalate into a situation that forces a woman to choose between her own incarceration or someone else's, or between a more severe sentence and sharing sensitive information that may compromise her safety at a later point. Consider, for example, the experience of nineteen-year-old Sam, bonded three years earlier to a man who facilitated her sex trading until they had a dispute when he refused to return her handbag, which prompted her to call the police. Sam was unaware that this man, with whom she was intimately involved, had been under investigation for trafficking in minors, and the events she unwittingly initiated by contacting the police promptly led to his arrest and subsequent prosecution in federal court:

> The cops were like, "Okay, the only way you won't go to jail is if you turn him in." I was like, "Okay." So, they asked questions: "Were you working with him?" "Yeah." "Were you posted [on an Internet escort site, by him]?" "Yes, I was posted at one point." They go, "Have you worked with him recently?" I said, "No, I came over here to talk to him and he ended up wanting me to work, I didn't want to so I tried to make it look like I was and I came back to get my bag and he wouldn't give it to me, and now no one's answering." They raided the hotel room after that.

In Sam's account, a dispute with an intimate partner over her handbag quickly evolved into a felony trafficking case against him due to her status as a minor at the time of his arrest. Women with more experience, particularly old school cougars, frequently bemoan young or inexperienced women's tendency to speak candidly to police officers because they fear arrest or other negative outcomes, or, like Sam, lack knowledge about the possible consequences of revealing information to police. In discussing this issue, African American old school cougar Pearlie candidly summarized the situation of a newly arrested woman who, in her haste to get out of jail, might accept a plea agreement and consequent lifelong criminal record:

> If they're only gonna give her [a relatively short sentence] dependin' how many times she's been arrested, then a lot of the time the girls who take the plea agreement just go ahead and plead "no contest," take the charge, so they can get outta jail, as opposed to waitin' for a speedy trial, which is like two weeks, sittin' in there and havin' to wait on gettin' the fuck outta there.

Pearlie's account concisely characterizes most street-involved women's circumstances, including the lack of adequate legal representation or clear explanation of legal charges and processes, and no opportunity to bond out of jail due to nonexistent or limited economic resources. In these circumstances, to some women, a long-term criminal record may quite reasonably appear more abstract than the more pressing desire to be released from jail. The often totalizing pressures of women's immediate circumstances likewise inform their understandings of the risks posed by those who enforce order or otherwise exert influence over their neighborhood surroundings.

Gendered Socioeconomic Relations

As in U.S. society more generally, men enjoy considerably higher status in the gendered socioeconomic relations that structure both the drug economy and the transactional sexual activities that revolve around it. Women almost universally depict street-based sex trading as the situational result of circumstances that coalesce in particular ways; as African American Kyra, an intergenerational, asserted, "It's not like you're just out here doin' it because it's what you wanna do or it's what you like to do, it's just 'cause you in a *situation*." Almost all women characterized their street involvement as the result of an almost linear series of events that occurred when they were already living on the brink of homelessness and absolute poverty. Responsibilities for small children only worsened such a situation, as African American caregiver Marie described:

> Rent, drugs, food, kids. One time I got knocked off of welfare—they took my food stamps for three years 'cause they found out that my boyfriend was in the house. I couldn't get a job and I had four kids and a man and all kinds of troubles. Back in them days it was really bad, that was the only way a woman could take care of family, and I mean for three years I took care of my whole family, drugs, motel, everything, and I mean it was really hard 'cause I couldn't get a job.

Women without children described equally constrained environments in which sex trading presented the best out of a very limited set of life options. Kay, who has worked under the radar since she arrived in Denver a decade ago from a reservation in the Dakotas, said that the street offered possibilities relative to some women's previous living situations:

> It's the promise of, you know, an easier life. I just think of a few girls I knew, they don't know anything but the reservation life, and that is no life. You know, suicide rate's so high, it's just drinkin' and then you get up here and you never been in the city, you have nowhere to go and somebody's gonna, you know, "Oh, you can come crash over here" and, before you know it, you're in it.

Once they had engaged in transactional sex for an extended period of time, many women felt that it became more and more difficult to find legal ways to make money, especially as they acquired sometimes-extensive criminal records. Even just keeping up with the daily tasks of survival, women reported, was exhausting enough to preclude women from seeking out other opportunities or potential sources of assistance. Marisol, who is Latina and works under the radar, describes street involvement as all-encompassing in ways that make pursuing alternatives nearly impossible:

> We just don't have a lot of options, and that is what the situation comes down to, is that we just don't have any more options left, and that's what my situation came down to. You put everything into someone else and they take it and fuck you over. And they take everything and then you're left to start all over from the beginning again, and what're you supposed to do about that? It costs a hundred dollars a day just to live, basically. Out here, that's cents. That's, y'know, a motel, maybe some food, maybe some cigarettes, and that's about it and in the morning you're stuck back in the same situation that you were in last night. So you have to go out and do it all over again. You don't have a chance to look for a job, because you're tryin' to survive.

While Marisol describes the dissolution of a relationship as precipitating her involvement in prostitution, many women with intimate partners or children characterize their relationships as playing a significant role in their transactional sexual activities. Women reported a set of intimate partner–related risks that had an added layer of emotional complexity because of cohabitation, long-term shared drug use, and other affective bonds. African American K'neisha, who is bonded, felt a painfully ambivalent tension between her and her partner after she returned home to share with him the money she earned on the street:

> It's hard when you come in your own house, too. PTSD, things like that are real, it's traumatic, and you're going back into your household and you're trying to act like everything's alright, and maybe the person doesn't accept you, or maybe they do, but you never know, and it's a hard transition just for that first hour, it hurts like hell.

Shirley, an African American old school cougar, characterized her situation as one in which her partner was "runnin' everything, especially when it comes to runnin' me," although she had supported him for several years with her street earnings. A number of women specifically likened their economic support of intimate partners and children to exploitative "pimp" relationships. Marie, a caregiver, succinctly stated, "I ain't have no pimp, my four kids is my pimp! 'Mama, we hungry!' That's my pimp." Krystal, a White frequent flyer, echoed this sentiment in her observation, "Ain't no real pimps out here, they're your husband and your fiancés and your boyfriends and your significant others." Women often contextualized these choices as inherently gendered, which prompted Marlee, who is Latina and bonded, to describe most men's limited income-generation options by saying, "The only hustle that they really have is trying to get dope for other people." Such small-scale drug sales are neither as lucrative nor as reliable as sex trading, and present the additional risks of felony drug convictions and violent altercations.

Caregivers, with their significant economic responsibilities for minor children or intimate partners, face a special set of contradictory challenges whereby sex trading becomes one of few options for quick income generation, particularly at the end of the month following the exhaustion of food stamps or other government benefits. This is further complicated for women in intimate relationships with men with whom they are forbidden contact by case workers or other alliance professionals with the power to revoke benefits or enact other serious consequences.

Such a situation initially pushed African American old school cougar Ms. Ella into street sex trading:

> If there's a woman who's working out here who's got kids, who ain't got nowhere to go, that's her only means, because I'm telling you that social services will kick your ass in a New York heartbeat and say, "We do not give a fuck." Excuse my French, but that's the damn truth. And when they caught my man in the bed, they said, "Oh well." And they did, they cut me off'a welfare for three years and food stamps for two. I ain't have no trade, honey, I *had* to do what I did.

Women who ally with one another to provide housing and other basic necessities for their children, as did caregivers Mary, who is African American, and Dion, who is White, sometimes find themselves feeling the kind of systematic exclusion that Ms. Ella describes. Mary emotionally recounted the time when Dion left her baby, who had a life-threatening liver condition requiring injections every few hours, with her in the motel room as Mary tried to care for her own child:

> She left the baby with me for like nine days. I couldn't fuckin' find her nowhere. I didn't know where she was. I'm calling everyone, and I'm like, "Great, I have to take her to the hospital, and I don't even know what I'm gonna do, and I'm gonna get in trouble." I had a two-month-old baby then. They [social services] ended up taking her [Dion's baby], and she had another baby, and then they turned around, they said the only way they would take the baby was if they had the youngest one, too. They said that they would give the baby a liver transplant immediately if she would terminate her [parental] rights. They said that they would save her life and give her a transplant immediately, that they'd bump her up the list just as long as she signed her name on that paper [terminating her parental rights].

The situation Mary and Dion faced, which led to Dion losing custody of both her young children under the coercive condition of offering one a life-saving liver transplant, speaks to the additional risks women face in forming relationships with other street-involved women. Indeed, women almost universally avoid any demonstration of emotional vulnerability that might cause an opportunistic person, especially another street-involved woman, to exploit them. As Julie, who is White and works under the radar, put it,

> A lot of people, they try to tell you every sob story in the world just so they can get a little something from you. Do that shit to me, I just turn around and do it right back to you. It ain't no lie, you gotta do your own hustle sometimes even if you've got somebody, because [eventually] that person starts relying on you.

An environment in which everyone needs to perform her "own hustle" is not conducive to the establishment of trust-based relationships. Women frequently reported avoiding other street-involved women whom they did not know because of the difficulties inherent in determining intentions in a resource-scarce environment where most individuals struggle with addiction as well as other mental health issues and face multiple forms of violence and social exclusion. Some women observed that they would actively avoid sharing information about themselves or other street-involved women due to the potential for negative consequences. Vanessa, who is Latina and bonded, and Traci, an African American intergenerational, shared their reasoning for avoiding exchanges with their peers, particularly in times of crisis or need:

> VANESSA: Call your family, call your Mom, talk to family or somebody, but these people out here ain't gonna care about what you gotta say. These people out here, they ain't gonna be your company, they ain't gonna be your confidante, everything you tell 'em, they gonna call your weakness, make you gullible. So anything that happens to you, all those sad stories and stuff, you don't tell nobody out here—that's part of your weakness, that's givin' 'em strings to pull. I don't tell nobody shit like that. It's none of their business.
>
> TRACI: If another woman out here said somethin' to me about a pimp, I'd be like "Go on ahead, I ain't gonna hear about it, and whoever he is, I don't wanna know who he is." I don't wanna, because I don't wanna make a mistake and say somethin' to him. I don't wanna know it. I don't wanna know about it, honey, so if she doin' that, that's her business, God bless her, if I see her with a Black guy, I'm like, "Okay, I already know what that is."

Self-protective forms of this avoidance behavior are also evident in women's characterization of peers who do not respect the rules of competition as "clock-blockin'" and "scandalous people." Clock-blockers, who disregard the time a woman has spent waiting on the street for clients by jumping in front of cars or engaging in other aggressive soliciting, present the risk of driving clients away completely. Noelle, a White intergenerational, describes an occasion when another street-involved women clock-blocked her:

> That was my spot, and she was across the street and it was like freezin' cold and this guy came across, and as soon as I got ready to see him she turned and she boned it across the street, and it was like kinda funny because he like locked the doors real quick. So that's kinda like with clock-blockin' and scandalous people, that they try to take your date before, you know, you actually get to your date.

It is partly in response to such behavior that women jokingly refer to East Colfax Avenue as "Crackville," often in the form of an explanatory preface, such as "out here in Crackville," a reference to the neighborhood's reputation as a resource-scarce socioeconomic environment where everyone is involved somehow in the illicit drug economy or its policing. Frequent flyer Mariah, who is Latina, described gendered drug-related vulnerabilities as endemic to the neighborhood and resulting in the low prices that some women charged for sexual acts:

> All they are carin' about is gettin' that next buck and that next high. And there's girls out here that, the lowest I've heard is there was this one she will suck a guy's cock for five dollars, go get her a five dollar hit, and the highest I've heard was really, about forty bucks, and that was for a quick lay. Out here, we scallywags.

In some cases, women's experiences with these gendered drug-related vulnerabilities began with parents or other caretakers who struggled with addictions and other mental health problems. Janeiece, a White intergenerational, first traded sexual services for money when she was a young teenager temporarily housed in a motel room with her younger siblings and mother, whose addiction and mental health problems incapacitated her:

> My first experience, when I first turned a trick, my mom was using. I was fourteen, and we stayed at a place on First and Broadway, my mom was crying about diapers. I took a walk, this White dude in a Lexus was lookin' at me. I was young. So they just honk, this and that, and I got in and showed him my little nipples and he gave me a hundred dollars. I bought diapers and food.

Janeiece's pragmatic description of using transactional sex to provide for her family at a very young age reflects the gendered expectations at work in a situation of extreme poverty and social isolation; rather than expressing outrage or frustration at these circumstances, Janeiece clearly recounts them as simple social facts. Yet adult street-involved women are far less sympathetic in their accounts of seeing or hearing about neighborhood adults who encouraged or forced their children or other young girls under their care into prostitution. These adults, all of whom suffered from severe addictions, mental health issues, or sociopathic traits, were subjects of the women's derision and, sometimes, intervention; in one case, several women anonymously called the police when they discovered that a neighborhood man was forcing his two teenage daughters to work the street.

Street-involved women's clients come from a variety of backgrounds, and the risks they face in dealing with these men accordingly span a continuum from nuisance behaviors to the threat of violent assault or even death. Part of this continuum involves the remuneration women receive for the sex acts they perform, such that on one extreme clients are men who insult women by offering very small amounts of money and on the other are men whom African American bonded woman K'neisha describes as "the good ones," who will pay any price:

> You got the rudeasses that are like "ten dollars" and, don't get me wrong, there've been some times, but most of the time, uh-uh, that's not right. And then you got the good ones that have wives and they're doctors and they got a livin' and their fantasy is to be with a Black girl or somethin'. They'll pay you whatever you say.

Women emphasized that this client diversity does little to assuage their safety concerns during sexual encounters with men they know little about. For instance, frequent flyer Krystal, who is White, regularly smoked crack with a man who also paid her for sex; it was only after he was sentenced to life in prison that she learned he had murdered several other street-involved women:

> Come to find out this fool had a torture chamber and had already killed like five chicks! He's in prison now, for life. I'm glad I never gave him the impression to attack me. I'm very skeptical about people bein' crazy, so, I might even mess it up and they might not even be tryin' to attack me. I might get scared and be ready to take off runnin', but it's a good thing I didn't second-guess myself, 'cause most of the time when you do that, you're pretty much right.

Instances of rape and being threatened with weapons take place with disturbing regularity among the women, and almost every woman I spoke with shared a story about a woman she knew who had experienced sexual assault.[5] In some instances, women recalled female acquaintances, friends, or family members who disappeared or whose bodies had been discovered hidden in dumpsters or other public places after persons unknown murdered them. Florencia, a Latina bonded woman, described the speed with which this could take place in recounting what had happened to her mother's friend: "She got into a car with somebody and they raped her and they beat her to death. And left her out there, like just trash, pretty much."

Sexual assault also takes place in the form of clients who do not pay or who use physical force or verbal threats to demand a woman return the money that they have paid her prior to commencing the sexual act. Clients often do this under the guise of moving to a different location; Carla, who is Latina and works under the radar, described an incident in which "he was like, 'let's move to the back of the truck' and I get out, he gets out, next thing I know he's taking off, no money." For women who are homeless or precariously housed and carry most or all of their belongings with them, knowledge of this practice provokes particular anxiety regarding clients who, as Latina caregiver Elena put it, "try to hurry up and take off with your shit in the vehicle."

Cultural norms widely shared among the women depict a constellation of occupational risks primarily tethered to policing and gendered socioeconomic relations in the neighborhood in which they live and earn money. To hear most of the women tell it, their biggest occupational risks derive from constraints that the criminal justice system, and to some extent the criminal justice–social services alliance more generally, imposes on their physical mobility, autonomy, and safety. These risks occur in the context of interpersonal and neighborhood relations that feature their own constraints and challenges as a result of scarce resources, women's limited abilities to protect themselves from harm, and sometimes extensive punitive social services involvement in the lives of women and their children. Yet the alliance ethos, as well as many of those tasked with its implementation, takes a different view of the risks women face in the course of their quotidian activities.

Alliance Professionals' Perspectives on Occupational Risks

The alliance ethos identifies a set of interconnected occupational risks the women face as part of a cycle of substance abuse and addiction compounded by traumatic experiences and intersectional vulnerabilities. This ethos conceptualizes a woman's involvement in prostitution and illicit drug use as an individual choice, albeit one inherently tied to her socioeconomic vulnerability and past experiences with traumatic events. In this view, a woman's negative life experiences have inhibited her from developing the wide range of skills, from culturally appropriate gendered social behaviors to money management, necessary for a successful life. In characterizing the women's ways of being in the world as intrinsically "unhealthy" for both their bodies and their inner selves, the alliance positions the women as physical manifestations of social ills stemming from structural inequalities that require and, from the alliance perspective, deserve, state intervention.

Alliance professionals fulfill this interventionist role by arresting, sentencing, and monitoring women's progress in court-mandated therapeutic treatment programs, correctional facilities, and supervision through regular meetings with those on probation or parole. These work responsibilities revolve around a threefold understanding of the women's risks that include the consequences of addiction and its criminalization, trauma-related impediments to psychological development and appropriate social functioning, and intersectional harms related to identity and community factors. Positioned as interventionists by the ethos that governs their work, individual alliance professionals describe facing three major attendant risks as part of their jobs, including feeling ineffective in struggling with the status quo, witnessing the operations of racism and sexism at work, and the potential for the abuse of power.

Alliance Perspectives on Occupational Risks among the Women

The alliance ethos holds that addiction creates the primary occupational risks street-involved women face, yet individual alliance professionals differ in terms of the causal forces to which they attribute this risk. Enforcers and bureaucrats, who advocate strict enforcement of the law and adhere most closely and uncritically to the alliance ethos, tend to regard women's choices, including the decision to use illicit drugs, as the primary causal agent in the production of risk. For instance, Calvin, a White diversion court evaluator with a bureaucrat orientation derived from years of experience working in problem-solving courts throughout the United States, characterized the women's lives as part of a "very simple, repetitive pattern" whereby "they became addicted to drugs, needed money, and, in their minds, prostitution was the means to acquire substances, then they would use the substance."

Idealists and transgressors, who are frequently young and work directly with street-involved women, tend to take a more nuanced view of the ways in which addiction creates risks for women. While all alliance professionals acknowledged or referred to some version of Calvin's assessment regarding patterns in the women's lives, police patrol officers and vice detectives consistently made the important observation that a woman's choices with respect to preferred substances and partners can dramatically impact the way she engages in street-based sex trading. Kurt, a White vice detective who shares a strong transgressor orientation with many of his colleagues, observed that

> [h]eroin being a depressant, it kinda knocks you out, and you probably need somebody there, but also somebody can manipulate you easier. Whereas something like crack, you use it, or even something like meth,

you're alert, but see meth is kind of a young person's drug too, so then you have pimps. And I've seen that most of the lesbians don't have pimps, and I think it's the idea of, "Okay, I can do this to get money. I don't enjoy it, but it's a job." And that's a job for them. "I go to work and do my job, but there's no way I'm going to have a man tell me what to do." So, they're probably more empowered in that way.

Kurt's knowledge of these nuances and contingencies reflects the sustained opportunities that those who work undercover have to observe and interact with the women, since their jobs require understanding (but not acceptance) of the cultural norms that frame the women's lives. These norms, as the women themselves note, directly shape both the risks women face and the way that they engage in their routine activities. The low status accorded to street prostitution by both the law, in which it is a misdemeanor offense, and the street economy, where it does not share the prestige of the illicit drug trade or gang involvement, contributes to the frequency and relative speed with which street-involved women cycle through the criminal justice system. In so doing, they often accumulate a lengthy record of convictions due to inadequate legal representation and a desire to plead guilty in order to leave jail sooner.

Janine, a Latina probation officer with an enforcer orientation, oversees a caseload of women with prostitution convictions and spoke to me at length on several occasions about her frustration with what she regards as superficial divisions between escorts and street-involved women. Rather than alluding to nuances and contingencies, Janine describes these different women's unwillingness to cooperatively participate in the same court-mandated programs as inhibiting their own collective awareness of their many mutual experiences, including trauma. This point is particularly significant because street-involved women face different treatment and options in comparison with women who perform sex work indoors as escorts, whose criminal cases tend to be more complex, often involving multiple codefendants in a jury trial and state or federal, rather than city or county, charges:

> The likelihood that escort cases go to trial is higher than street prostitution. The street women may just admit to it, and sometimes they're a little bit more open about street life, versus the [escort] women that

were caught through an undercover sting. So they're equal and the same, just different personalities. I've learned that you can't put them in the same groups, there's a dynamic that they view each other differently but whether it's budgeting or saying "no," you could peel away street prostitution, you can peel away escorting and the trauma's still there for both of them, the substance abuse is still there for both of them.

Janine argues that while all prostitution is essentially the same, this refusal on the part of women from different sex industry sectors to share this view negatively impacts therapeutic group work by necessitating separation, as well as different types of criminal justice system encounters.

I witnessed an escort engage in the kind of disassociation from street-involved women Janine describes while observing in prostitution diversion court, where almost all participants are street involved. A well-dressed and very embarrassed White woman in her early thirties sat among the predominantly African American and Latina women in the courtroom before being called before the judge to announce her intentions with respect to her case. "Your Honor, look around you," she said with deliberately careful diction. "I don't belong here. I'm not like these women: I'm not an addict. I'm not homeless. I just need to pay the bills. Let me do my thirty days [in jail] and pay my fine. I don't need this program." The judge agreed and a deputy led her out of the courtroom for transfer to county jail.

Arrest and incarceration temporarily disrupt women's involvement in street prostitution and illicit drug use, and yet accruing criminal convictions simultaneously increases the likelihood that women will continue these activities. Prospective landlords and employers routinely engage in criminal background checks in Denver, as in other U.S. cities, and pervasive discrimination against women with prostitution- and drug-related convictions places them at a further disadvantage in seeking housing and employment. Hence it is unsurprising that almost all alliance professionals lament the frequency with which street-involved women move through the criminal justice system without experiencing meaningful changes in their lives. Diana, an idealist White public defender who works with a prostitution diversion court, noted that this lack of real change stems from a system that accords little attention to

the deeper structural issues that inform street-involved women's decision making:

> The first jail sentence [in this jurisdiction] is typically thirty days, a sixty-
> day suspended sentence, but then we see them again in six months and
> they have the sixty days they're sitting on, so that's a problem. Jail just
> incapacitates them for a little while. I don't think this should be a criminal
> justice issue; it should be a community issue. People living on the streets
> are mentally ill and using drugs. Our police officers aren't trained to deal
> with people who are mentally ill, and we continue to arrest those buying
> crack for ten dollars or selling their bodies for ten dollars of crack, not the
> person bringing the crack to the streets.

In a separate interview, the judge who presides over the diversion court
where Diana works also iterated this assessment in his observation that
mental illness and traumatic events combine to create challenges that
can prove insurmountable for women without assistance:

> The incidence of trauma, early trauma, is really remarkable. This isn't
> unique to this program. In the lives of these women, trauma is huge: be-
> ing gang-raped, beat repeatedly, being forced to do things. This involves
> early initiation of sexual behavior, and substance abuse, mental health
> issues. I think there may be one or two women without an active diag-
> nosis, but most have bipolar, schizophrenia, major depressions. Even for
> someone with a lot of resources these things would be challenging, and
> these women don't have resources.

The type of trauma-informed approach the judge describes here aims
to sensitively attend to women's past experiences while simultaneously
encouraging them to address the root causes of their present behaviors.
The trauma-informed approach advises professionals to proceed with
empathy and sensitivity as they work with individuals who have suffered psychological damage from a violent or grief-generating event
(U.S. Department of Health and Human Services, 2014). This approach
contends that experiencing such an event can create psychological and
emotional after-effects that can inform or impair individual functioning
to such a degree as to require expert intervention to help the individual

recover. Yet, as Elizabeth Bumiller (2008) argues, this well-intentioned approach can also function to infantilize women who are already struggling with significant restrictions on their autonomy.

The alliance interpretation of the trauma-informed approach holds that trauma's overwhelming power over the women who have experienced it necessitates that professionals take great care not to create circumstances that "trigger" the women by causing them to relive painful events.[6] Andi, an idealist Latina social worker at a drop-in center for street-involved women, describes how her agency attempts to maintain this fine balance:

> We try to be a very trauma-informed agency where we understand that at any point women could be triggered by anything that we're doing here so we try to create a very safe environment. Unfortunately that's not necessarily something that a lot of women understand very well, what it looks like to be safe, what it means to treat someone else with dignity and respect, in a way that doesn't cause them to feel unsafe.

The trauma-informed approach that Andi describes, and that prevails among many social services providers, positions women's everyday lives prior to their involvement with the criminal justice–social services alliance as essentially unsafe, disrespectful, and undignified, a condition many alliance professionals seek to correct by creating what they regard as encounters that have the opposite effect. Doing so proves very challenging, if not impossible, in the coercive environment that surrounds court-mandated treatment or incarceration. Street-involved women often have no choice regarding the type, duration, or tone of most encounters they have with alliance professionals, and yet these exchanges require that women openly disclose—or at least convincingly fake open disclosure of—information about events alliance professionals regard as sufficiently traumatic to have prompted their involvement with illicit drugs and prostitution.

Even the most well-intentioned alliance professionals exercise considerable discretionary authority and power to determine their clients' futures, resulting in a situation with a high potential for misunderstandings and cultural insensitivity. Diego, a Latino court-mandated therapist with an enforcer orientation, took great pride in explaining his approach to working with women sentenced to meet with him weekly in exchange for a suspended jail sentence. He, like a number of alliance professionals who provide therapeutic services, attributes many of the women's struggles to low self-esteem and self-image issues that prevent them from achieving their full potential.

Diego offered an example of what he termed a "breakthrough moment" with one of his more challenging clients, Shondra, a young African American woman who, following culturally normative practices among many of her neighborhood peers, favored long, straight-haired wigs. Diego recalled how Shondra had wept when he initially met with her in jail, where she could neither wear a wig nor afford the commissary's expensive hair products. At their subsequent meeting in his office, he called his African American colleague, Dee, into the room and informed Shondra that she should remove her wig in order in order for him to "see the real Shondra." Shondra initially protested, informing Diego, "You obviously don't know that you don't tell a Black woman to take off her hair." As Diego and Dee continued to prompt Shondra to remove the wig, he noted, she grew increasingly annoyed:

> She goes, "Fine. I'll take it off." When she took it off, you just saw her facial features come out. She started getting teary-eyed. So when we asked her, "What's going on?" she said, "No one has said that I'm beautiful and made me believe it like I feel it today." And so for that good forty minutes that she was in my office talking to me she didn't put the wig back on. That's where they're at, it's very objectifying. It's very sexualized, but that's what's true to them. That's cognitively where they're at.

Diego expressed great confidence in the belief that he had succeeded in increasing Shondra's self-confidence in her appearance, and it is, of course, impossible to know how Shondra experienced this encounter. Yet in making claims to knowledge about Shondra's inner cognitive state and his ability to enable her to see her true self, Diego's account comes dangerously close to replicating the very forces the trauma-informed approach purports to subvert. Many alliance professionals of all ethnoracial backgrounds observe that African American women and Latinas face unique sexualized vulnerabilities as a result of the structural violence wrought by what they characterize as entrenched poverty and ghettoization. Steve, a White detective, speaks to intersectional factors at work in the lives of young African American women and Latinas he encounters during his criminal investigations in neighborhoods that surround or resemble East Colfax:

> I think it's a complete, total problem when you look at our society, at neighborhoods and impoverished communities, we see a disproportionate number of minors that are minorities. It's because of all of those different backgrounds and factors that lead up to it [sex trading]. So you're coming from an impoverished environment, you're coming from a broken home, say mom has different boyfriends and things like that, and the different men that come into their lives, those are the ones that are sexually abusive. I think that that's part of the dynamic.

Steve, as an enforcer, does acknowledge the oppressive structural forces, such as poverty, that he and his colleagues observe in neighborhoods they intensely police. Yet his overall portrait is one of a dysfunctional community populated by individuals in need of outside regulation by the criminal justice system and the alliance more generally.

Roxanne, a Latina corrections officer with a transgressor orientation, described the impact that these exclusionary social forces have on her work by using an example of a graduation event for incarcerated women who successfully completed an addictions-treatment course. As she looked around the room, proud of the women's progress in the program, she began to notice some stark ethno-racial differences between program participants and the general jail population:

> I was like, "Okay, there's one Black female," there wasn't any Hispanic females, and it typically gets like that. There's times that there might be two or three Black females and then there might be two or three Hispanics. The court will sentence the White women more towards treatment, and then the minority women just get the 165 days [jail sentence] for prostitution, and then we have to try to engage them and look for them. Or they have to say something to somebody, and that's when we hear who they are, and their name, and that's when we contact them. The Black women in jail, I could hear them saying things like, "Oh, that's a White program." I could really hear that.

Roxanne's job forces her to witness ethno-racially discriminatory sentencing practices, the difficulties African American women and Latinas experience in accessing drug treatment while incarcerated, and the almost arbitrary ways in which correctional facilities determine the women's potential interest in treatment. She highlights some of the pervasive and systemic barriers African American women and Latinas face as a result of these practices, which is particularly significant when considered in conjunction with the reality that many street-involved women are mothers, sometimes of very young children.

Most of the alliance professionals who participated in this study cited intergenerational criminal justice system involvement as a risk women face, both with their parents and, as they age, with their own children. Doris, an African American probation officer with a bureaucratic orientation, spoke from her decades of experience working with street-involved women when she said, "You can just see that their hearts break when they say, 'Oh my son just committed his first felony and he's nineteen. I didn't think it was gonna happen to him, because he saw how hard it was for me.'" Kate, a White social worker and idealist, prefaced an account that brought her to tears by stating, "There's a lot of dynamics between kiddos and moms":

> They're not all success stories, but I can say that with one woman, my success story was that her baby was safe, and unfortunately parental rights were terminated, but my work played a role in that baby being adopted, having a loving family. She's continued to be on the street and continued in the sex industry and we gave her a chance three times to be a mom and even though it was unsuccessful and it ended in a lengthy jail sentence, that baby was safe so, in my mind there are success stories that someone else may not see as a success.

Kate's example highlights the sometimes-sharp disconnects between alliance professionals and street-involved women with respect to definitions of "success." This particular case, which still caused Kate to cry years after the event despite her classification of these events as a "success," underscores both the limited time street-involved women have to make comprehensive life changes and the difficult legal and moral decisions alliance professionals must make when women cannot achieve goals the alliance has set for them.

Precarious housing and homelessness dramatically impact a woman's ability to make any changes while simultaneously exposing her to a number of risks. Knowledge about these risks and the frequent inability of shelters and transitional housing facilities to meet women's needs for housing present alliance professionals with a frustrating set of dilemmas. Consider the experience of Shelley, a White county jail employee with a transgressor orientation who is tasked with assisting women in finding housing and other basic resources they will need on their release:

> I am so irritated with homeless shelters! To get somebody in there is like an act of Congress. I call and I call and, "No, we don't have a room," and we pay them a hundred and ninety-nine dollars a week, but I can't get them to agree to hold a bed or two for me. [One shelter] changed their whole process and they have to do this little matrix and so if you're too much on the negative, on this side that you have all these issues, you can't get in there and I'm like, "Are you kidding me?"

In such circumstances, it is understandable that the often constrained and overburdened alliance professionals feel that they face their own set of occupational hazards.

Alliance Professionals' Perspectives on Their Own Occupational Risks

Identifying and interpreting the women's occupational risks within the alliance ethos is an important task for all alliance professionals irrespective of their work orientation, such that they must encourage, or even mandate, that women share (or at least convincingly fake adherence to) the system's values. Yet even as alliance professionals come to know at least some aspects of the women's lives through their encounters with them, they face particular occupational risks of their own. These perceptions of occupational risk involve individual sensitivities and preferences but, as with women who are street involved, commonalities do exist, specifically in the areas of feeling ineffective, struggling with limited resources, experiencing racism and sexism at work, and the potential for the abuse of power.

"Burnout" is the evocative term all the alliance professionals who participated in this project use to describe colleagues who can no longer perform their jobs because they have become too overwhelmed by exhaustion and feelings of inefficacy. In extreme cases, these sentiments can even involve the belief that street-involved women they attempted to assist have betrayed them by making choices they regard as ill advised. Alliance professionals experience burnout differently according to the type and duration of interactions they have with the women, such that police officers may feel emotionally battered by the suffering and interpersonal violence they see on a daily basis and have few resources to deal with these feelings.[7]

Probation officers and those who provide court-mandated therapeutic counseling interact with street-involved women in more sustained and controlled settings where they are less likely to be under the influence of illicit substances. In forming and sustaining these inherently coercive relationships, which make claims to therapeutic intervention, alliance professionals must support a paradox whereby they engage in attempting to assist a woman against her will. This assistance, which necessarily takes place on alliance terms, often has little relevance to what street-involved women regard as major issues in their lives. These realities, along with the sometimes-painful disclosures the women make to them, can constitute a heavy emotional burden for alliance professionals.

The situation is somewhat different for police officers, whose patrol or investigative work regularly puts them into contact with women who are actively engaging in street-based sex trading and illicit drug use. A police officer who leads a raid on a motel room and sees a malnourished toddler playing on a floor littered with drug paraphernalia while his mother is in the shower with a trick has a very different set of experiences than a court-mandated therapist who, in a controlled office setting, listens to the same mother grieve after losing custody of her child. As Peter, a career police officer with a bureaucratic orientation, concisely stated, "Most police encounters are negative. If I have my house broken into, the cop might be the best cop in the world, but it's a negative encounter, 'cause my house was broken into. So imagine if you're being arrested."

Alliance professionals who have regular contact with the women in a court, office, or correctional setting generally attempt to maintain what they regard as mutually respectful relationships with them. Such a relationship is at best difficult and perhaps even impossible, when women's futures are at stake and their life priorities may differ considerably from what the criminal justice–social services alliance demands of them. Reconciling these issues presents significant challenges for alliance professionals; consider, for instance, the intricate and ever-shifting power dynamics that Ellie, a Latina diversion court worker with a transgressor orientation, describes experiencing with her clients:

> Some of the women will tell me, "You're getting played by *all* of us, you know we're lying." And I'm like, "Well, what do we need to do to where you don't have to lie about this?" So we kind of like work on that, 'cause I know when they're lying to me, but I'm not gonna like full out call them out on it. I kind of expect it, which is very cynical. I always tell 'em, "I'm not stupid. Just because I'm not acknowledging that you're lying to me doesn't mean I don't know. And it's only gonna be harder for you in the long run because lie after lie after lie, it's heavy on the heart, and it's hard to keep up. I don't want to be wasting your time; you don't want to be wasting my time. And I know we respect each other enough to not want to do that." I could just say, "Fine, I'll go ahead and check off [boxes on a form documenting group attendance for court purposes], say 'you're here' but if it's gonna be nothing but lies, we can go ahead and be done now," and that's when a couple of the women have been like, "Oh, well, I did go see *the* guy [a regular client]. When I was joking saying I was gonna go the block, I was really going to the block." And I'm like, "Well, of course, we know you were!"

Ellie expresses a range of complex sentiments regarding the challenges she faces in her work with women who engage in what some might view as interpersonal intrigues, one of the few resistance measures they can undertake in a system that offers them few alternatives in their interactions with alliance professionals. Yet this resistance may feel like manipulation to an alliance professional who regards herself as deeply invested in helping the women to achieve particular goals, especially if the professional is unable to acknowledge that the women may not share these goals.

Scarce financial, political, and professional resources, combined with a lack of political will to make long-term and substantive changes to the status quo, present dual occupational risks to alliance professionals. This is particularly true for alliance professionals who regard themselves as advocates for women who otherwise receive limited alliance support despite being subject to its purview with great frequency. As Anne, an African American detox staff member with a bureaucrat orientation concisely stated, "We cannot do the work required with these women with the resources that we have." This is particularly challenging for alliance professionals who interact with both the women and those who set the funding and policy priorities that have a direct impact on their lives. For instance, Sofía, the Latina director of a drug treatment program in a Denver-area jail, evinced a transgressor orientation in expressing resentment toward city officials who, in her estimation, did not share her concerns about what she regarded as the misguided and inequitable allocation of resources:

> I couldn't understand why they [women convicted of prostitution] could receive up to a year in the county jail. It's not even a misdemeanor; it's a city ordinance, like urinating in public or public intoxication or loitering, ten days. I could understand that they wanted to change the behavior by giving them more of a sentence, but that's not working and I don't know why we continue to do it that way. We have this Johns TV[8] thing, those guys pay these huge fines and I'm like, "Why isn't some of that money coming to treatment and to help these women get off the streets?" And of course nobody wanted to answer me. I kept asking, "Where is this money going and who is it benefiting? Why isn't it going towards the women?" I couldn't get a straight answer.

Such frustration with what Sofía regarded as city officials' lack of willingness to provide "a straight answer" about funds can be compounded by professional rivalries. For instance, Alan, a White idealist detective who frequently coordinates with social services agencies to help find safe accommodation for women testifying against (typically male) street-involved figures who may seek to harm them, described a pattern of interactions with services providers that cast him in an adversarial position. Alan recounted what for him was a particularly frustrating instance of a social worker refusing to allow her client, whom he had referred and transported to the social worker's shelter, to speak with him due to her concerns that additional police contact might further traumatize her. In his view and in this particular case, the opportunity to speak with the woman in shelter would have provided valuable information in the case against a man he regarded as her abusive pimp. He reported telling the social worker, "I'm not looking to harm your client, I'm looking to help her out of the situation!" only to be refused entry and the potential to gather evidence to strengthen a federal case against the man who had violently abused and sexually exploited this woman (as well as a number of others) over an extended period of time. Yet, as Carrie, the White idealist social worker who denied him entry, put it, "Cops don't understand that just because someone says something out loud doesn't necessarily mean they're okay with it being too discussed."

Individual professional orientations can clash in what both, or even multiple, parties regard as a high-stakes situation, and such negative encounters only compound what alliance professionals characterize as the everyday challenges inherent in their work. It is a bitter irony that as alliance professionals attempt to prevent women from engaging in what the alliance ethos regards as dangerous individual choices rooted in traumatic experiences, the professionals often experience negative psychological consequences of their own. Throughout the research for this book, African American and Latina/o alliance professionals most consistently and readily acknowledged the impacts that witnessing the operations of racism and sexism at work had on their professional lives and inner emotional states. Their experiences and perspectives as people of color tasked with enforcing the law in a predominantly White city may make it easier for them to acknowledge how the criminal justice system in particular, and the alliance more generally, reinforces and perpetuates existing ethno-racial inequalities.

All alliance professionals recognize that particularly difficult work-related experiences, which social services providers in particular refer to as "vicarious trauma," are a real and ever-present occupational risk, and everyone I spoke with shared at least one account of a case or incident that presented especially tough challenges. Sometimes these events involved experiencing violence first-hand, as was the case when Alejandro, a Latino patrol officer with an enforcer orientation, told me about being surrounded by armed young men who threatened to kill him before reinforcements arrived. Although alliance professionals who work in a therapeutic capacity with the women are far less likely to experience violence or the threat of violence in such a direct way, they also suffer emotional consequences from their therapeutic engagement with the women's experiences.

César, a Latino prostitution diversion court counselor and idealist, expressed anger, grief, and deep sorrow as he told me about the struggles he faced after a court-mandated client disclosed that she had experienced a particularly demeaning form of childhood sexual abuse. Her disclosure impacted his ability to function in both his professional and personal lives to such an extent that he had to seek out his own therapeutic support:

> Her stepdad forced her to have sex with the dog to get sexual pleasure. He watched her perform with the dog and he would masturbate watching her. I remember sitting there, looking at her like, "My mind is not able to fathom, I cannot comprehend that." I told her, "This is it for today." I took it home. I didn't know how to let it go. Who does this to an eight-year-old, who? I couldn't sleep. I didn't want to eat. I was very cautious; super cautious about how older men would look at girls. My [intimate] partner asked me, "What's wrong with you?" Every time we would go out, for weeks, I was like, "What the fuck is this man doing with this girl?" And my partner told me, "You have no control over it" and I was like, "How dare you say that to me?" But then I realized I'm trying to rescue everybody. And I can't. Then I sought out therapy and I realized that I can't save everybody and I need to take care of myself.

Here César vividly recalls the consequences he faced in his personal life following the woman's disclosure of a painful event from her past, as well as the struggles he experienced in recognizing his powerlessness to help others in potentially abusive situations. This account also underscores the social isolation or even marginalization alliance professionals may feel as a result of their work with morally charged and socially taboo issues that can be difficult or even impossible to discuss with those outside the field.

Danielle, a White social worker with a transgressor orientation who counsels women in an addictions-treatment program, felt that "guilt by association," as she put it, prompted strong reactions among some individuals in her social circle. Echoing some of César's sentiments, Danielle expresses disdain for those she regards as too insensitive or coddled by life to handle the realities of her work:

> People are like, "How do you have your hands in there? You must have a jagged past to be able to do that kind of stuff." Even with people that I normally interact with in social settings, it's still very taboo, 'cause there's a lot of people who want to rescue the world without really understanding. It's the whole white privilege kind of thing, like, "Oh, well, let me give you a hand 'cause I have my shit together so that means that I know how to tell you how to put your shit together."

Stigma surrounding transactional sex and illicit drug use, white privilege, and patronizing attitudes combine in Danielle's sophisticated connections between her own work with the women as well as her peers' perceptions of her as a person and a professional with a potentially "jagged past." Veronica, who is a Latina transgressor and works at a Denver-area jail, shared equally complex sentiments regarding the unique issues facing alliance professionals of color tasked with policing, monitoring, or controlling other people of color under the criminal justice system's purview. Here Veronica speaks disapprovingly about the behavior of the deputies, most of whom are African American or Latina/o, who staff the jail:

> The majority of the deputies are minority, they're Hispanic, they're Black, less White. They make comments to the women on their way out, to push their buttons "Oh, you're not gonna make it. You'll be back." Or when they come back, they're like, "Oh, I knew you would be back, what did you do this time?" Things like that.

Veronica alludes to the potential for alliance professionals to abuse their power through dismissive or disrespectful comments and lack of empathy. Adam, a White patrol officer who previously worked in a correctional setting, described a fine balance between needing to maintain a cool, emotionally distanced demeanor in a correctional setting replete with human suffering and interpersonal intrigue while not dehumanizing those incarcerated there. Adam's detached bureaucratic orientation allows him to rather clearly surmise how an individual who spends an extensive period of time working in a correctional facility might become desensitized as a coping mechanism:

> I think they just get hardened. I really think in a prison or jail type of setting, there should be a limit on the time that you spend in there, and then move on to something else in the department, or something. I think you become too callous, you become really disheartened, not caring, because in that type of job you can't be too caring.

The risk of abusing or exploiting professional authority is even more complex for officers and detectives who regularly work undercover, which requires special skills and personality traits that allow an individual to successfully "pass" as a street-involved person. Several vice detectives explained the potentially explosive combination undercover officers face while immersed in adrenaline-charged activities related to illicit drug use and prostitution. This immersion can be long-term in criminal investigations of large-scale narcotics operations that take months or even years to build, and some officers may face what one undercover officer described as a situation in which "you work around it nonstop and you hear about it and you think, 'Oh man, I could do that and get away with it' kind of thing." As Kurt, a senior vice detective with a transgressor orientation, concisely stated,

> When it comes down to it, this job is about men, women, money and sex. Guys that're around it that much, something clicks in their head. I think there is a difference between men and women with the sex thing; it's a bigger issue for men. I would hope that there are not that many cops that are engaging in that, but they do so. Being around it, it's one of those things, that's why some agencies don't let you be in those positions for that long.

Similar characterization of a moment when "something clicks" emerged particularly strongly among male officers in their twenties and thirties, especially those who self-identified as heterosexual, often through casual mention of a wife or female intimate partner as we conversed to build rapport. These officers framed this as a complex issue, frequently mentioning that male officers require strong character traits to resist the temptation to engage sexually with street-involved women, profit from the illicit drug economy, or push permitted procedural limits to make an arrest. This creates an ever-present dilemma for those officers, who must remain mindful not to cross boundaries that may become increasingly blurry, just as they do for the women themselves, with the passage of time.

The boundaries can be even blurrier for outreach workers and other direct social services providers, particularly those who share experiences of substance abuse, addictions, or sex trading.[9] Compounded by limited funding and consequent job insecurity, alliance professionals with these shared experiences can struggle to practice self-care due to encouragement they may face from colleagues to self-present as a success story. Peer-to-peer interventions, with their roots in harm reduction and the anti–violence against women movements, place great stock in the ability of individuals with lived experience of addiction or sex trading to exert a positive influence on the lives of those still engaged in these activities. Yet without adequate support, these front-line services providers can be highly vulnerable to relapse and other negative consequences when they return as outreach workers to neighborhoods that, in many of the women's views, exerted a destructive influence on their lives.

Concluding Thoughts

Academic, policy, and legal perspectives often approach the issues street-involved women face in their everyday lives by focusing on risk in ways that overemphasize the importance of individual decision making, sometimes to the exclusion of any consideration regarding the structural forces that inform these decisions. We have seen that, from the perspectives of women who are street involved, risk is a complex and contextually defined concept that is both a product of, and a reason for, engaging in transactional sex. Street-involved women report that their biggest risks stem from policing, the criminal justice system more generally, and the gendered socioeconomic relations that regularly force them to make very difficult choices, all while evading police detection. Alliance professionals clearly recognize that addiction (and its criminalization) creates very serious risks for women, including exclusion from housing and employment as a result of drug- and prostitution-related convictions. These professionals likewise position addiction and involvement in street-based sex trading as consequences of a set of intersectional harms related to identity and community that result in trauma-related impediments to full social functioning. Yet the solutions and interventions proposed continue to focus on women as individual problems.

This disjuncture leads us to question the utility of criminalizing street-based prostitution and illicit drug use, particularly since street-involved women and alliance professionals alike clearly recognize that arrest and its consequences constitute one of the biggest risks women face on the street. Decriminalization would remove this risk while still allowing women to report violence to the police, creating safer living conditions, and yet this possibility remains highly unlikely in any U.S. city due to prevailing ideological conditions. At the time of writing, street-involved women remain lucky if they are able to receive any kind of assistance that does not involve court-mandated oversight or incarceration. As the next chapter will illustrate, much of this help remains predicated on a woman's willingness to abide by very narrow parameters for success. The terms of such assistance can appear almost Orwellian at times, such that the best a street-involved woman under the alliance purview can hope for is an alliance professional who will say, as a probation officer did to me while we role-played how a typical client encounter might unfold, "Help me help you. Help me help you get this off your record. The more you open up to me, the more you share, the more I'm able to provide you with assistance."

Corinne's Decision

Corinne perches on the chair's edge, her knees touching mine, as we consider the implications of the last twenty-four hours' events. It is four in the morning and we are both staring at each other, unselfconscious with exhaustion and slightly disturbed by the way that the cheap lamp's greenish glow renders our faces grotesque. We are surrounded by six black garbage bags containing everything Corinne owns, which we just retrieved from a storage facility under the cover of darkness to avoid encountering anyone, especially Jayda, her intimate partner of many years. We are waiting for other transitional housing facility residents to wake up before we drag the heavy bags upstairs to one of the bedrooms Corinne will share with other women who, whether by court order, individual decision making, or some combination of both, have decided to end their involvement in street-based sex trading and illicit drug use.

Jayda and Corinne have been working the streets together for almost a decade as a means to procure the money they need to pay for their motel room, crack cocaine, and other basic needs. The years have been punctuated by periods of separation caused by Jayda's two short prison sentences, jail time served by both of them, and the birth of several children who now live with adoptive families. Corinne loves Jayda deeply and resents the weeks Jayda spends living with neighborhood men who enjoy prominence in the street-level drug economy. During these times apart, Corinne does not know whether Jayda is incarcerated, on a binge in a motel with a man, or dead. Last night Corinne confronted Jayda when she saw her on the street with one of these men, and Jayda assaulted her so severely that Corinne thinks one of her ribs may be broken.

Corinne cannot count the number of times that she and Jayda have previously fought this way, and Corinne often ends up seriously injured. When things are going well in their relationship, their joint engagement in transactional sex doubles their income, offers protection since they can look out for each other, and maximizes the amount of time they can spend together. Corinne resents that Jayda seems to enjoy the affective and sexual bonds she cultivates with regular clients as well as other men with whom she smokes crack cocaine. "If we keep goin' like this," Corinne says of their relationship, "one of us is gonna kill the other, and I'm prob'ly the one who's gonna end up dead."

Alert to the seriousness of this statement, I ask Corinne the standard set of questions transitional housing facility staff pose to women to help them feel safe in a crisis situation. Staff members are acutely conscious of the very fine line between informing a woman of her options in a given situation and advising her to take a particular course of action; we often remind ourselves not to give advice because we do not have to live with the consequences. Ever wary of this fine line, I address Corinne's safety concerns by emphasizing the transitional housing facility's confidential location, engaging her in the creation of a safety plan for avoiding Jayda, and asking Corinne if she wants to file a protection order with the county court that will legally prohibit Jayda from contacting or being in close proximity to her.

Corinne sighs and shakes her head at the last option, hesitating slightly as she looks at the garbage bags that contain all her possessions. Newcomers to the transitional housing facility often delay disclosure about their criminal justice system involvement, fearing that it will exclude them from receiving the housing and other services that they desperately need. After a few moments of silence, I take the initiative and ask Corinne if she has any outstanding warrants that make her hesitant to interact with agents of the criminal justice system in any form, then reassure her that this will have no bearing on whether she can stay at the facility. Corinne estimates that she has between four and seven different active arrest warrants in different Denver-area counties, all for misdemeanor drug paraphernalia and prostitution charges. Our eyelids heavy with exhaustion, we agree that court is clearly not the place to go to resolve her problems, at least not today.

3

Harm Reduction and Help Seeking

By midafternoon on a dusty summer day the large black shoulder bag I am carrying feels like a sack of heavy stones. Inside are at least one hundred small plastic bags that contain condoms, hand sanitizer, shampoo, tampons, and a card with the transitional housing facility's mission statement and contact information. Leelee, my outreach partner,[1] who used to work the streets in this neighborhood, and I had to be careful not to include more than three condoms because the women tell us that police officers will use these as evidence of their intent to engage in prostitution. Police officers tell me that this is untrue, but we do it anyway, just in case. We encounter different people each time we visit, and so we never know what to expect; when police cars enter or a fight erupts, people scatter into motel rooms or around the block, off the main street.

"These crackheads are like a buncha damn cockroaches," an older African American man once told me disapprovingly at a bus stop as we sat together watching the street empty as a siren ripped through the evening air, red and blue lights flashing. His comment underscores his own annoyance with drug-related neighborhood activities as well as the way in which the criminalization of illicit drug use and street-based sex trading forces people in this neighborhood to live, irrespective of their personal choices. When there are no police in sight, we can see people engaging in open-air crack cocaine and methamphetamine sales; those who want to purchase heroin have to travel at least another twenty blocks, to a predominantly Spanish-speaking neighborhood.

A sharp sob pierces the afternoon silence, immediately drawing our attention to a woman we recognize as Keanna, who is crying inside a small group of women who have surrounded her. My outreach partner, who knows Keanna well, immediately approaches the group. "I've been raped!" Keanna sobs as the women try to restrain her from running away. We lead her and the other women back to the motel room we rent to interview women who are interested in talking to us, although we also use it to provide a place to rest for those who do not want to participate in the research. Keanna sits on the bed, shaking and crying. Everyone knows not to ask her if she wants to call the police or the rape crisis center; her assailant was a date, she doesn't know his name or anything else about him, and she may have warrants out for her arrest. Almost all the women in Keanna's family have engaged in street-based sex trading at some point, and her aversion to the police consequently runs deep.

We are sitting with her on the bed attempting to console her when the motel room door swings open without a knock and two police officers enter. The women freeze, so I take the lead, addressing one of the officers in a higher-pitched voice that I hope will indicate my submission to his male authority. "Well, hello officer!" I say, as if I'm genuinely pleased to see him. "How are you today?" His partner silently scans the faces of the women in the room, as if visually recording the scene. I think they probably recognize Keanna, an intergenerational who has lived in the neighborhood her entire life, and I am very worried that they may search the women, knowing that at least one of them probably has drug paraphernalia, most likely a crack pipe, in her possession.

The small group of women watches me intently as I pull out a card bearing my name, university position, and address and hand it to the officer with my driver's license, which he looks at for a moment as I awkwardly tell him that my father spent his career as a police officer in New York. His expression softens as he tells me, "I applaud your efforts, Susan, but this is a very dangerous neighborhood. At any moment someone could come in and take everything you own, or even hurt you." He turns to leave and I thank him for his concern for my well-being, wanting him to leave as quickly as possible without talking to the women. Keanna's face, still swollen from crying, is blank as she stares into space, looking at nothing in particular and not at all surprised by any of this.

Conceptualizing Help and Harm Reduction

Keanna and her peers are well aware that their street involvement tends to make police patrol officers and other criminal justice professionals habitually regard them as suspects. This is particularly true for women whose female family members have a history of sex trade involvement, and who socialize them into extralegal means of protecting themselves.

Keanna's silence, which deflected the patrol officers' attention to me, is just one of the self-protective strategies street-involved women employ in ways that reflect the exclusionary forces that shape their lives. Street-involved women develop these strategies with the knowledge that alliance professionals cannot provide assistance on terms that contradict the alliance ethos, which positions the women as individually flawed products of traumatic experiences, unhealthy families, or other social arrangements that require alliance intervention.

Women who cannot, or do not wish to, seek alternatives to street involvement are well aware that the alliance ethos follows a clear-cut practical script that many have experienced themselves or witnessed secondhand. This script holds that alliance intervention typically precedes or encourages a woman's convincing demonstration of readiness to change and demonstrate compliance with the alliance ethos while expressing accountability for her individual actions. Such intervention, which almost always begins with arrest, is a regular and dominating feature of daily life for women working the street to the extent that women orient a significant majority of their activities around avoiding police encounters. Almost all the women who participated in this study described arrest and its consequences as their primary occupational risk; accordingly, the harm-reduction[2] and help-seeking strategies most women employ to navigate this and associated risks dissuade women from involvement with alliance professionals.

The force with which the alliance exerts power and control over street-involved women on a routine basis dramatically exceeds the assistance measures provided by small and poorly funded harm-reduction or rights-based organizations. A street outreach worker, most often a volunteer, periodically offers empathic conversation and condoms or other small tokens that women will use within hours. The countless amounts of time I have spent engaging in street outreach work taught me that the majority of women genuinely appreciate the small gesture outreach workers provide in offering referrals to service providers. Yet most women also quite reasonably regard outreach as wholly inadequate for addressing even a partial aspect of their needs.

Unlike the outreach worker who prioritizes harm reduction practices and open, nonjudgmental conversation with women working the street, a uniformed and salaried police officer cruises the street armed with both a gun and the power to enforce the state's will. Women are well aware of the gulf in politico-economic power and authority that exists between these various actors, and engage with them accordingly. Hence while the women can and do develop their own harm-reduction strategies to minimize the risks that result from the criminalization and stigmatization of their sex trading and illicit drug-related activities, they realize that the alliance's vast power and scope ultimately dooms these strategies to failure once an officer decides to make an arrest. In this context, it is unsurprising that Keanna and her peers remained silent until the police patrol officers left our motel room.

Findings presented here juxtapose what street-involved women generally describe as their needs with corresponding measures alliance professionals use to regulate the women through a highly circumscribed set of sanctions and services. Street-involved women almost universally identify their major needs as housing, safety, mental-health and substance-abuse treatment, legal forms of paid work, and culturally sensitive services. The alliance ethos, with its focus on prostitution as inherently harmful to both women who engage in it and the familial and social groups of which they are a part, conspicuously ignores the fact that sex trading *is* a help-seeking strategy for the women in that it meets their immediate needs as they struggle with homelessness, addiction, and related challenges. The dearth of assistance available to the women combines with their stigma-related exclusion from employment and housing to make street involvement the best, if not the only, option to meet their basic needs. While alliance professionals may also recognize this reality, the ethos governing their work forces them to minimize and often condemn the creative strategies women employ to meet their needs on a daily basis.

Alliance professionals, particularly those who work directly with street-involved women in sustained ways, readily acknowledge the limitations of prevailing approaches. Idealists and transgressors in particular characterize alliance professionals' socioeconomic distance from the women as inversely proportional to the possibility for real and meaningful insight into their lives. Bureaucrats and enforcers, conversely, tend to attribute these disconnects to lack of appropriate funds and training that they describe as necessary to do their jobs effectively. Despite these minor differences in attribution, alliance professionals of all work orientations express frustration with the difficulties they experience in applying the blunt force of the law to the nuanced realities of street-involved women's individual lives.

Research in the social sciences, criminology, and social work conducted throughout the urban United States clearly demonstrates the lack of services for street-involved women relative to their needs. Researchers throughout the United States contend that women's struggles with addiction and homelessness work in tandem with their involvement in criminalized and stigmatized activities to exclude them even from existing services.[3] For instance, a large-scale interview- and focus group–based study conducted in Miami, Florida, found that both structural and individual barriers, such as limited office hours, lack of transportation, stigma, and mental health problems, all constrain women's abilities to receive services they need (Kurtz, et al. 2005).

Likewise, interviews with New York City street-involved individuals and services providers found that the vast majority of those who trade sex struggle with addiction and homelessness and receive no substantive services as part of their involvement with the criminal justice system (Thukral and Ditmore, 2003). A national interview-based study that compared the experiences of women who received drug and mental health treatment over the course of a year indicates lower rates of engagement in street-based transactional sex and substance abuse following receipt of therapeutic services (Burnette, et al. 2009). Researchers in each of these respective fields take different approaches to assessing women's needs and the challenges they face in attempting to meet them, and yet the results of most studies echo the lack of meaningful services for street-involved women.

Substantially less agreement exists among researchers regarding women's reasons for seeking out particular services, and what types of services provision programs might best assist them in meeting their needs. Many studies start from the premise that leaving street prostitution is a desirable goal, a view certainly shared by the vast majority of women who participated in this project. Sociologist Sharon Oselin, for instance, conducted a four-city, interview-based study of organizations assisting women who wish to leave street prostitution. Oselin argues that women come to inhabit a role as a street-based sex worker over time, and that such programs assist women as they attempt to take on a new social role (Oselin, 2014). In Denver as nationally, many services-provision organizations for women leaving street-based prostitution entail approaches that encourage participants to accept the alliance ethos of rehabilitation and accountability in making significant changes to their lives.

Studies that present models or predictive theories of women's ability to leave street-based sex trading acknowledge that doing so involves a complex process replete with social and economic barriers to starting a new life (Cimino, 2012; Baker, Dalla, and Williamson, 2010; Dalla, 2006). Our findings expand on these studies by offering an ethnographic portrait of how these forces operate and influence women's everyday decision making with respect to help seeking and harm reduction, and suggest that including women's perspectives in a sustained and meaningful manner would increase the effectiveness of services.

Quantifying Help Seeking and Harm Reduction

Ethnographic research, which necessarily involves long-term engagement in people's lives, lends itself to the development of rapport bonds that often prove formative in the final presentation of results. Since this ethnographic rapport privileges particular perspectives, it is useful to juxtapose this qualitative data with quantitative material that highlights key trends among a larger number of women. Examining quantitative data on variables related to trends in the women's circumstances with respect to help seeking and housing, education, legal work histories, and health outcomes results in the emergence of clear patterns. The purpose in identifying such patterns is not to obscure meaningful differences in women's personalities, orientations, and other individual characteristics. Rather, this analysis aims to demonstrate how particular issues, addiction being foremost among them, commence a mutually reinforcing series of events that ultimately place street-involved women under increasingly severe state control.

Critically examining these patterns demonstrates how the totalizing impacts of homelessness, incarceration, and problems with substance abuse work together to compromise women's health. For many women, the result is a kind of vortex from which it can be exceedingly difficult to emerge and begin a new life due to criminal records and lengthy periods away from legal employment. Such exclusion is even more meaningful when considered in conjunction with the women's relatively high levels of education and almost universal experience with legal employment.

Housing

Data obtained from coding the transitional housing facility's intake files depicts women's housing situation on entrance to the facility and demonstrates that the vast majority of women were either homeless, precariously housed, or incarcerated prior to entry, as depicted in figure 3.1. Yet unlike the qualitative data collected throughout the research, this graphic format does not clearly show the pattern of economic need, the interpersonal conflicts, or the speed with which women can move from precarious housing into homelessness. Hence while the "friends/relatives" category presented in figure 3.1 is salient and worth reporting because it is meaningful to the women, it warrants mentioning that this broad social category can (and often does) include those who sell them illicit drugs, pay them for sexual services, or attempt to profit from their sexual labor. It can likewise include parents or intimate partners who provide the women with financial and emotional support in ways that mirror U.S. cultural ideals.

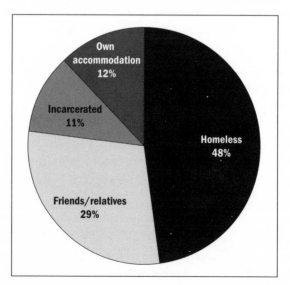

Figure 3.1: Housing

Formal Education and Employment

Data presented in figures 3.2 and 3.3 illustrates that despite their struggles with addiction and homelessness, the vast majority of the women have experience with formal education and legal forms of employment. Most of this work is in legal feminized occupations that offer far less flexibility and lower wages than transactional sex, including service sector work in retail, food service, and cleaning, office work in telemarketing, customer service, or other clerical work, and caregiving work in childcare, eldercare, or drug and alcohol counseling. A small number of women have trade-related experience in factories, salons, or the U.S. military or management experience in food service or retail, and a very small minority self-identified as being unable to work.

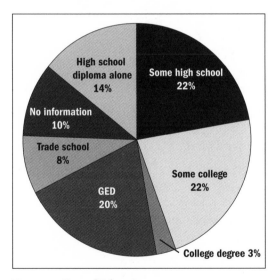

Figure 3.2: Formal Education

Substance Abuse

Figures 3.4 and 3.5 illustrate the illicit substances women struggle with in their addictions, with crack cocaine predominating among the single-substance users. About half of the women are polysubstance

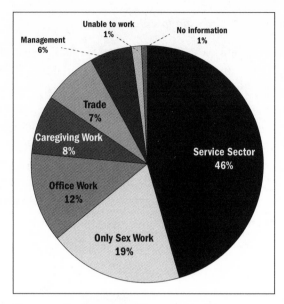

Figure 3.3: Employment

users, meaning that they smoke, ingest, or inject a preferred substance, generally crack cocaine, methamphetamine, or heroin, together with a mitigating substance with the goal of such mixing being to reduce undesirable effects while enhancing pleasure. Polysubstance use, like almost all other pleasure-seeking activities, is highly contextual and individualized in that it depends on a woman's personal preferences as well as what substances are available at a given time.

Health

Many researchers, practitioners, and people who struggle with substance abuse regard addiction as a mental health issue. Assessing mental and physical health involves a number of subjective indicators of well-being within a particular cultural context as well as an environment conducive to overall well-being. As Latina frequent flyer Layla said while describing her health, "I get sick a lot. It is difficult to eat properly and regularly without safe and stable housing." A full 40 percent of women characterize their health as "good" and, excluding a rate of

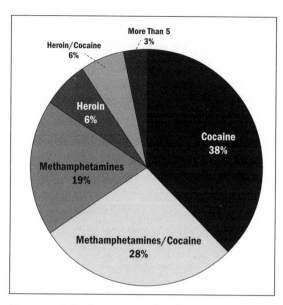

Figure 3.4: Polysubstance Users' Preferences

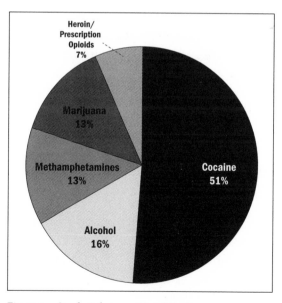

Figure 3.5: Single Substance Users' Preferences

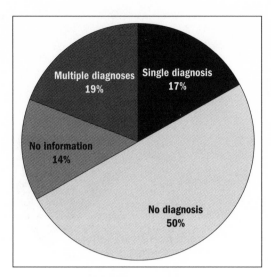

Figure 3.6: Mental Health

hepatitis C seropositivity that is higher than the U.S. national average, those women who do describe health problems, particularly physical problems, generally do not significantly differ from women who are not involved in street-based sex trading and illicit drug use. Physical health problems reported by the women include diabetes, chronic pain/ migraines, cancer, reproductive health issues, asthma, dental or vision problems, pancreas, kidney, or gall bladder problems, and digestive tract disorders.

Women describe their access to healthcare as largely inadequate, and 56 percent take medications of some kind, 90 percent of which are pre-scribed mental health medications. Of women taking medications, 20 percent take only one medication, 25 percent take two, 25 percent take three, 15 percent take four, and 15 percent take five or more. Women report taking prescription medications to treat various physical health problems, including the circulatory system (57 percent), pain (21 per-cent), bacterial infection (21 percent), thyroid problems (21 percent), gastrointestinal issues (14 percent), HIV/AIDS (14 percent), heroin ad-diction (14 percent), diabetes (7 percent), and asthma (7 percent). Most of these physical health issues also occur commonly among women who

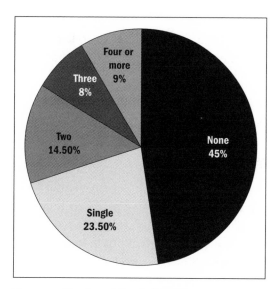

Figure 3.7: Number of Physical Problems

do not engage in illicit drug use and street-based sex trading, underscoring that women confront a complex set of collateral health issues that may worsen as a result of their struggles with homelessness, addiction, and related harms.

Prescribed Medications

Women most commonly receive medication to treat a mental health diagnosis following a crisis situation, such as incarceration or an emergency room visit following a severe mental health episode or incapacitating physical health problem. When they leave jail, women receive a thirty-day supply of medications prescribed by healthcare providers during their incarceration, but these can be difficult to refill while homeless or precariously housed and struggling with addiction. As depicted in figure 3.8, these typically include antipsychotic/antimania medications that treat bipolar or schizoaffective disorders (74 percent), antidepressants/anti-anxiety medications (95 percent), and prescription sleep aids (6 percent). Women who receive psychiatric medications in a correctional or other alliance-controlled context accordingly transition from illegal to legal controlled substances that often significantly alter their moods and inner states.

This transition receives only nominal medical supervision due to understaffing and variable healthcare budgets at correctional facilities, and many alliance professionals who provide therapeutic support readily acknowledge the subjective nature of the mental health diagnoses women receive in crisis contexts. Women may regularly use illicit substances to cope with sustained pressures on the street and periodically consume larger quantities as dictated by money, availability, or mood. Illicit drug markets' almost nonexistent regulatory oversight with respect to purity or chemical composition means that while a habitual crack cocaine smoker knows how her body typically reacts to this drug, she usually cannot know whether an individual has cut the powder cocaine with additives other than the usual baking soda and distilled water prior to crystallizing it in rock form.

Mental health diagnoses, and the subsequent prescription of medications, accordingly occur in a context where women have limited control over the chemical composition of the controlled substances in their bod-

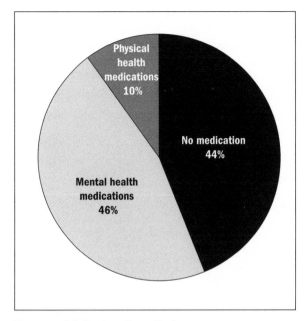

Figure 3.8: Medications Prescribed

ies and how they react to them. This is compounded by the reality that women are often experiencing extreme stress following arrest, incarceration, or a violent or otherwise distressing event (or all three) when they receive a diagnosis and prescription. Considering these realities, it is unsurprising that greater numbers of women reported taking prescription medications to treat mental health conditions than reported taking medications for physical health problems.

These data were helpful in analyzing findings related to help seeking and harm reduction because they clearly document, albeit in discrete form, the totalizing impacts of substance abuse, mental and physical health problems, and homelessness or precarious housing. The frequency with which these commonalities occur in the lives of women seeking services at the transitional housing facility is particularly striking when compared with the relatively high levels of education and experiences with legal forms of work reported by the women. Taken together, this quantitative material suggests an iterative process whereby women's struggles with addiction or related mental health problems intervene in their ability to stay housed or employed, making street-based sex trading in the neighborhood where they purchase and use illicit drugs the most readily available means by which they can generate an income.

Street-Involved Women's Perspectives on Their Needs

Street-involved women who participated in this project consistently articulated a need for accommodation, safety, mental health and substance abuse treatment, legal forms of paid work, and culturally sensitive services. Despite differences in their sex-trading orientations, the pressing and fundamental nature of these needs resulted in the women's consistent reference to them. With few exceptions, most street-involved women could recite all of the shelters, free or low-cost healthcare providers, drop-in centers, subsidized addictions-treatment programs, and other agencies that could provide them with desired services. Such extensive and widespread knowledge stems from both the concentration of prostitution and illicit drug use in a limited geographical area, where information about services rapidly circulates among individuals with shared life circumstances, and the fact that there are a very limited number of organizations that offer these necessary services. Most women use the relative anonymity of the emergency room as their primary healthcare provider and often delay help seeking until the situation is severe in favor of staying with peers or clients whose intentions they can assess before making a decision regarding whether they can heal without seeking out a healthcare provider.

Accordingly, the women's generally extensive knowledge of available social services does not mean that they regularly interact with alliance or other professionals at these services-provision sites, or even that they access them at all. Staying at a shelter, unlike with an acquaintance in a motel or other location, does not allow women to exert any control over those who will sleep next to them at night and potentially exposes them to individuals who may have a severe mental illness or even the intention to harm them. Likewise, seeking out a regular healthcare provider risks stigmatizing treatment for those women who do not wish to end their drug use or sex trading. Cultural norms operative among the women position most existing services as excessively restrictive or even punitive, a sentiment neatly encapsulated in the women's frequent use of the term "the system," a powerful reference to the complex intersections between the social services and criminal justice mechanisms that frame their lives and that generally refuse assistance to all but those who fit a narrow model of being drug free, law abiding, and subservient to authority.

Women of all sex-trading orientations position the multiple risks posed by street involvement as preferable to services-provision conditions that deny their realities while providing them with far less autonomy than street involvement does. Frequent flyers, old school cougars, and intergenerationals particularly dismiss existing services as unlikely to help, a view at least partially informed by their extensive experiences with alliance professionals through their numerous experiences with arrest and incarceration or sheer number of years on the street. Caregivers, women working under the radar, and bonded women tend to regard services segregated by gender or age, particularly shelter or transitional housing, as completely impractical because these often require them, as a condition of services provision, to separate from children or intimate partners they support.

The need for accommodation, safety, mental health and substance abuse treatment, paid work, and culturally sensitive services constitute mutually reinforcing and totalizing issues in most street-involved women's lives. Hence a woman experiencing homelessness may quickly accrue a criminal record for a variety of misdemeanor offenses such as prostitution, loitering, or possession of drug paraphernalia, which in turn may bar her from employment and particular social services, creating a situation that further compromises her health, safety, and ability to make substantive life changes. At the risk of oversimplifying the complex interplay between these forces, it is analytically useful to separate these issues as a means to explore the constituent elements of how women discuss their individual experiences with, and perspectives on, available services.

The need for affordable long-term housing is all-encompassing and comprises issues related to income, safety, punitive measures, and stigma. Homelessness exacts a totalizing negative impact on women's abilities to find work or feel secure in the world, and limits their abilities to handle other problems until they obtain housing, which is not only an immediate need but also a drain on their income, due to the nightly cost of motels, and a drain on their time, due to the need to constantly search for ways to make money to rent a room. Eileen, a White caregiver, concisely noted,

> First of all, that's the most important fuckin' thing, that's what we're out here workin' for! We need a place to live. We don't care about food stamps, we don't care about some motherfucker handin' out some benefits, what we care about is having a place to go. Somewhere to lay your fuckin' head down, that is *ours*. Period. I mean, at the end of the fuckin' night, everything else can be taken care of.

Eileen's keen summation that ultimately "everything else can be taken care of" speaks to the primacy of homelessness or precarious housing–related concerns, particularly for women with economic responsibilities for children or intimate partners. In the absence of a safe place to sleep or store one's belongings, it is very difficult for the women to tackle other pressing issues.

While caretakers may face additional special challenges in finding shelter and often difficult decisions regarding housing for minor children, women without these responsibilities also struggle to find temporary accommodation. Frequent flyer Layla, who is White, said that one of her goals when engaging in transactional sexual exchanges involves persuading a client to help her "to pay for a room, to just get somewhere to sleep" whether through allowing her to remain overnight in the motel room he may rent for their sexual encounter or by providing her with extra money to pay for a room of her own. Women frequently mention this as a desirable outcome, particularly given their concerns that staying in a shelter might expose those with active warrants to the threat of arrest.

Bonded woman Marlee, who is Latina, describes the ideal situation as a facility where there were "no questions asked when you come in, and you can sleep for a minute, shower, without fear of the law." Women regard mixed-gender shelters as dangerous and to be avoided at all costs; as Latina frequent flyer Magdalena put it, such facilities are "like a warehouse full'a men, and you want me to sleep right there? Oh, no! No, man, I'd rather just walk the streets." For most women, the profound sense of physical insecurity created by a male-dominated shelter dramatically increases the potential risks they face, especially with men of uncertain mental health status. In the street context, at least women have the opportunity to screen, however briefly, prospective clients or others with whom they may spend part of the night.

Many of the women lack social or family support, which at least partially results in their precarious housing situation. A majority of respondents who chose to share personal information about their own life trajectories report a chain of events, starting with poverty and precarious housing as prevailing concerns, followed by a dispute with family members, intimate partners, or others with whom women reside, that pushes women into homelessness. This shift, in turn, often precipitates what almost all women regard as a system of surveillance in which they did not want to involve themselves. Deb, a White old school cougar, offered a dismal portrait of an intractable situation in which social services providers serve a punitive function almost indistinguishable from that of the criminal justice system:

> They get more involved in your life, they only shut your ass down, they don't help you. It's like bein' in prison. They don't wanna help you. They don't help you. Any money you make over a dollar they shut your fuckin' insurance off, they'll shut your food stamps off; they'll shut your fuckin' everything off. Even if you make four hundred dollars a month regular [legally earned] money, they don't care. I had a part-time job, because as long as I make under $999 when I was applying for Social Security, it has to be under that. But like I said, they don't care. It's all about the profit they make from prosecuting us.

Deb's description of unsympathetic social workers who are unwilling to assist women with meeting the numerous requirements for receiving healthcare, housing, and Social Security benefits makes an explicit connection between seeking social services and "bein' in prison." Deb, like a number of women I spent time with in motels or on the street, effortlessly outlined what she regards as the parameters of the criminal justice–social services alliance. Her assertion that "it's all about the profit they make from prosecuting us" underscores a cultural belief, shared by most of the women, that street involvement is an obviously more desirable choice than the systemically negative treatment they receive from alliance professionals as criminalized and stigmatized women.

Some women presented specific accounts of their own experiences with the punitive treatment they received when attempting to seek assistance. Lexi, who is White and works under the radar, spent several hours in a motel room with me one afternoon drinking from a plastic liter bottle of vodka. Every thirty minutes or so she stopped her narrative to remind me, "I could be out there makin' money, but I'm in here with you because I want you to tell people how it fuckin' is out here." Lexi recounted leaving an abusive intimate partner in a state hundreds of miles away, taking their two children with her, to stay with an aunt in Denver. After just a few days at her aunt's Section 8 apartment, a visiting social worker informed them that the unit was designated for one person, not four, and told Lexi and her children that they would need to find alternative accommodations.

Lexi's aunt, afraid of losing her own housing, told Lexi in no uncertain terms that she had to leave, and the two women then had an argument in which Lexi expressed her keen sense of betrayal after having uprooted herself and her children to move across the country to stay with her aunt. They began to shout at each other, and neighbors called the police. Officers who arrived on the scene transported Lexi and her two young children to a shelter for homeless families, which promised to accommodate them for a few days. Depressed, afraid, and without money or a support system, Lexi began drinking to excess and, within days of her arrival in Denver, both her children were in foster care and she was turning tricks on East Colfax. Lexi attributed this chain of events to the state surveillance that she and her children faced once they became homeless:

> They don't help you do shit. I can get a job, I got skills, I got experience. But will anybody fuckin' help me? Can I get into shelter, can I do anything? No! Instead, I lost everything that I loved. My life, my kids, my belongings, my values, my morals, everything went out the fuckin' window when I got in these fuckin' shelters. They won't help you, their only aim is to take mothers away from their children, and keep criminals off the street for the night, that is it.

While Lexi's account is unique because of the speed with which it transpired, many women describe a similar path into homelessness or precarious housing. Reeling from the shock of losing things or people they previously regarded as constants in their lives, these women find that the street, with all its problems, differs sharply from available social services in that it offers the women opportunities to make money and use illicit drugs in the company of others with a shared set of experiences.

Street cultural norms also provide women with a level of psychological autonomy that existing social services restrict by positioning them as troubled deviants in need of control. All the women I spoke with were highly sensitized to what they regarded as the uniquely gendered social stigma they face as women who do not adhere to socio-sexual behavioral norms and who lack culturally valued forms of stability like a fixed address, a job, and co-residence with their children. This heightened awareness made some women even more likely to avoid seeking services due to a desire to separate themselves from those who they felt were even worse off. Shirley, an African American old school cougar, explained her reasons for avoiding shelters or other social services targeted toward people in need by stating, "It's a pride thing for me. . . . I ain't about to be fittin' in with them derelicts down in shelter." For Shirley, this means occasionally sleeping behind a convenience store's dumpster when she cannot earn enough money for a motel room or rely on the kindness of others when she needs a place to rest.

In addition to individual women's own senses of propriety, practical constraints also discourage women from seeking services. Mandatory drug testing, for instance, presents a significant obstacle to obtaining assistance, as many programs or overnight shelters refuse admittance to individuals whose urine tests positive for controlled substances or who fail a breathalyzer test for alcohol. This requirement seems counterintuitive to most of the women, all of whom use illicit drugs and many of whom drink alcohol, leading K'neisha, who is African American and bonded, to note, "You're coming off the street, of course you're not going to be clean and sober, hello!" Joyce, an African American frequent flyer, expressed frustration at shelter requirements that result in *de facto* exclusion of those they aim to help:

You have to do a drug and alcohol screen when you first go in and if you have any drugs in your system then they tell you, "Well, we can't accept you, and come back in thirty days." Where does that put a woman? If they're comin' from the street, you have to figure that they've been doin' somethin' to try to survive. Then you gotta be there at a certain time and they kick you out at five a.m.

Existing services likewise neglect or disregard women's difficulties with meeting appointment times while actively using drugs and being homeless and without transportation. Corinne, who is White and works under the radar, used a high-pitched, syrupy voice as she pretended to be a well-intentioned social worker, saying, "Oh, just go over to this building at this time" before switching back to her lower-pitched and serious voice to respond, "Lady, I don't fuckin' know where I'm gonna be in two weeks!" Providers do not always acknowledge that women's difficulties finding even low-wage service sector jobs or accessing available government benefits stem from a number of interconnected sources, including lack of a fixed address, lost or stolen identity documents, and cognitive impairments related to addiction and other mental health issues. Criminal records of both misdemeanor and felony convictions for prostitution, theft, possession of drug paraphernalia, and possession of a controlled substance only further compound these barriers.

Many women feel that the stigmatization related to sex trading, illicit drug use, homelessness, and other prevailing issues actively informs services providers' interactions with them. At best, this results in women's need to perform gratitude in return for services and, at worst, it results in further destabilization. Marie, an African American caregiver, characterized this situation as one in which she walked into services providers' offices fully prepared "to swallow my pride, and then they hit you with, 'We're just gonna take your kids and the rest of whatever you got.'" Women attribute this to the stigma associated with street life generally and street prostitution specifically; as Julie, who is White and works under the radar, stated, "We have such a bad rap. You know, we're not the disgusting people that people think we are, a lot of us have good hearts."

This stigma is just one more heavy weight the women must carry in the course of their everyday struggles, and most consequently express a feeling of being overwhelmed by their problems. These sentiments combine with various other constraining factors that resign many women to avoiding social services whenever possible in favor of the street. As Traci, an African American intergenerational put it, "Who has time for all them forms and waitin' in line and all kinds'a who-knows-what nonsense when you're out there livin' on the streets?"

The almost total absence of harm reduction–oriented services and social policy due to the alliance ethos' near-absolute dominance prompted some women to clearly articulate the limits of prevailing approaches and suggest alternatives. Women all report a lack of harm-reduction services to protect or maintain their health and well-being, which they described as threatened by violence, inadequate mental health treatment or medications, and limited access to condoms. The everyday and almost inevitable nature of violence for women who spend the majority of their time in a neighborhood dominated by the illicit drug economy and heavy policing led Layla, a White frequent flyer, to observe that improved access to nonjudgmental medical services and social support would be "good, you know, cause the rapes happen, the beatings happen." Ms. Ella, an African American old school cougar, summarized the women's safety concerns by simply stating, "We need bodyguards."

Overall, the lack of compassionate emotional support from services providers, who may themselves be exhausted and overburdened by shrinking budgets and unrealistic agency expectations to engage in holistic and highly individualized care while working with an extensive caseload, emerged strongly in my conversations and interviews with women. Women consistently acknowledge their unmet needs for accommodation, safety, mental-health and substance-abuse treatment, legal forms of paid work, and culturally sensitive services. In the absence of these meaningful services, women develop and implement their own harm-reduction strategies, all while attempting to avoid arrest and meet their basic needs.

Women's Harm-Reduction Strategies

Street-based social networks, intuition, streetwise self-presentation, and invoking gendered social norms comprise the four major harm-reduction strategies women utilize in the absence of adequate legal or social protections. As described at length in chapter 1, arrest indisputably constitutes a major concern among street-involved women, and all of the strategies women use to avoid it are necessarily extralegal because they require evading law enforcement. Regardless of their orientation to sex trading, the women's cultural norms position similarly extralegal means of interacting with clients and other street-involved figures as the most effective means to reduce harm.

Harm-reduction strategies discussed here primarily address challenges posed by various interpersonal encounters in a socioeconomic context that forces individuals to be creative in their search for money, illicit drugs, a place to sleep, food, and other basic resources. In highly individualized ways, women juggle numerous relationships as part of their efforts to procure things they need to survive and meet their needs. Women's harm-reduction strategies are rarely mutually exclusive, just as the regular cast of street-involved characters in women's lives, including client, intimate partner, dope buddy, or aspiring intermediary ("pimp"), are not always clearly distinguishable from one another. Thus a woman's primary reliance on intuition in her interactions with others may inform her choice to self-present as a tough, independent street hustler to protect herself or exert her authority in a particular situation. Invoking gendered social norms, particularly by appearing weak or needy, may likewise allow a woman to extract more money from a client, a skill she may learn from her participation in street-based social networks.

Women employ these primary self-protective mechanisms in a highly uncertain environment with few legal or social protections, the absence of which forces street-involved women to rely on themselves and, when they are unable to solve a problem alone, other street-involved individuals who may be able to assist them. Cultural norms position three primary figures as the most likely agents of assistance: the dopeman, as various neighborhood purveyors of controlled substances are known, intimate partners or others with whom women share their income, and, less frequently, other street-involved women. Women generally alternate between these figures depending on the nature of the problem, the status of their relations with particular individuals at the time the problem occurs, and the impact that the request for assistance will have on their future interactions.

These three figures generally serve different roles depending on a woman's orientation to sex trading and the type of assistance she wishes to receive. For women without an intimate partner willing or effectively able to perform this role, the dopeman is the primary agent of retribution against street figures who cause them harm, including clients who do not pay women the agreed-upon amount for sexual services. The dopeman plays this enforcer role as part of his own income-generation strategies, since women can only pay him for illicit drugs if they have money from their clients or other sources. Yet the dopeman, like other street-involved actors able to enforce their will against clients who refuse to pay or others who deceive or harm the women, will not perform these services for all women. Frequent flyers, with their troublemaker reputations among both people on the street and police, are far less likely to receive such assistance despite the regularity with which they purchase illicit drugs from the dopeman. As thirty-three-year-old African American Marcellus, to whom women universally ascribed dopeman status, put it, "I ain't about to get caught up in nobody's mess if I can avoid it."

The "mess" to which Marcellus refers could involve a range of negative consequences following a violent altercation, police intervention, or damage to his street reputation. To avoid these consequences, the dopeman tends to intervene only in cases where he knows the woman in question well enough to trust that a client or other street-involved figure has in fact cheated or otherwise harmed her. Despite the existence of numerous neighborhood men who sell illicit drugs, standard street linguistic usage always refers to such individuals in the singular ("dopeman" rather than "dopemen") because individuals who use illicit drugs typically cultivate a single point of contact from whom they purchase all or the majority of their preferred substance. A woman will often seek out a friendly or otherwise intimate relationship with the dopeman in order to ensure her access to a regular supply of illicit drugs, although even the dopeman himself has little control over the latter due to his low status at the bottom of the drug economy's hierarchy.

Intergenerationals and old school cougars are most likely to call on the dopeman for assistance because of their particularly deep bonds of trust, which sometimes span many years and may even precede his involvement in the illicit drug trade. These women's family entrenchment in neighborhood street involvement means that the dopeman may be a relative, a current or former intimate partner, or a childhood acquaintance. Old school cougars, some of whom are also intergenerationals, command the dopeman's respect as a result of their age and extensive street experience. These women, whether partnered or not, invoke the dopeman's authority because they know that their ability to do so likewise commands respect and minimizes the likelihood that anyone will cross them in the future. Street-involved women who are in intimate partnerships with other women or self-identify as lesbian also tend to enlist the dopeman's support due to gendered street social norms that position men as more effectively able to violently enforce their will.

Bonded women, caregivers, and women working under the radar also use illicit drugs but often prefer to request assistance from male intimate partners or other men with whom they share money because of the moral imperative that this economic and affective bond imposes on the men. Bonded women also enlist support from men who are connected to them through shared gang membership or other mutually agreed-upon economic-affective ties of loyalty. The balance of power between men and women varies in these relationships and can dramatically shift over time in response to changes in their access to resources, personal priorities (including illicit drug use), and involvement in the criminal justice system.

Caregivers and partnered women working under the radar navigate a particularly fine balance with male intimate partners they support because these relationships so often raise the racialized and culturally loaded specter of the "pimp" among their peers. Street-involved women who participated in this project eschew the term "pimp" because they insist that the neighborhood's economic deprivation and intense connections between sex trading and the drug economy preclude local men from filling the protective role that the majority of women regard as a requirement for true pimp status (Dewey and Epler, 2015). During participant observation at a neighborhood motel one afternoon, I experienced a particularly poignant example of the struggles that the racialized pimp stereotype presents for caregivers with dependent male intimate partners.

Eileen, a White caregiver, looked as though she had been crying for a long time when she approached me on the motel's shared second-floor outdoor landing, which serves as the entrance to all the upstairs rooms and provides an ideal vantage point from which to observe activities on the street below. Eileen and I always enjoyed our friendly conversations, which sometimes became emotional as she shared more difficult aspects of her life, and that afternoon she wanted me to meet her long-term partner, who was nowhere in sight. "Fred's ashamed," Eileen said. "I want you to talk to him and tell him there's nothing to be ashamed of. We're out here doing the best we can." To make Fred feel welcome and put Eileen at ease, I moved the motel room's single plastic chair to a desirable location under the heating vent and sat down on the bed, which was everyone's least-preferred place due to its sexual connotations and the insect infestations endemic to neighborhood motels.

Fred, a gaunt African American man who appeared to be in his early sixties, at least a good fifteen years older than Eileen, averted his eyes from mine as he entered the room. "What's happenin', Fred?" I said as I leaned back against the wall and inhaled deep to light two menthols, one of which I quickly passed to him.

Eileen stood in the doorframe with her arms crossed as Fred sat in the plastic chair opposite the bed, staring at the floor as he smoked in silence. Suddenly he burst into tears and covered his face with both hands, his shoulders shaking; as I got up and put my arm around him, he looked up and said, "You prob'ly think I'm a goddamn *pimp*. I hate that she has to do this." He almost spit with contempt as he pronounced the word "pimp."

Eileen responded directly to me with a message clearly intended for Fred. "He knows that if I didn't have him I'd still be strung out. He's my only reason for stayin' clean."

Eileen raised her eyebrows and shrugged from the doorframe as she looked at me, clearly frustrated by this ongoing problem in their relationship. Eileen and Fred sat together for several hours that afternoon in the motel room, talking about their struggles with long-term homelessness and occasionally involving me as an intermediary when Fred grew especially upset about his disability, which made him unable to work. They left before dark because one of Fred's nieces had promised him that he and Eileen could sleep in her garage if they arrived before seven that evening. Although women's caregiver relationships with male intimate partners take many forms, Fred's acute sense of shame at not being able to earn an income took at least some form among all the men I met in such a situation.

Unlike caregivers, whose affective-economic ties resemble a marriage or other long-term intimate partnership with the men they support, bonded women tend to describe their income-sharing arrangements with men, whether gang involved or not, as essentially pragmatic in orientation. Bonded women readily acknowledge that men and women have gendered responsibilities to each other contingent on the exchange of money and other scarce resources, although they vary in terms of their expectations as to what these responsibilities entail. Some women believe that giving men all or part of the money they make by trading sex obligates these men to protect or otherwise support them. Florencia, who is Latina and bonded, described the confidence she felt in her ability to invoke the support of gang-involved men, whom she regarded as obligated to her as a result of the money she provided to them:

> You gotta break 'em off somethin', like money, or somethin'. Attention is not free. I will break off a chunk of my money for attention at any minute of any fuckin' day that I feel like I need it. And don't think I can't go out on the street and be like [snaps fingers], "You, you, you, you're comin' with me, I'm hiring you for protection," don't think they don't have my fuckin' back.

Bonded women did not all evince the same faith in men who, whether gang involved or not, offer to protect women from aspects of street life universally regarded as dangerous or uncertain. Sam, who is White and bonded, offered a more cynical interpretation of such arrangements and questioned the motives of men involved in them. "The ones that say they're your homeboys," she explained, "those are the main ones that take advantage of you, unless you knew 'em before you were in the business." Here Sam alludes to the kinds of trust bonds often shared between the dopeman and women who are intergenerationals or old school cougars, in which women and men have longstanding relationships that predate their involvement in the illicit drug and sexual economies.

Sam's concise evaluation of these gendered street vulnerabilities underscores how women must carefully weigh such offers of such protection—made by men, from men—with consideration of the exploitative terms they might involve.[4] All of the women share persistent concerns related to homelessness or precarious housing, and many women accordingly regard an intimate partnership with a man as desirable for the sole reason that men may be able to offer more material resources than other women. Even if such a relationship involves intimate partner violence or the expectation that a woman have sexual relations with the man's friends, these conditions are still preferable to the women spending extended periods of time outdoors in the neighborhood, sometimes in extremely cold or hot weather, while carrying all their belongings with them.

Street-involved women tend to position men, in their various roles as clients, intimate partners, and purveyors of controlled substances, as most able to provide them with reliable forms of both financial and other benefits. None of the women I spoke to described the general social climate among street-involved women as supportive, a fact that almost all participants attributed to life in a criminalized and highly competitive social environment. Many women feel that the numerous immediate needs for money, drugs, and shelter have compromising impacts on women's abilities to engage in altruistic behavior toward one another; as Wanda, an African American old school cougar, put it,

> When you find two women who look after each other, there ain't really nothin' better than when you out here on the street. But that's few and far between, because usually a trick don't want both of you. He wants one'a you. He tryna pull y'all apart, or he wants to have you up in the crackhouse smokin', and leave your girl outside.

Wanda paints a vivid portrait of the elaborate social calculus that women must engage in as they attempt to meet their everyday needs while protecting themselves. Women carefully weigh the benefits of sharing motel rooms, illicit drugs, and other tangible resources with another street-involved woman against the potential for such a relationship to incite conflict or otherwise worsen their circumstances. Sustained relationships of mutual support are also rare among the women because they are in direct competition for clients and neighborhood men whom they regard as potential sources of money, illicit drugs, housing, and other coveted resources.

In this context, intuition becomes an especially important skill to cultivate, particularly when interacting with potential clients, who are the most variable actors in women's lives due to their relative anonymity as individuals who do not always live in the immediate neighborhood. Intuition, which women variously describe as "instinct," "readin' folks," "vibes," or "pickin' up on energy," involves the interpretative process through which women assess physical-environmental cues and interpret various sensory phenomena that allow them to avoid dangerous clients or situations. Women frequently couch their intuition-based responses to such behavioral and environmental cues in language that emphasizes their abilities to instantly determine the most likely potential outcome of a particular situation.

"You can just tell by the way he's actin'," Italian American frequent flyer Gianna advised with respect to gauging a potential client's likelihood of causing harm, while African American caregiver NeNe advised, "Just go with your first instinct. You feel he actin' funny, you feel he bein' too pushy, get out, as long as you get the money first in your hand." Women universally report faith in their abilities to sense others' intentions, which they often attribute to previous experiences both on the street and in life more generally. Sometimes women state this very generally, such as African American caregiver Mary, who asserted, "I am very good at reading people's personalities. Like you can tell if somebody's a little weird or a little psycho. I have enough life experiences to know all of that crap."

Brandy, a White intergenerational, described how her fear after a client sexually assaulted her was instrumental in heightening her intuitive powers: "After that, I was workin' on pure instinct, so if I didn't feel right or if it seemed like it was too good to be true, I didn't get in the vehicle." Women are keenly aware of the high potential for violence in their neighborhood, which necessitated the development of what African American frequent flyer Joyce described as "that instinct, knowin' when somethin's gonna happen." Others were more graphic in their depictions of intuition's role in combating what could potentially go wrong with clients, as with African American intergenerational Traci's assessment:

> Women can feel that he's safe or he's not safe, if he's goin' to take them and strip them and beat them and fuck them up or is he goin' to you-know-what, it's all about energy. When I get in a car, I go off their energy within that car. It's all about energy.

Once a woman intuits that she may be in danger, she must make a choice about how to respond, sometimes with threats or force of her own. Many women take pride in their ability to clearly assert autonomy in their interactions with others in the street environment, particularly by cultivating a versatile, independent approach to sex trading. One aspect of this involves setting very clear rules—and being prepared to enforce them—with clients around the issues of acceptable illicit drug use, sexual behaviors, and the corresponding prices of both. The price of sexual acts is a particularly contentious subject among women, who deeply resent clients who try to bargain with them, or to receive additional sexual services without paying. Emphasizing that rates are nonnegotiable is a common approach to this nuisance behavior, as described by Florencia, who is bonded:

> I hate to say it, but the ten-dollar [for sex] people are usually the Mexicans and they always try to drive you down to flea market fuckin' price. This ain't no flea market pussy. You want pussy, you pay for it. I have to explain to them in Spanish, because I speak fluent Spanish [as if speaking to a small child], "Either you pay this price or you can't have it, it's like goin' to the store to buy somethin.'"

Florencia's account emphasizes how she explains to clients why price is not open to discussion by drawing a direct analogy with another, more explicitly commercial exchange. Other women describe how clients try to "switch up on" them in the course of an agreed-upon sex act they have already paid for, such as relatively inexpensive oral sex, by attempting to engage in vaginal sex, thereby necessitating a firm or even physically forceful response from the woman. Indeed, a number of women recalled being with a client during a moment or encounter wherein they transitioned from a fear-based response to one of righteous anger, typically when a client crossed what the women consider an unacceptable behavioral line. Consider, for instance, how African African old school cougars Pearlie and Ms. Ella reenact the ways in which they both successfully self-actualized in situations they felt held threatening potential:

> PEARLIE: There's that bad person that comes along, like, [raises vocal pitch to mimic terror] "Girl, I was so scared and I thought he was

gonna kill me 'cause he was on drugs" or, "Every time he'd take a hit [from the crackpipe] he'd be all crazy and shit, like [mimics angry man] 'Bitch, sit down and shut up, you can't go nowhere!'" and at first it scares you and then it really pisses you off and you just turn into like, "What the fuck, quit smokin' dope if you gonna act like this!"

Ms. ELLA: You don't know what they gonna do. When I come across one like that, you know, I gets very aggressive with them. "Where your damn money? Don't put your fuckin' hands on me! Where your damn money?" [Mimics man's voice] "Oh, calm down." [Deepens her own voice] "*You* calm down with the touchy-feely, you ain't paid for that." You gotta be more aggressive with them because if you show that you're weak, they gonna take advantage of that.

Pearlie and Ms. Ella vividly depict how a woman might exert power and control in an initially intimidating or coercive situation, showcasing the intuitive and interpersonal skills that street-involved women must develop in order to protect themselves. Women also describe such streetwise self-presentation as facilitating both improved self-protective strategies and income generation. Many women believe that enacting a streetwise persona makes it easier to garner more money or other benefits from clients, whom they regard as less likely to contest the cost or terms of their sexual encounter when these are presented as nonnegotiable.

For instance, the frequency with which clients want to use illicit drugs with them prompts many women to mandate that shared drug use take place following the sexual act due to the erectile dysfunction and/or dramatically delayed ejaculation that women report as common among men following the use of illicit drugs, particularly cocaine. Quite a few women report clearly explaining this to clients using some variation of what African American Jayda, who works under the radar, concisely stated: "I ain't workin' myself to death here." Clients from outside the neighborhood who wish to use illicit drugs as part of the transactional sexual exchange are highly sought after because they present a significant opportunity for women to capitalize on their superior street connections. Such instances allow women to reduce the amount of time they spend with the client by restricting drug use until after the sex act, and to charge considerably more money by stating an artificially inflated price for drugs the women obtain from a local purveyor.

Women also acknowledge the need to defend themselves should a client turn violent or demanding. When I asked about how a woman might protect herself in such a situation, many women responded by wordlessly reaching into a bag, bra, or other concealed location to show me weapons, including switchblades, small guns, pepper spray canisters, screwdrivers, miniature electronic stun gun devices, and, in one instance, a makeshift blowtorch devised from a small can of aerosol hair spray and a lighter. Women with extensive street experience, particularly old school cougars and frequent flyers, express their readiness to assault clients who attack them; as Annette, a White frequent flyer, put it, "It's like this, either you gonna whup my ass or I'm gonna whup yours. It's me or you." White intergenerational Noelle spoke proudly of her readiness to fight any man who threatened her or demanded money she earned: "I'm not gonna pay you when I got a switchblade in my pocket, fuck that! Why would I pay somebody when I can already protect myself?"

Violence is an ever-present concern among the women, many of whom first attempt to resolve conflicts with clients through more neutral means, such as by invoking gendered social norms. Most interactions between street-involved women and their clients reflect heteronormative exchange practices that position women as essentially beneficent, emotionally driven caregivers who require economic support from men. Establishing trust is especially important with nervous or inexperienced clients, who may fear robbery, assault, arrest, or other negative consequences that could ensue from their decision to seek out transactional sex. Deb, a White old school cougar, noted that reassuring conversations between the woman and her potential client are an integral part of the trust building necessary for a mutually beneficial exchange that may result in a regular income source for the woman:

> There are some like, "Oh, I've never done this before" and you try to talk 'em through that. "It's okay if you're not ready. If you are ready then I'm glad you picked me cause I'm not gonna try to get over on you," and that's how you get a [regular] clientele, especially if it's somebody new to the game.

Some women describe cultivating relationships of regularity with clients as desirable because of their perception that better treatment by clients seems to occur in direct proportion to their knowledge about individual women's life circumstances. The means to create these regular relationships often follow a heteronormative courtship script in which a man provides economic resources to a woman with a tacit understanding that she may agree to sexual intimacy with him at some future point. Yet, as in the heteronormative courtship script, increased familiarity also leads to greater pressure for sex without a condom, or for sexual acts the woman may regard as unpleasant or painful.

Soliciting other forms of support, such as food, from potential clients is a strategy that also helps women to minimize the risk of a prostitution-related arrest by an undercover officer (Dewey and St. Germain, 2014). Consider, for instance, the ways in which Latina bonded women Vanessa and Marlee embark on the negotiation process:

> VANESSA: I always start off with food. So the first thing I do is, if he does not want to get me food, a ninety-nine cent Tuesday at Popeyes, something, a bag of chips, a drink, if he doesn't want to do that, then I don't feel like I'm gonna deal with 'em.
>
> MARLEE: I kinda ease my way into that, maybe mention somethin' about a phone bill or "I need a room." Somethin' like that, like, to help, like [higher-pitched, sweet voice], "Can you help me out with this?" or "I need my electricity bill paid."

Women also invoke gendered social norms when dealing with difficult clients who persist in requesting sex acts that women do not wish to perform, often by making direct reference to the client's female relatives of a similar or younger age. This point of immediate comparison often serves to rapidly disrupt the fantasy space of the transactional sexual exchange while simultaneously inspiring empathy. African American caregiver NeNe reported that "I freely tell 'em, the ones that's bein' just pure assholes, 'How would you feel if your daughter chose this particular profession? Would you like her bein' treated like how you doin' me at the moment?'"

The competitive, fast-paced, and resource-scarce street context rarely offers women the opportunity to share valuable trade-related knowledge with one another in a sustained manner. Instead, women often learn these strategies while incarcerated with other street-involved women and experiencing what some regard as a temporary respite from the frenetic pace of life on the outside. As African American frequent flyer Joyce said, "You don't have time and energy out there [on the street]. In jail you get your mind back—because you been out there hittin' it hard, and you're tryin' to get rested up." White intergenerational KelliAnn characterized jail as "nothin' but time to think," while African American old school cougar Shirley noted that it is "a relief of havin' to walk the streets, with the three course [square] meals and a bed to sleep in."

Some women indisputably regard incarceration as a respite from the street's numerous pressures and uncertainties, and one that potentially facilitates their acquisition of valuable harm-reduction skills they can implement on their release. Once incarcerated, however, women must confront a set of prevailing beliefs about their needs that derive from the alliance ethos and accordingly may sharply diverge from their own perspectives. These prevailing beliefs, dominated by the alliance ethos, regard a commitment to abandoning prostitution and illicit drug use as essential for women to improve their lives. While a number of individual alliance professionals clearly recognize the inherent contradiction in detaining women to prevent them from engaging in survival behaviors, the alliance ethos nevertheless mandates implementation of this approach.

Alliance Professionals' Perspectives on Street-Involved Women's Needs

Alliance professionals must abide by the alliance ethos as they structure their individual responses to street-involved women in the course of their everyday interactions. The ethos mandates that alliance professionals position street-involved women as targets of intervention who must convincingly demonstrate readiness to change and take accountability for their own actions. Both of these requirements entail ending all street-based income-generation activities and abstention from illicit drug use, which alliance professionals monitor through mandatory, and often random, urinalysis and breathalyzer tests for illicit substances and alcohol coupled with regular meetings in which women must report on aspects of their lives of interest to alliance professionals. Even though individual alliance professionals sometimes acknowledge that the restrictive conditions of their jobs skew their abilities to accurately evaluate whether or not a woman has effectively met these criteria, occupations across the alliance spectrum rely on professionals' discretionary authority.

Alliance professionals mobilize a variety of strategies, depending on the specific parameters of their jobs and individual orientations, to make discretionary determinations about street-involved women they encounter in their work. A city attorney may review the criminal history of a woman with multiple drug paraphernalia and prostitution charges and convictions and decide that she may be a good candidate for diversion court, rather than another jail sentence. A probation or parole officer may tell one of her clients to end an intimate partnership with a man on the grounds that the relationship is "unhealthy" and hindering the woman's progress toward freedom from correctional control. A police officer who sees a woman he has previously arrested for a prostitution-related offense loitering at a bus stop may choose to ignore his suspicions that she is soliciting because he knows she just regained custody of her children, or even just because he does not wish to make another arrest before the end of his shift.

Yet despite their general consensus on the women's needs to stop trading sex and using illicit drugs, most alliance professionals acknowledge the systemic limitations that result from differences between individual women's priorities and the alliance ethos' rather superficial approaches to deeply embedded socioeconomic issues. Alliance professionals fulfill multiple and complex roles in positioning themselves as agents of intervention in women's lives, whether through arrest, legal assistance, or providing programming to incarcerated women. These professionals, particularly those who work directly with the women through street-level policing and various forms of legal or therapeutic assistance, are well aware of the women's everyday activities as they pertain to their need to obtain money, drugs, and basic needs.

Many alliance professionals, particularly those with an idealist orientation, characterize their work as playing a critical intervening, or even life-saving, role in women's lives. Diana, an idealist White attorney who works with a Denver-area diversion program for women charged with prostitution-related offenses, stated that for the women she works with, "arrest means safety, a warm place to sleep." Kevin, a White detective who regularly organizes large-scale undercover policing operations likewise explained that women may seek out arrest as a means to obtain assistance from law enforcement, particularly in leaving an abusive situation he characterizes as "pimp control":

> They seek out arrest to get help. They just don't know where to go to get this help, some are under pimp control, they don't want to be there anymore. It's a strange mental state where it's almost like a domestic violence situation where it's that cycle that they're going through and they want to get out, but they don't know how to get out, they don't know what else they would do. They think, "Maybe if I'm arrested I can cry out for help. Then that's my excuse to get out and I can go from there."

Kevin's enforcer orientation employs the cycle-of-violence model that originated decades ago in the anti–domestic violence movement[5] to justify arresting women as a means to provide them with necessary assistance. In drawing explicit parallels in his analysis between what he terms "pimp control" and "a domestic violence situation," Kevin positions alliance professionals as agents of rescue while omitting the harmful consequences that a criminal record inevitably causes in the women's lives.

The alliance ethos likewise characterizes intervention through arrest and subsequent entry into what can be a lengthy period of monitoring by agents of the criminal justice system as essentially beneficial to women and society as a whole. Like Kevin, César, an idealist Latino diversion program officer, described arrest-related outcomes as providing women with "a sense of relief," as he claimed it did with one of his clients:

> I'm working with a woman now who's had four pimps. She was done [ready to stop prostituting] mainly because this last pimp threatened to kill her. She was scared for her life so she was actually happy that she got caught and she felt relief, a real sense of relief.

The alliance ethos holds that arrest is necessary for women to receive services that they need in order to make substantial changes in their lives with respect to street prostitution and illicit drug use. Calvin, a diversion court evaluator with a bureaucratic orientation, noted that arrest can constitute "a turning point, in the sense that if they don't do something to change their lives, they're going to end up dead." Calvin's sober assessment derives from the alliance perspective that the criminal justice system plays a powerful role in producing what alliance professionals often characterize as "cognitive shifts," such as those described by Shelley, a White jail program administrator:

> If you're interested in treatment services and follow-up services, I'm able to help you and guide you through those systems and help you break down some of the barriers that are maybe in your way and some of the things that continue to get you in trouble and in jail.

These beliefs about intervention place the onus on women to convince alliance professionals of their readiness to change and demonstrate compliance with a variety of sociolegal requirements. Foremost among these is the "desire to succeed," as described by a prostitution diversion court judge who convenes every Wednesday with street-involved women:

> So long as they maintain a desire to succeed in the [diversion court] program, our job is to work with them. Seeing the sense of accomplishment in the eyes of the women is exactly what I hoped for. They know they couldn't have done this on their own. Even things like basic hygiene: many women have to have their teeth worked on, because they've been lacking the hygienic routine. So many of the women have neglected themselves, and then they see themselves succeeding in the workplace. Usually I leave work exhausted, but on Wednesdays I leave work excited at how much the women have accomplished. That's their reward, and my reward.

The judge's characterization of mutual rewards underscores the discourse of shared community responsibilities that informs alliance professionals' interactions with the women. In this view, the women lack the essential abilities to appropriately perform gendered roles as responsible members of society and accordingly must enter the criminal justice system's purview to become "ready" to make what the alliance constructs as appropriate life choices.

Consideration of these status quo operations develops an added layer of complexity when considered in light of some alliance professionals' recognition that the ethos they implement holds women to a standard that many of them would fail to pass in their own lives. Three social workers I came to know relatively well throughout this research cast this reality into sharp relief for me during one celebratory evening after their agency had unexpectedly received a much-needed grant that would allow them to continue their work with street-involved women. Ana, Deedee, and Kylie were delighted when they learned the news and invited me to accompany them after work for drinks at a nearby restaurant, where we promptly sat down at a high round table with a mixture of exhaustion and elation, and ordered several rounds of cocktails.

"Are you writing case notes, Deedee?" Ana laughed, her words slightly slurred, as she watched Deedee write something down on a cocktail napkin. We all burst into laughter, thinking of how much time the three women regularly spend writing detailed accounts of their meetings with women as a means to document the women's progress toward meeting agency goals.

Kylie put her arm tightly around my ribs, emphasizing her point's importance as only an intoxicated person can. "Wait, wait, wait, wait—everybody wait!" she said. "I'm going to write case notes about *Susan!*" Kylie and I quickly slip into role play, with me effortlessly performing the role of the client since at this point in the project I have attended more therapeutic groups with the women than I can count. She looks at me seriously and says, "Susan, what are we doing to address your workaholism?"

Before I can suppress my laughter long enough to play along, Deedee pretends to be me and bursts into mock tears, emotionally stating, "I'm not doing anything, Kylie! I relapsed and wrote like three books this weekend, and *I need help!*"

"Oh, please," Ana says firmly to Deedee, readily slipping into group facilitator mode. "You need to confront your own issues in this group. You are clearly in an unhealthy relationship and yet you refuse to acknowledge this."

Deedee quickly regroups and says, "You better stay in line, Ms. Garcia, or I'll write you up for disrespect." We continue laughing at ourselves and each other, hoping to dissipate some of the helplessness engendered by our own daily personal struggles in addition to attempting to assist other women with solving their own much more serious problems.

Eventually the server returns and says, "Okay, I think you ladies've had enough for tonight. I'm gonna go ahead and bring the check," and Ana's slurred clarification that three of our group members provide addictions counseling only makes us laugh harder.

The social workers' drunken mockery of the system underscores their keen awareness of the contingencies that compromise their ability to simultaneously adhere to the alliance ethos and provide meaningful individualized services to street-involved women. Their fundamental ambivalence about the contradictory tasks their jobs demand of them emerges powerfully as they intentionally employ the language of their work to satirize their own lives. Yet ambivalent or otherwise, alliance professionals nonetheless find themselves forced into making judgments about whether particular relationships or activities among the women they supervise are "healthy" or "unhealthy," with the former indicating progress toward long-term sobriety and legal means of earning an income. Such judgments inherently involve the powerful exercise of discretion, as noted by Janine, a Latina probation officer with an enforcer orientation who supervises a caseload of women with prostitution-related charges and convictions:

> I don't think we can make a cookie cutter approach. Five women can have the same charge but they're each gonna have a different treatment plan because their needs are different. I have a woman that had severe substance abuse issues and mental health issues, and I never thought she would be successful. We had to get her on the right meds, have the proper mental health evaluation, and once we got that, step two was to address the substance abuse. So once we had her stable and had treatment and then after that, it was trauma, street life, and everything else so, for her that was very different. Someone else who had the same charges as this woman, her treatment plan was very different. And then there are women that've had trauma, that are in fear for their life. So one woman we had to assess the situation, we had to get a restraining order [against a man in her life] immediately. So, there's no set of, if you get this charge, you're gonna have to do x, y, and z.

Some alliance professionals feel more comfortable than others in making definitive judgments about what women need to do in order to change their lives for the better. Ultimately, however, such alliance-mandated change must involve compliance with a cultural belief system that positions the feminized ghetto of low-wage service sector labor as an acceptable alternative to what the alliance ethos regards as the inherently pathological conditions that accompany street involvement. A Denver-area diversion court judge followed this line of thinking in his description of the essential challenges facing the women who weekly stand before him in court to report on their progress:

> The women have to make their own choices, to be ready for normal living. Last week in court, one of the women said, "I'm ready to get an apartment and move out on my own." I don't want to insult the person, my role is to congratulate them, but, let's look at the reality of living on their own. In my own mind, I'm picturing what it's like for them to enter the normal workplace and normal living.

The type of "normal workplace and normal living" available to the vast majority, if not all, of the women the judge sees in court will involve a minimum-wage service sector job and a subsidized apartment in a neighborhood where illicit drugs may be readily available. Yet, as part of their readiness to change, successful women will eschew illicit drug use and opportunities to earn a little extra money through small-scale hustles in favor of the minimum wage earned under conditions they may regard as far more demeaning than trading sex. The diversion court judge's job, in cooperation with the judicial team, is to assess whether each individual woman is prepared to live on these terms and, if she is not, recommend that she be subject to intensified forms of correctional control.

Street-involved women's relationships also become the target of intense alliance scrutiny, as progress toward success involves women's willingness to embrace, or at least convincingly fake adherence to, a discourse that positions particular ways of being in the world and engaging in relationships as essentially pathological. Enforcers, as well as the idealists who genuinely believe in their work's potential to positively impact people's lives, generally feel most comfortable in offering guidance to women about how they should conduct their personal lives. Kendra, a White probation officer with an idealist orientation, expressed pride at her success in coordinating with a district attorney's office in encouraging a woman to press felony assault charges against a man with whom she was in an intimate partnership as a means to demonstrate compliance with the terms of her probation. In Kendra's view, the woman demonstrated great progress by reinterpreting this relationship as exploitative and deserving of criminal justice system intervention:

> She has done an amazing job; she got away from her abusive boyfriend–drug dealer–pimp. It was just a very awful situation, she went through a relationship that we told her wasn't healthy but she learned for herself and saw it, which was great. That's one case where it took her four times in and out of jail, not complying. She would get a warrant, she'd get picked up on the warrant, we'd give her another chance and finally with her having [criminal charges in] multiple jurisdictions, she had to be held accountable.

Kendra's assessment highlights the totality of power and control that even well-intentioned and idealistic alliance professionals hold over the women. Kendra's job authorizes her to characterize a man she has never met as an "abusive boyfriend–drug dealer–pimp" on the basis of her impressions of conversations with her client, and gives her the power to demand that her client terminate the relationship. Furthermore, her assessment of a woman's success or failure determines the amount of time that the woman will remain under the criminal justice system's surveillance.

Positioning alliance intervention and sustained monitoring as essentially beneficial requires the assumption that alliance professionals ultimately have the abilities to effectively assess the best course of action for a woman. Sometimes this can mean an extended period of criminal justice system involvement through various forms of correctional control framed as essentially positive and supportive. As César, a Latino diversion court worker, noted regarding the uncertain duration of correctional control for street-involved women,

> There's no statute of limitations. They can be in diversion for two years, three years. Right now I have a girl that's been on with us for a year and

half going on two. But she needs that additional support, so we are the additional support. Remember, our goal is not to enable, it's to empower.

At times this perspective seems almost parental, as in the case of Elena, the idealist Latina probation officer who described sentiments among the prostitution diversion court's judicial team as "a genuine love, so that we want people to be successful, but it's important that we hold the women accountable for their actions." Ellie, a Latina diversion court worker, likewise described this balance between caring about the women and adhering to the accountability model as "a juggling act":

> We try to provide them that time to get things done while at the same time still holding them accountable for coming to their groups and treatment. So it's a big juggling act, with prioritizing things. It's a very delicate time for them, that's why we're seeing a lot of the relapse, a lot of the suicidality, because they're starting to understand what it means to deal with trauma.

Ellie describes working with women to make what alliance professionals and the women alike regard as substantive life changes that, in turn, force them to confront the significant struggles that they have often faced throughout their lives. In so doing, she, like many of her alliance colleagues, acknowledges the limitations of the prevailing approach within a system that everyone I interacted with acknowledged to be imperfect due to limitations on funding, lack of political will, and the reality that the criminal justice system alone cannot tackle the substantive injustices that, in many cases, generate the circumstances that prompt women's involvement with the system.

Many alliance professionals acknowledge that the assistance measures they can offer women are at best a superficial approach to some much broader social issues impeded in part due to restrictions on funding and lack of political will. As Diana, a White public defender with an idealist orientation put it, "The real problem is flawed legislation, and to break it down to an act between two strangers on the street isn't accurate. . . . There should be a women's community center where they can get the resources they need." A number of alliance professionals pointed out that an individual's socioeconomic distance from the women's own life circumstances is inversely proportional to his or her ability to provide assistance, as did Andi, an idealist Latina drop-in center worker:

> I think as a system, having all the P[robation] O[fficer]s and the city attorney, the public defenders and the judge all go to some extensive training on what it means to be working with this population would be helpful. I wish I could just say, "All of you guys just go for a week, learn what it means to be interacting with someone who's not your socioeconomic status."

Andi speaks to the reality of living in a society powerfully stratified by race and class, where those with real and meaningful decision-making authority over the women's lives often lack knowledge about the dynamics at work in those lives. Such a situation is compounded by a lack of funding, community support, and available training, as well as difficulties coordinating among agencies. Consider, for instance, a detective's description of the challenges inherent in maintaining cooperative relations across the various fields comprising the criminal justice–social services alliance:

> The biggest thing is that as a city, we need to kinda come together. One of the D[istrict] A[ttorney]s said it this way the other day. . . . We were sitting in a room and everybody's in there arguing and the D.A. just said, "We all have the mission of the best interest of the victim. The problem is that we all come from different arenas." So my best interest, maybe I'd like to see them go to treatment and testify to put my bad guy away so he doesn't do it to them or to anybody else. Something human services might say, the best interest is to maybe get them back in treatment, stabilize, go to school. As a cop, I don't care about the bad guy.

Alliance professionals likewise acknowledge that not all women are equally well served by programs or approaches because women's priorities differ in seeking help. Aaron, a White public interest lawyer who works for a Denver legal aid services provider noted that "rarely do clients actually want to go after whoever abused them. . . . Usually it's they just want to get themselves out of this situation, get stable, and get some help."

Given these perspectives, it is unsurprising that street-involved women with particular characteristics and abilities are able to meet alliance definitions of success while others almost never do. Alliance programs intended to assist the women strongly emphasize quantifiable markers of demonstrable success through program completion, obtaining stable housing and legal work, and adherence to the alliance ethos. This predisposes providers toward selecting women whom they deem as having the necessary traits to succeed, which effectively means excluding women who cannot completely dedicate their time and energy to therapeutic and other programming, such as those women with caregiving obligations, severe mental illnesses, and, of course, women unwilling to stop engaging in sex trading and illicit drug use. In conversation among themselves regarding the selection of particular women and rejection of others, services providers often describe women they regard as able to meet program criteria by using oblique language that characterizes them as "a good fit," "ready to do the work," or "committed to focusing on herself and making changes."

In the alliance programs to which courts, providers, or peers funnel street-involved women, staff members' case notes and other evaluation forms generally reflect how well a woman is able to espouse alliance rhetoric and, by default, submission to authority. A woman who clearly states, "I need to work on myself" or "I need help" while affirming her willingness to trust in the expertise of services providers and other alliance professionals is highly likely to receive preferential treatment in accessing a program. This trust involves, from the very start, completing sometimes extensive application forms, assessment tests, and other documents that correctional facility or other alliance workers vaguely describe as "paperwork" and that often mandates women's disclosure of mental health diagnoses, sexual and other forms of abuse, addictions, and other information deemed necessary for alliance professionals to determine women's suitability for particular programs.

Rarely do women know the purpose of completing these documents, who will read this material, or how alliance professionals will share it with others; in the case of women with cognitive impairments, even completing this work presents a significant (and perhaps impossible) challenge. Women may accordingly feel a sense of conspiracy among alliance professionals, who often have more access to information about a woman's criminal record, pending court cases, and likely outcomes than the woman herself. An applicant to a program may not fully understand the process alliance professionals will undertake in assessing her application, even in instances where a case worker or other services provider carefully explains these procedures to women, due to highly specialized legal language and the prominent role discretion plays in these selections.

Alliance professionals may regard women who actively challenge or question this secretive system as difficult to work with and accordingly deem them a poor fit for services. An exhausted and underpaid services provider visiting a correctional facility, shelter, or other site to meet with women who apply to her program may have little patience for women who cannot complete a required application or other written materials, or convince someone to help them do so, or for women who appear to contest the terms of services provision. Conversely, women who express unquestioning willingness to abide by a program's terms and to wait patiently for available space may rather easily convince a services provider of her "good fit" status. The ability to patiently wait, on other people's time and decision making, occurs in sharp contrast to the culture of immediacy that prevails on the street, where women necessarily live in the moment through their relentless search for money, illicit drugs, and basic needs.

Waiting for available program space co-occurs with the myriad other forms of waiting that women must do in their everyday lives with respect to the criminal justice and social services systems. Court-involved women must wait in jail until their hearing because they often do not know anyone with sufficient funds or property to bail or bond them out, homeless women must wait for a caseworker to process forms that evaluate their suitability for shelter or transitional housing, and chronically ill women must wait in emergency room lobbies or lengthy lines outside free clinics for the indigent poor.[6] Emphatically, women only find themselves in this situation once they are under the alliance purview, as in the street context they can often meet their needs for money and other desired things within a matter of hours.

Incarcerated women face particularly intensive forms of scrutiny regarding their suitability for a program, due in part to the sheer amount of information about them made available by the criminal justice system either publicly or via file sharing with services providers. An alliance professional visiting an incarcerated woman she has never met will already have reviewed, at a minimum, information posted about the woman on the correctional facility's website, along with her booking photograph, including her birthdate, height, weight, pending criminal charges, and convictions. She will have reviewed this information in conjunction with program-specific documents completed by the woman (or on her behalf) containing a detailed account of her experiences with abuse and negative life events. When she speaks with the woman in a semi-private correctional facility room reserved for meetings between incarcerated women and alliance professionals, her job requires that she document her assessment of the woman's suitability for a particular program. The only tools available to her in making this assessment are her own professional discretion and alliance-produced documents that present a partial perspective of the woman's experiences. Incarcerated women also mobilize their knowledge of the system in such encounters, and those who can convincingly describe their desire to change their lives receive rewards in the form of "good fit" status.

Few other spheres of social interaction in the United States allow a complete stranger access to so much information about another person. This extends from the mundane, such as women's whereabouts, to other alliance professionals' intuitive projections about women's futures that underlie case plans and other alliance documents intended to record women's pathways through the system. Women's complete and total self-disclosure, or at least a convincing performance of it, remains a requirement of addictions-treatment or other therapeutic programming, such that women must repeatedly recount instances of abuse or other grief-generating life events to complete strangers in group or, less frequently due to resource constraints, one-on-one settings. Sometimes they do so as their only alternative to staying out of jail, but this self-disclosure always occurs under the guise of alliance professionals' abilities to somehow fix problems inherent to the individual woman.

Women who succeed in this measurable outcomes–driven approach must be willing to submit their blood, urine, and other bodily fluids to tests for illicit drugs and sexually transmitted infections, with the former occurring on a daily basis in some cases. They must likewise agree to endorse the tenets of personal responsibility and accountability inherent to the alliance ethos, and abide by the implementation of rules and discretionary authority as practiced by alliance professionals. At its most fundamental core, then, a woman's likelihood of succeeding in an alliance-endorsed program is determined by her willingness to abide by, or convincingly fake adherence to, alliance professionals' complete surveillance over her body and inner state.

Concluding Thoughts

As we have seen, sharp disconnects remain between street-involved women and alliance professionals regarding the constituent components and definitions of "help." Disconnections presented here clearly illustrate the difficulties that both street-involved women and alliance professionals face, albeit in different ways, with respect to the criminalization and stigmatization of street-based sex trading and illicit drug use. We have seen how prevailing approaches necessitated by the alliance ethos unintentionally encourage or even force women to rely on street involvement by entrenching them within it because they cannot meet the requirements for legal forms of income generation that pay enough to support them and their dependents. Having multiple criminal convictions likewise makes it difficult to find legal forms of work, which often pay considerably less than street-based sexual exchanges and offer none of the street's freedoms.

The alliance ethos regarding readiness to change and demonstrate accountability is at odds with the women's everyday life realities in ways that actively work against their ability to meet any of these benchmarks for "success." This is especially apparent in the sharp divides between women's expressions of what they regard as the constituent elements of "help" and those described by alliance professionals. Each group's definitions are fundamentally different, such that alliance professionals strongly focus on women's accountability whereas the women themselves almost universally express a desire to simply meet basic needs. This speaks to the reality that, for many women, street involvement *is* the solution to their problems in that it provides cash while allowing them the relative freedom they need to navigate their struggles with addiction and homelessness. Alliance professionals also recognize this reality, and accordingly the next chapter tackles the complex and nuanced means by which both individual and systemic discretionary forces shape encounters between street-involved women and alliance professionals.

Two Sides of the Same Dirty Coin

Julie smiles wryly at me as she cradles her new phone, her long silver and light blue acrylic nails sparkling as she stands under the streetlight outside her apartment. Feeling ambivalent about our plans for the night, I sit down on the curb and light a cigarette, watching the smoke dissipate into the cold mountain air. Everyone out here always seems to gets a little weird before Christmas, when the artificially cheerful music, Salvation Army Santas, and advertisements featuring happy heterosexual couples with children become difficult to ignore. This is a hard time of year for women who cannot see their children, and especially for those who do not know their children's whereabouts. Although we don't talk about it very much, last summer a judge terminated Julie's parental rights to her four children, who range in age from six months to eleven years, recommending "no contact" with her until they turn eighteen. Unlike other women who know that they can probably regain custody of their children from foster care or relatives if they stop using drugs and get into stable housing, Julie has reached the end of the line.

Julie and I met three years ago at the transitional housing facility, where she stayed for six months before returning to the street. When five separate shift managers at fast food restaurants and gas stations said that her felony theft convictions made her ineligible for employment, Julie decided that all the talk about personal transformation she heard in group meant very little in the outside world. Now that Julie is busy working under the radar, she is constantly on her new phone operating a series of ever-changing hustles that generally involve trading in stolen merchandise, illicit drugs, and, of course, sexual services if the price is right. I admire her as I sit smoking in my second-hand clothes on the pavement, noticing how she is wearing her newfound income because she does not trust banks. She looks fantastic, with long hair extensions that cascade past her shoulders, elaborate makeup, and new clothes. I hope I will not embarrass her tonight with my plain appearance.

Julie hangs up after twenty minutes of cajoling punctuated with cryptic statements like "Susan's down, it's cool," followed by long periods of silence as she listens to the person on the other end of the phone. She shakes her head dramatically and says, "Kara's bein' all kindsa weird. Man, she thinks you're like the ghost of Christmas past or somethin'. Anyway, she's gonna come by later. I've got something she wants." Julie's casual reference to Kara, whom I do not think I know but who I gather may want to buy some of the narcotics Julie recently procured by prescription, makes me think that I should know who she is, and I quickly conduct a mental inventory of the street-involved women we both know. Since I often only know women by the street names they use, I'm not sure who Kara might be and I don't want to offend Julie if Kara is one of her close friends and I've previously met and spent time with her. The only Kara I remember meeting was a senior addictions counselor many of the women regarded as tough but understanding and who rapidly left her job after developing an addiction to prescription pain pills.

As we walk up the stairs to her Section 8 apartment, Julie stops and asks, "You really don't remember Kara? It was like knowing all'a us made her wonder what she was missin' out here." My heart sinks as I think about the shame Kara is going to feel if she arrives at Julie's place before I can make a graceful exit, and how Julie may have purposefully staged this encounter to show off her newfound power over Kara. Julie does not know that Kara was instrumental in allowing me access to the addictions-treatment program where she used to work, and that she confided in me on numerous occasions about the emotional upheaval she was experiencing while going through a divorce and the unrelenting pressures of her work.

Kara arrives very quickly and, before I can get up to greet her, she pulls Julie into the back bedroom, avoiding eye contact with me. She leaves quickly after completing the transaction, which takes less than a minute. I hear Julie say to her in the hallway, louder than she needs to, "I'm glad I could help you out tonight, Kara. Call me anytime." Julie turns to me as she closes the door, doubling over with laughter. "Shit, I never thought I'd sell pills to my fuckin' therapist, man, but it just goes to show, right?" she says. "All this shit's just two sides of the same dirty coin." Sitting silently on the couch as the snow falls outside, I realize Julie is right.

4

Discretion

The air feels charged as Leelee and I slowly stroll past motels and used cars lots, carefully observing the activities going on around us, as we always do before we settle into our motel room to spend the rest of the evening talking with women who work the surrounding streets. The street scene has a luminous quality under the full moon, which casts into sharp relief the figures of young men leaning against various motel gates, looking otherwise occupied to deflect police attention as they wait for customers who want to buy small amounts of illicit substances. Women walk slowly up and down the street, as we are doing, or sit on bus stop benches, their eyes keenly scanning passing cars for potential clients. Everyone is on alert, searching for trade while attempting to avoid the appearance of doing so.

A single city police squad car is parked facing us with its lights off, on Yosemite Street, where Denver County's jurisdiction ends and neighboring Jefferson County begins. As we get closer we can see that the officers are deep in conversation, their faces tense in the squad car's dim light. Leelee is gazing intently at the officers, who seem to only be aware of each other, her expression tense and concerned. After all the years I have known her, I can tell that she thinks something is about to happen. The entire atmosphere feels electric, and Leelee looks uncharacteristically serious as she pushes me toward the squad car. "Go tell those cops what we're out here doin," she says, and I nod, careful to walk slowly to the passenger side to avoid surprising the police officers sitting inside. Leelee stands almost directly behind me, and I can see her face, serious and concerned, reflected in the squad car's window.

A very young officer sits on the passenger side, deep in conversation with his older, and presumably more experienced, partner, who is in the driver's seat. Neither officer notices us, and I knock once on the passenger side window, concerned that if we continue to stand there silently, they might think we are intoxicated, seeking to harm them, or both. The younger officer jumps a little at the sound as he turns his head sharply, his eyes narrowed and expression guarded as he cautiously rolls down the window. I realize that he is afraid. I smile as brightly as I can and explain why we are here, telling him our organization's name, and how we provide housing and other services to women who want to get off the street. He appears not to know how to respond, so I deferentially add, "Officer, sir, we just wanted to let you know, in case you see us hangin' around." His partner, whom I know from previous encounters, leans over and makes eye contact with me as he says, "Be careful, Susan. Full moon tonight." Leelee nods sharply, adding, "He's right. All the crazies come out the woodwork when it's a full moon."

Leelee and I make our way to our second-floor motel room, which provides an ideal vantage point to observe the street as we talk with women in a more private setting than the street allows. The motel room and the second-floor landing just outside it are a zone of relative safety for the women because Enrique, the motel owner, strictly forbids people to be on the premises without paying for a room. Enrique likes me and Leelee because he knows we won't cause him any trouble, which makes some of the women joke that I must be intimately involved with him to receive such special treatment. They intend this as a compliment, since Enrique cuts a very stylish figure with his snakeskin cowboy boots and ornate turquoise belt buckle, an image only enhanced by the widespread assumption that he is a prominent figure in the neighborhood's illicit drug economy.

Following our usual practice, during our stroll down the street we quietly inform a few key people that we are in our motel room and happy to welcome women who need a break. Word spreads quickly, as Joyce and Dion arrive within minutes to ask if they can stay with us, and we welcome them inside. "Somethin' don't feel right out there," Dion adds, capturing the general sentiment. "I ain't about to get arrested tonight."

We make space for ourselves in the small room and settle into conversation about mutual acquaintances and recent neighborhood activities. Within an hour our mundane conversation abruptly comes to a halt when we hear men shouting and police sirens wailing outside. Leelee and I look at each other, remembering how the older officer cautioned us, and his young partner's fearful expression. Joyce shakes her head as she looks out the window. "Shit," she says. "Whole block's goin' to jail tonight."

We open the motel room door, and Leelee and I go out onto the motel's second-floor outdoor landing, surveying the chaotic scene of six squad cars, lights blazing, and a dozen police officers with at least as many young men handcuffed face down on the ground. The bright moon's constant light and the red and blue squad car flashers erratically illuminate the squad car hoods, which are completely covered with overstuffed plastic bags. Two of the police officers, charged with adrenaline and quite likely the thrill of completing what may have been a months-long narcotics investigation, high five one another, clearly elated with the large quantity of controlled substances they have commandeered from the handcuffed men. This is a big achievement for them, and possibly will lead to their promotion.

Joyce passes me a cigarette we are sharing and says, "Lord, it is *Wild Kingdom* out there tonight."

Dion laughs, "Girl, you remember that show?" and I nod my head a little, vaguely shocked at their nonchalance regarding the scene transpiring just a few hundred feet away.

Leelee leans over the railing, quietly speculating about how much dope the bags contain, then laughs out loud at Joyce's popular-cultural reference. "Yeah" she adds, taking the cigarette from me, "that's that TV show, the one with the lions and tigers eatin' the antelopes and shit down by the watering hole. *Man.*"

Conceptualizing Discretion

Discretion comprises the dynamic combination of personal judgment and procedural norms that individuals employ to navigate their everyday encounters, whether on the street or in more explicitly alliance-dominated contexts. Alliance professionals and the street-involved women they police or otherwise regulate each employ discretion in their interactions, often in strikingly similar ways. Leelee's insistence that I inform the police officers of our intentions on the street, the young officer's fear, and Dion's "somethin' don't feel right out there" are all examples of the complex ways in which individuals use their intuitive powers to guide their interactions with others in a fraught and potentially dangerous street social context.

As we have seen, women employ an extensive arsenal of fundamentally discretionary strategies to obtain money, shelter, and other basic needs, avoid arrest, form protective relationships with other street-involved individuals, and ensure their safety in an environment that offers them few sociolegal protections. This chapter focuses on discretionary forces and processes operative in prostitution-related policy formulation, intra-alliance relationships, everyday encounters between police and women suspected of sex trading, and criminal and problem-solving courts-based interactions that take place among alliance professionals and women charged with prostitution.

Prostitution-related law and policy take shape on the basis of prevailing ideology in a marketplace of political sensibilities informed by electoral and budgetary concerns. Significant federal, state, county, and city financial support endorses this prevailing ideology, which relies on a particular definition of, and appropriate responses to, street prostitution as a social issue. The alliance ethos predominates throughout the United States and, in turn, enjoys support from both entrenched political forces and the funds that these forces divert to agencies or organizations adhering to the ethos. The alliance ethos focuses on women's involvement in sex trading and illicit drug use as inherently harmful, mandating sociolegal intervention, and requiring the women to claim personal responsibility for their own situations. Irrespective of whether or not alliance professionals explicitly acknowledge the powerful cultural and politico-economic forces that inform the conditions in which they—and the street-involved women under their purview—earn a living, the alliance ethos remains unassailable.

Nevertheless, alliance professionals enjoy sometimes-significant discretionary latitude in their interpretations of the prevailing alliance ethos. Here we accordingly address four major explanatory and ideological frameworks that alliance professionals use to position women's sex trading as problematic for both society and the women themselves. All four frameworks justify alliance interventions in street-involved women's lives by envisioning their sex trading as a public nuisance, an ancillary result of addiction, a product of women's maladaptive social circumstances, and an intractable social issue that the law can police but never stop. These ideological frameworks, none of which are mutually exclusive, influence individuals at all levels of the political hierarchy, including state and municipal legislators, police patrol officers tasked with everyday street-level enforcement, district attorneys and judges who handle the women's cases, as well as social workers who provide services. Taken together, these alliance frameworks and those tasked with their implementation constitute a systemic force such that discretionary decision making at one level impacts all others as part of an interconnected sociolegal mechanism that imposes powerful punitive constraints on women's lives.

Individual alliance professionals also employ discretion in their relationships with one another, particularly agencies or individuals with whom they resent being forced to work or otherwise coordinate with due to considerable differences in orientation and approach. The exercise of intra-alliance discretion is particularly significant given increased legislative and policy emphasis on coordination efforts in the provision of services to criminalized women under the alliance purview. Hence it is notable, while not surprising, that alliance professionals who work most directly and explicitly within the criminal justice sphere, such as police patrol officers, correctional and probation officers, and members of the judiciary, deemed such intra-alliance coordination most successful, an impression that social services providers shared far less often. We attribute this general characterization of successes in alliance coordination among criminal justice professionals to the hierarchical cultural norms of their jobs as well as the fact that the alliance ethos itself emerges from punitive criminal justice paradigms with which they are familiar.

Such coordination efforts indisputably create conflict, as in instances where some criminal justice professionals resent social services providers who refuse them access to clients, withhold information, or otherwise appear to obfuscate their investigative efforts despite the providers' professional duty to protect women's confidentiality while serving as their advocates. Simultaneously, most social services providers adhere to a dominant professional discourse that celebrates collaboration and mutual respect, which can make it more difficult (albeit still obligatory) for some individual providers to accept that the alliance ethos mandates nonnegotiable adherence to the punitive approach. Such providers express frustration with alliance professionals who seem less invested in women's autonomy, abuse their authority, or seem unprepared or unwilling to grasp the complexities of women's lives. The exercise of discretion is a significant means by which individuals navigate this complex and contradictory work environment.

Individual discretion and professional procedure operate simultaneously in everyday police encounters, where officers must implement the political will of the jurisdiction in which they work. Beholden to citizen complaints as well as neighborhood, police district, and city-wide political priorities, patrol officers must constantly employ some of the same types of intuitive interpersonal assessments that street-involved women do while ensuring that they obtain sufficient evidence before making an arrest. Being unable to act on these intuitive assessments can leave officers feeling trapped by legal and procedural limits in adrenaline-charged encounters that can unfold very quickly.

Discretionary forces continue to profoundly impact street-involved women post-arrest, when they face sentencing and often subsequent monitoring by criminal or problem-solving courts. Alliance professionals who work as public defenders, judges, or probation officers, or in other court-sanctioned capacities, must regularly assess women's motivations and inner states in ways that significantly determine their futures. In problem-solving courts, such as prostitution diversion court, the judicial team's discretionary decision making occurs over a period of months, even years, before a woman is free of correctional control. Probation officers face numerous discretionary responsibilities, including case plan formulation and recommendations to the court regarding women with whom they have spent very little time.

The interplay among these complex factors raises profound questions about the intersections of public opinion, law and policy, and everyday alliance activities as they pertain to street-involved women. Criminologists and social work scholars have illustrated the co-constitutive nature of prevailing public opinion and policing or other forms of criminal justice oversight, which reinforce the outsider status of street-involved women as unruly bodies in need of containment. Ethnic studies scholar Lisa Sanchez, for instance, argues that antiprostitution laws and zoning ordinances constitute a contemporary form of banishment and exclusion from protective social forces (Sanchez, 2004). Criminologist John Scott likewise underscores the historical frequency with which criminal justice, public health, and other regulatory forces have socially demarcated women involved in prostitution as unhealthy, immoral, and fundamentally in need of regulation and control (Scott, 2011).

In this context, it is perhaps unsurprising that many alliance professionals experience competing realities regarding what their jobs require of them and the everyday dynamics of encounters that they have with street-involved women. Criminological research demonstrates that alliance professionals tasked with executing law and policy derived, in significant part, from prevailing public opinion experience conflicting sentiments about their work that inevitably impacts their exercise of discretion. Criminologists Mary Maguire and Thomas Nolan found that the majority of vice officers they surveyed in a city in the northeastern United States believed that sting operations and other forms of anti-prostitution policing were ineffective deterrents and served solely as a form of neighborhood and city-wide appeasement (Maguire and Nolan, 2011). Criminologist Mary Dodge, in an article coauthored with two Denver-area law enforcement officers, noted the ambivalence that many undercover female officers faced during their participation in sting operations, which caused them to feel pity, contempt, or some combination of both sentiments toward those they arrested (Dodge, Starr-Gimeno, and Williams, 2005).

Social work researchers who have addressed prostitution diversion court also observe the ambivalence, among both alliance professionals and street-involved women, characteristic of criminal justice interventions in the women's lives. In their study of a Baltimore prostitution diversion court, social work scholars Corey Shdaimah and Shelly Wiechelt found that participants had resoundingly negative experiences with a criminal justice system that failed to address their reasons for sex trade involvement, and described diversion court as a positive alternative despite the restrictions it entails (Shdaimah and Wiechelt, 2012). These restrictions vary from program to program, but generally require restricted movements and regular drug testing; an Ohio prostitution diversion court program mandates that participants wear an ankle monitor to track their movements and only visit their loved ones as an "earned privilege" (Begun and Hammond, 2012).

Diversion courts, which position women in the sex trade as victims of their addictions, abuse, and other compromising life circumstances, subscribe to the alliance ethos that mandates women submit to long-term correctional control. Since women enter diversion court as the only alternative to jail time, some researchers and practitioners view this form of problem-solving court as just another form of coercion the women face in their lives. Social work scholars Stéphanie Wahab and Meg Panichelli caution that endorsing any form of increased criminal justice oversight in street-involved women's lives violates core ethical and human rights principles of social work and related fields (Wahab and Panichelli, 2013).

In this fraught context, alliance professionals' abilities to exercise discretion serve as a lifeline by allowing them to employ at least some elements of their own individual orientations and personal beliefs. Yet alliance professionals remain fundamentally beholden to the ethos that governs their work and that accordingly impacts all interactions they have with street-involved women. The women are well aware of this reality and accordingly use their own beliefs and knowledge about individual alliance professionals and the system of which they are a part as they attempt to advocate for themselves. Women's self-advocacy is particularly evident as they share stories about their lives in the hope of receiving services, while recognizing that alliance professionals will critically evaluate the ways in which women represent their own choices and experiences.

Emergent Patterns in Women's Life Story Narratives

Critical evaluation of self-presentation comprises a central means by which alliance professionals make decisions about how to proceed in their interactions with street-involved women. Review of 131 case files from the transitional housing facility identified consistent patterns in the way women depicted the sociolegal situations at work in their lives, particularly in their written narratives. Each case file contains a one-page, handwritten, and often very high-impact account of the woman's life prior to her seeking services, which she submits along with her application to the program. While self-reported and hence inevitably informed by each woman's individual perspective and orientation, this large number of personal narratives are extremely valuable because they reveal patterns in the narrative forms women choose to employ while seeking services.

Women who apply to the transitional housing facility sign a release that explicitly permits the use of this material for research and publication purposes, yet they often do so in a crisis context that does not encourage them to contest the terms of services provision. Hence, generalized analysis of these emergent patterns serves an ethical function by ensuring against the use of women's narratives for purposes they did not intend. I open coded the personal narratives using a series of key events and narrative structures that clearly emerged from multiple readings of these documents. While women write their own life story narratives when completing their applications, which often occurs months prior to entering the program, my own experiences of completing intake forms with new clients at the transitional housing facility complemented this analytical process by cautioning me to remain mindful of the significant challenges that women face prior to their arrival.

The facility makes every effort to welcome women by providing food, toiletries, clothing, and a comfortably furnished (albeit shared) room, yet almost all women arrive directly from the streets or correctional facilities and are accordingly experiencing extreme stress and exhaustion. Yet the stress and exhaustion they experience at the point in their lives when they write their life history is even more acute as a result of their residence in a correctional facility, a shelter, or a motel where they are actively using drugs and trading sex. The women are well aware that the stakes are high in compiling their narratives, and these are accordingly important cultural texts that, while produced by individual women, reveal significant insights about how the women generally feel they must self-present to services providers.

Coding the narratives provided valuable insight into choices that the women make regarding self-presentation to facility staff, since these written accounts sometimes precede their initial meeting by months. Once a woman enters the program, the life story narrative becomes just one aspect of her case file, which grows exponentially in size the longer a woman stays at the facility due to accumulated case notes and extensive criminal or problem-solving court and other institutional records. A case file, with its wealth of information highlighting particular aspects of a woman's life, is the primary means by which staff members come to know the women as clients and accordingly determine the actions they must undertake. Keenly aware of this fact as a result of their previous encounters with social services more generally or the alliance specifically, women understandably feel pressure to self-present in ways that evoke staff sympathy by highlighting their status as victims of multiple exclusionary forces while emphasizing their need for assistance.

Women's narratives consistently stress the uniquely gendered dynamics they face, including entangled struggles with economic difficulties and troubled or even volatile relationships with families and intimate partners. Financial problems feature prominently, including the often-catastrophic need for money caused by a sudden and dramatic change to a woman's family structure or living situation. Women variously attributed this shift to a primary income earner's departure, a woman's decision to leave her living situation, or a sudden transition from precarious housing to homelessness. Every single one of the women's narratives characterized their relationships with family members and intimate partners as deeply framed by loss, violence, and their own (and sometimes their loved ones') addictions.

Certainly many individuals, including the women's own family members, struggle with these issues without becoming involved in sex trading or illicit drug use, and women's narratives frequently highlight their desire to develop new strategies for living that will allow for family reunification. A striking number of narratives employ therapeutic discourse commonly employed in correctional settings and at twelve step meetings, such as Narcotics or Alcoholics Anonymous, as well as other groups in which the women participate through their encounters with various services provision agencies. Describing their addictions and sex trading as "dysfunctional coping mechanisms" or activities that lead to "repeating trauma," women employ the language they have learned in other services provision contexts in the hopes of receiving assistance at the transitional housing facility.

Women consistently juxtapose their use of therapeutic discourse to interpret their life circumstances with clear statements regarding how their illicit drug use and sex-trading activities have become untenable. Sometimes women attribute this to age, frequently making statements such as "I'm too old for this" in their narratives, or to fatigue, often expressed through "I'm tired" or "I want a new life." Approximately half of all women highlight particularly transformative, and often recent, events as pivotal in their decision to seek services at the transitional housing facility, such as an overdose, sexual assault, or the threat of long-term incarceration.

Critically analyzing these life stories with the intent of determining patterns at work in the women's lives is particularly challenging since it risks questioning the women's thought processes and motives in presenting their narratives. Instead, this analysis positions the remarkable consistency in women's narrative accounts as a product of their individual decision making within a U.S. cultural context. Dominant American social norms highly esteem a narrative arc that describes individual triumph over adversity, and this discourse of personal transformation and redemption accordingly holds great salience in addictions group discourse.[1] As we have seen, trauma discourse, with its focus on how a violent or grief-generating event can irrevocably and negatively alter a person, also holds great sway in alliance and other services provision contexts that the women regularly encounter.

Women's near-universal decision to present themselves in their narratives as trauma victims who need assistance on their journey to personal transformation reflects their knowledge that subscription to the alliance ethos constitutes their strongest currency when seeking services. None of the 131 women's narratives emphasized the individual resiliency and creativity that allowed them to navigate what they characterized as difficult life circumstances. In fact, women's representations of their lives "on paper" often differed dramatically from what they shared with me privately (Dewey, 2014a). Women are fully aware of the unequal and often restrictive terms of their relationships with services providers, and their narrative self-representations as victims in need of assistance attempt to balance the scales by unequivocally stating their worthiness as clients.

Women's life stories accordingly follow a narrative sweep that highlights pivotal moments and patterns that they identify as having resulted in their sex trading and illicit drug use. It often hits a nadir at the end of each woman's account in emphasizing a desire to change and their need for help in doing so. This emphasis often occurs in both words and style, with many women capitalizing, underlining, or otherwise drawing the reader's attention to the pressing nature of their need. Pivotal moments, defined as sudden changes after which life cannot ever return to its former state, typically include entry into a violent relationship, long-term repeated abuse as a minor, a change in living situation, incarceration, or an especially dramatic relapse.

Women's narratives most often situate these pivotal moments within recurring patterns or cycles that they identify as inhibiting their abilities to make what they regard as significant and meaningful changes to their lives. Such patterns, like the pivotal moments that punctuate them, often feature similar circumstances surrounding relapse or intensified periods of illicit drug use, repeated involvement with intimate partners struggling with addiction, and the need to care for others in severely economically constrained circumstances. Women juxtapose these patterns with what they regard as choices they have made that have led to particularly negative consequences, with the most common situations involving intensified drug use leading to child custody loss, homelessness, or trading sex more frequently and for smaller amounts of money.

Women's construction of their life history narratives demonstrates their sophisticated knowledge regarding alliance requirements, and hence the women's self-portrayals deliberately conjure the "ideal client"—a woman who has struggled with abuse by her family or other loved ones in ways that led her into a life plagued by more violence and abuse while addicted and trading sex on the street. Women present themselves as ideal clients in various ways through emphasizing aspects of their lives that they know have currency and that maximize emotional impact on the reader, particularly victimization and negative sex-industry experiences. They likewise minimize other facets of their life experiences that an alliance professional would likely construe as involving more volitional culpability than sex trading, such as their own involvement in small-scale illicit drug dealing, shoplifting, assault, and other criminalized activities.

The result is an echo chamber in which the women present themselves in particular ways by attempting to capitalize on victimization's cachet while emphasizing their need for alliance assistance in changing their lives. In so doing they draw on prevailing, and deeply conflicted, U.S. cultural norms that sexualize women and girls while simultaneously (and, perhaps, accordingly) positioning them as uniquely vulnerable to sexual assault or other forms of coercion.[2] Women accordingly adhere to a cultural script that much more readily interprets sex trading, rather than other criminalized activities in which they almost always engage as well, as indicative of victimization and accordingly meriting assistance, empathy, and other benefits. Simply put, women write their narratives with the knowledge that emphasizing their street reputation as a fighter, or an accomplished shoplifter, will not result in positive treatment in the same way that emphasizing their experiences with sex trading will.

By depicting themselves as downtrodden and victimized by a series of events resulting in abuse, grief, and loss, women deemphasize all aspects of their individual personalities and life experiences that helped them to navigate the street environment. Their life history narratives effectively erase the many challenges women have successfully confronted in their lives by engaging in criminalized or otherwise stigmatized activities. This occurs precisely because the women know, whether from previous alliance encounters or from more explicit discussions with other street-involved women, that the alliance demands this of them as a condition of services provision. Yet women also understand, as a result of their socialization in the United States, the power inherent in a potentially redemptive narrative that aspires to upward mobility through individual hard work and self-reliance.

Hence when women include a statement in a life history narrative along the lines of "I want to change, but I need help," they draw on deeply embedded norms that they share with alliance professionals by virtue of shared membership in a culture that emphasizes individual accomplishment. It is particularly significant that women consistently do so by positioning the alliance as the agent of intervention that will help them to transform into independent and self-reliant citizens, thereby indicating the women's fluency in alliance-endorsed discourse and their readiness to abide by its associated terms to program staff who review their applications. This consistency does not strike alliance professionals or the women under their purview as odd or insincere precisely because of the tacit understanding between members of both groups that the alliance ethos and associated practices remain unassailable.

I felt extremely disconcerted, particularly during my initial months of transitional housing facility residence, by the stark differences between these rather one-dimensional narratives' striking similarities and the significant differences in the individual women's personalities and orientations to life. The brave and resilient women I came to know and, in some cases, deeply admire, as they shared with me their justifiable pride in various hustles they worked while still on the street, bore almost no resemblance to the sad and victimized cases they described on paper. As we sat smoking cigarettes on the facility's front porch or waiting in line for various social services and healthcare benefits that almost inevitably exhausted us by requiring women to self-disclose very personal information while simultaneously appearing grateful, I slowly began to realize that the women's narratives were less reflective of their lives as they saw them than they were of the demands that poverty and criminalization place on women.

These narratives, as cultural artifacts produced as a means to a particular end, force women to maintain a delicate balance between claims to victimhood and self-determination, while emphasizing their willingness to take accountability for their individual actions. It is particularly significant that women do so as a means to obtain housing and other services that they hope will eventually minimize or eradicate alliance intervention in their lives. Their discretionary decision making with respect to their self-presentation in narratives demonstrates a keen awareness of the alliance ethos that shapes their lives and the terms under which they can receive desired assistance. While the stakes are inevitably higher for street-involved women, alliance professionals also struggle with decisions they make within a hierarchical system that employs an ethos that can cause more problems than it solves.

Policy Formulation

All alliance professionals are obligated to the political, ideological, and associated financial pressures that combine to frame prostitution as a social issue that requires alliance intervention. Individuals in every type of alliance occupation noted that legislators and policymakers ultimately respond to prevailing public sentiments and voter demands, sometimes with little regard for, or knowledge about, their actions' implications for everyday encounters between alliance professionals and street-involved women. A judge who presides over a Denver-area diversion court described how prosecutors and judges in his jurisdiction respond directly to influential citizens' complaints in issuing harsher sentences to those convicted of street-based sexual and illicit drug exchanges:

The feeling of the community, or City Council rather, is that the original [city] has been taken over by criminal elements to such an extent that people don't want to go there at night, and that hurts merchants. It doesn't sound good to say "it's the money," but it is the money. It is the money, taxes, and people spending money in retail establishments. One of the beliefs is that prostitution is a magnet for criminal activity, therefore prosecutors and judges in this community do sentence perhaps a little stronger than other communities might. It's a basic rule of justice that the purpose of punishment is to discourage criminal activity.

While this judge was uniquely candid in his concise synopsis of "it's the money," most alliance professionals acknowledged the prominent role that legal and policy approaches to prostitution played in their work. Legislative or policy-related commitment of financial resources for particular alliance approaches results from the economic and cultural vicissitudes that inform popular sentiments among voters. While sometimes these sentiments and associated actions prioritize the "tough on crime" approach summarized by the judge, they can also result from economic concerns about the high costs of maintaining the criminal justice status quo. Alliance professionals are all highly cognizant of the prominent role that such political will plays in their work lives.

Calvin, a White diversion court evaluator with a bureaucrat orientation derived from years of working in problem-solving courts throughout the United States, positioned the origin and spread of problem-solving courts, which he terms "therapeutic jurisprudence," in the 1990s as the product of an overburdened and costly system:

The revolving door of jail and prison has really got people thinking, "Maybe there's another way to conceptualize this." It's a very adversarial system and the outcome is such that people continue to cycle through the system and not much changes. The idea behind therapeutic jurisprudence is that we can address underlying factors leading to crime, such as substance addiction, then we can reduce their criminal behaviors. In the 1990s, we were locking people up right and left, Rockefeller drug laws, three strikes—they were leading to incredibly expensive confining of people with criminal behavior. Research showed drug court works, and then the recession hit and state agencies said, "We can't afford to incarcerate people at this rate!"

Calvin highlights how the economic recession led individuals of all political persuasions to recognize the unsustainably high costs of incarcerating those imprisoned as part of the war on drugs. Indeed, it was conservative former Miami-Dade County prosecutor (and subsequent U.S. attorney general) Janet Reno who started the first problem-solving court in response to the massive costs that county incurred by incarcerating individuals with drug convictions.

While legislators and policymakers may differ in their political motivations for advocating particular responses to prostitution and illicit drug use, the systemic impacts of both these social issues often mandate increased coordination between alliance professionals. Sofía, the Latina director of an addictions-treatment program in a Denver-area jail, described the 2005 city ordinance that established the Denver Crime Prevention Control Commission as instrumental in facilitating collaboration between criminal justice and social services agencies. The commission is a larger and better-funded version of numerous other Denver-area task forces that, like their counterparts throughout the United States, attempt to unite alliance professionals (often termed "stakeholders") around particular social issues.[3] Sofía concisely summarizes the political and financial mechanisms at work in such collaborative endeavors, which fund her jail-based addictions-treatment program:

> Money has a lot to do with it. Mayor Hickenlooper, he's governor now, and his administration pushed toward that stuff. The director he appointed to the commission, she's very powerful and has the backing of the mayor's office, and the dollars that come with that. It's pretty much a struggle trying to work with the people in criminal justice because they've been there for so long—thirty, forty years—so they're used to doing things their way and not very open to thinking outside the box.

Sofía's keen synopsis of the significant political and financial support criminal justice professionals enjoy in such collaborations underscores the powerful role played by the ideological framing of prostitution as a social problem. Alliance professionals generally emphasize street-based sex trading as inherently problematic for both women engaged in it and the society of which they are a part by referring to some combination of public nuisance, addictions, and socioeconomic inequalities. In many instances, individual alliance professionals who work directly with street-involved women readily acknowledged that these factors comprise a deeply entrenched and even intractable set of social problems that existing law and policy are poorly equipped to address.

Denver was one of the first U.S. cities to adopt, in 1994, the End Demand approach, often referred to internationally as "the Nordic Model," which imposes criminal penalties on men who attempt to buy sex (Dodge, Starr-Gimeno, and Williams, 2005). While the Denver Police Department, following national practices, does not disaggregate prostitution arrests by the venue in which they took place, interviews and extensive participant observation with both street-involved women and alliance professionals indicate that many clients are arrested in sting operations that target escorts rather than street-involved women. Likewise, none of the street-involved women I spoke with reported ever having a client arrested or hearing about the arrest of another woman's client, although they did acknowledge that officers frequently use neighborhood men's impounded cars to pose as potential clients in undercover operations.

Steve, a White detective with an enforcer orientation, expressed his frustration with the public nuisance approach, which disproportionately focuses on arresting women who publicly solicit clients, by arguing that the women's clients should face harsher penalties:

> We have a public nuisance abatement unit that impounds Johns' vehicles when we do street-level operations, and I think that's great. You have the supply side and you need the demand side for this to be an industry, and when the Johns are arrested, their fines and sentences, I don't think it's enough. That's not to say that the females shouldn't be punished for committing an act, but I think that if you look at the demand side as well, it's obvious that the whole area with the penalties needs to be really overhauled and addressed.

This prevailing focus on women who solicit publicly as a greater nuisance than the individual men who pay them for sexual acts also influences the parameters of alternatives to incarceration. Diana, an idealist White public defender who works in a Denver-area prostitution diversion court, expressed concern regarding the city attorney's decision to focus diversion court participation exclusively on street-involved women, rather than women who work indoors or solicit online via Backpage or a similar website:

> We're mostly dealing with women waving at cars to stop, women coming into contact with undercover officers and making deals for very small amounts of money—ten dollars, twenty dollars. Women involved in Backpage, they're not a part of the program. When designing the program, the city attorney described the program participants as "street prostitutes," not "sex workers," but they have a lot of the same needs.

Some amount of ideological framing and concomitant financial support for alliance efforts to curtail prostitution does acknowledge the prominent role that struggles with addiction and socioeconomic inequality play in women's street involvement. Kurt, a White vice detective who shares a strong transgressor orientation with many of his colleagues, alluded to the multiple restrictive forces that inform decision making among women who become street involved:

> The street-level prostitution revolves around some sort of addiction, whether it's alcohol or narcotics. They've reverted to this from just not being able to have a job, maybe being abused, and the addiction. I think that once some of them are looking at maybe getting out of that life, and they get a job at McDonald's where they are making five bucks an hour, and you get your paycheck at the end of the week and it's as much as you would get in a few dates, and they look at that like, "What am I doing? I could have made ten times this much." Those are some huge issues.

A judge presiding over a Denver-area diversion court echoed Kurt's description of women facing a set of challenges that make street involvement the most feasible and readily available choice:

> They have essentially two very difficult problems to overcome. One is psychological illness and the second is a behavioral problem. In many of the cases, these women have been on the streets since early childhood and don't have other experiences. They have limited job skills, transpor-

tation, clothing, in the sense of appropriate clothing for job interviews. If I was to draw a picture, the movie *Monster*[4] very accurately showed these obstacles. It showed the obstacles she faced in applying for a very entry-level position. It was a situation ripe for failure, starting with her clothing, her diction, her lack of knowledge and experience, and it just goes on and on.

Juxtaposing these statements from the vice detective and the judge reveals important experience-based perspectival differences that, in turn, reflect their respective social class backgrounds and the type of contact they regularly have with street-involved women. Kurt, who regretted that he never had the opportunity to go to college, entered the police force after serving in the military, and rose through the ranks as he garnered extensive on-the-ground experience coordinating large-scale narcotics and prostitution investigations as well as posing as a client in sting operations. He positions the women's struggles as essentially economic as a result of their addictions; in Kurt's account, abuse is an ancillary factor. The judge, conversely, with the significant expertise conveyed by his job title and prestigious university degree, uses a popular-cultural reference to characterize the women's central problems as essentially medical and behavioral as a result of their membership in a particular class group.

Despite the recognition of the complex factors at work in street-involved women's lives, alliance professionals almost universally subscribe to the alliance ethos' individualization of women's addictions and the sex trading that finances them. This approach offers little opportunity for women to find an alternative and sustainable means of support for themselves, all while they accrue a criminal record that makes it even more difficult for women to find legal ways to earn an income.[5] Individual alliance professionals certainly recognize this contradiction; Aaron, a White idealist public interest lawyer who works for a legal aid services provider, describes how he balances his own individual desire to advocate in particular ways and the limitations imposed by his professional role:

You're trying to work within the system to try to do good rather than necessarily change anything for the most part. There's a lot of tricky grey area in the middle, between doing legal work and speaking to the media to say that "we need to have this such-and-such law passed," or "this law is bad because of this reason." We can't take positions on whether we think prostitution should be legal or not legal.

Such individual conflicts with the system at large can become even more pronounced when alliance professionals share their perceptions with higher-ranked or more powerful officials who disregard them. Steve, a White detective with an enforcer orientation, recounted what happened when he and some of his colleagues from vice spoke to a Denver-area judge about penalties they regard as unfair:

> We were like, "This is crap. These guys should be getting penalized just as much as the women." But then when the judge would talk about it, he'd say, "Well, you know, I fine the guys this huge amount and if I do that to the women, they have to go back out and work [the streets] to pay it. So it might be easier for them to do a night in jail, whereas it's easier for this guy to pay a thousand dollars." He was real good at talking about it, but it's still a bunch of crap.

Police officers, like Steve, often expressed their frustration with what they regarded as misplaced priorities that they had no choice but to enforce. Their knowledge about other criminalized activities they felt were more serious only compounded their resentment about the need to respond to citizen complaints about prostitution. Kurt, a White detective with a transgressor orientation, acknowledged that public demand drives the work he and his colleagues undertake, such that they must focus their energies in areas that they may not agree are the best use of resources:

> All we're doing right now is raiding massage parlors. Why isn't forced labor being included? The public doesn't care, so we don't care. We don't get phone calls about the sheep herder [who may be a victim of labor trafficking] in the [rural Rocky Mountain] Front Range. We get phone calls about the sex worker standing on the corner who's an eyesore and brings down property values. If we are receiving a citizen complaint in either an area or maybe a specific person who may be in a specific area, we need to

get the citizen complaint handled and do our due diligence in investigating as best we can.

Kurt's astute "the public doesn't care, so we don't care" neatly captures the dilemmas alliance professionals face as they go about their daily implementation of prevailing political will. Interactions among alliance professionals sometimes cast these dilemmas into sharp relief.

Intra-Alliance Relationships

The policy intentions underlying coordination between alliance professionals emphasize the importance of services provision to women under correctional control as a result of their street involvement. Such coordination efforts appear to be somewhat easier for criminal justice professionals because of the hierarchical environment in which they work and the prominence the alliance ethos enjoys in such efforts. These combine to account for the frequency with which criminal justice professionals said in interviews, or noted to one another during my participant observation, some variation of the phrases "that's not our role," "it's up to the judge" or "those are the probation terms" to reinforce that they are bound by the terms of higher-ranked authorities.

Janine, a Latina probation officer with an enforcer orientation, expounded at length on "how well we work with the D[istrict] A[ttorney]'s office and the County. I love our [law enforcement] agents, even though the women don't, because they're so great in communicating and letting us know stuff." Emphasizing collaborative information sharing about women's cases as a strength, Janine strongly positioned herself and her colleagues as interventionists working in street-involved women's best interests. Alan, a White idealist detective, likewise emphasized that he attempts to play a positive role, akin to that of a social worker, in the lives of street-involved women he encounters through his work:

> I like to think that the encounters they have with me are hopefully positive enough that they're like, "Yeah, I don't have to be involved in this." Regardless of who it is, woman or child, when we're done interviewing, I always tell them, because it's true, "Hey, you're better than this. You can

do anything you want to do. I believe you are better than this. You need to believe you're better than this." You can't B.S. that, you have to believe it.

Yet coordination with actual social workers proved to be another thing entirely for some criminal justice professionals. Kurt, a White senior detective with a transgressor orientation, contrasted his previous work in vice with his current role on a Federal Bureau of Investigation task force that addresses prostitution-related issues by emphasizing the coordination it requires:

> In vice, the coordination wasn't as much because you work internally in Denver, so while you need to know some of the service providers and things that are out there, it's not as much your role. Here on the [FBI] task force, we work with multiple law enforcement agencies, a massive amount of nonprofits, victim advocacy groups, human services, public defenders—people that I would never have had to deal with before. So a lot of that is building trust for us. It's a ridiculous amount of coordination now, and we've had our hiccups and mistakes.

This "ridiculous amount of coordination" demanded of Kurt and his colleagues entails treating women charged in prostitution-related cases as victims, which necessitated involving social services providers. Many of these providers, who face increased pressures to provide wrap-around services with reduced resources and vague measurements for client success, expressed their own struggles with attempting to advocate for clients in an essentially punitive system.

Sofía, the Latina director of a jail-based drug-treatment program, described her surprise at learning that the jail sergeant, whom she had previously dismissed as unsympathetic to incarcerated women, had no choice but to self-present as tough and uncompromising as part of her job:

> When I first started at the jail I went to a training with the deputies and we were doing this exercise and I was paired up with the sergeant. So the facilitator wanted us to turn our backs to each other and we both said at the same time, "I'm not turning my back." And I thought that was really interesting because they are afraid, too, but they can't display it. They can't show emotions because it puts them at risk.

Sofía's low opinion of the sergeant stems in part from the sergeant's reserved professional demeanor, in direct opposition to the emotions that Sofía frequently displays in addictions group. Shelley, a White county jail employee with a transgressor orientation who is tasked with helping women to find housing and other basic resources, felt frustrated that corrections officers and other jail staff members sometimes behaved toward the women in ways that Shelley regarded as dismissive. Nonetheless, she empathized with the numerous pressures such alliance professionals have even as she explained why she takes more time meeting with women than her colleagues typically do:

> When you have two hundred women trying to get your attention and needing something, because women can be very needy, especially when they're in a crisis situation, and being incarcerated is a crisis. So I can see both sides of it, but I still think people should be treated with respect. You don't have to yell at 'em and call 'em names. You can just say, "You need to wait, I can help you," or something. In the court system, the women don't understand what's happening—things happen so quickly in there and of course a lot of big words are used and nobody's really explaining in detail. So sometimes when I ask, "So what was your sentence?" they're like, "Uh, not sure" because they're not clear about what really happened. So I make it a point to go through every document with them, and I probably take more time with women than anybody.

Shelley, who demonstrates an understanding of both why the women appear to be demanding and why correctional facility staff may disregard them, evinces pride in her ability to work as an advocate in this context. Sofía, the jail-based drug-treatment program director, took a different approach in dismissing corrections officers and other uniformed staff who she felt treated her as a naïve and potentially subversive force in the jail:

> They tend to think we're a security risk, and so that's been pretty challenging in the last couple years. I just say "hi" to everybody and if they don't answer me, that's fine. I don't chitchat with them very much, and that keeps me out of any kind of nonsense because there's a lot of cliques. We go through a day training, like a "Scared Straight"[6] kind of thing. It's

funny, because they come up with all these scenarios, like a riot, to try to scare you. I've been around a long time and I don't scare easily. They think we're not trained because we don't view the people that we work with as "inmates," like they do. I always call them "clients" or "participants," or I just say "individuals," I just can't bring myself to say that word, "inmate." That and they think we're bringing things in, like contraband.

Many social services providers felt that this environment of mutual disrespect and mistrust does little to foster collaboration in meaningful ways. Some services providers held criminal justice professionals in such low esteem that they withheld information, as did Carrie, a White idealist social worker, during a visit to an incarcerated client, and Ellie, a Latina diversion court worker with a transgressive orientation, when confronted with what she regarded as an inappropriate request from a woman's probation officer:

> CARRIE: She [the incarcerated woman] started talking about hearing voices, and so I immediately came out on the unit and I told the deputies that I really felt she needed to be seen [by a mental health professional], but I limited what information I shared. I said, "She's hearing voices, she's psychotic right now," so the sergeant took her down to medical. Other than that, I don't like to talk to them much; I think it's a gossip thing with them. I could see them using that against the women.
>
> ELLIE: The probation officers want to say, "Ellie, tell us about this kind of history that they have with their family so we can deny them a pass to visit them." It's not my responsibility to say, "Your family has a history of constantly subjecting you to abuse, and you're gonna see your uncle who totally abused you." Instead I say, "This is gonna be a trigger for you. Let's talk about what it means that you're going to their place for Christmas." That's not the approach the P[robation] O[fficer] wants to take.

These sentiments are not unknown to criminal justice professionals. Kevin, a White detective who organizes large-scale undercover policing operations, lamented this lack of intra-alliance trust, which he felt inhibited his ability to act as an advocate for women despite his desire to do so:

> We all come at this from different avenues, and it would be nice if we could get to the point where we respect each other and say that the victim-centered approach is the best for all, looking at their needs and then subsequently we can look at our needs. It used to be that I could go to a treatment facility but now you have to jump through a lot of hoops, not like before—part of those visits were professional, for my case, but 80 percent of those visits were because I cared about them and I wanted to make sure that they knew somebody cared about them. You can't do those things anymore, you're just not allowed to—there's too much distrust.

Some criminal justice professionals attributed this lack of trust to the hierarchical system in which they work, and were often careful to note that they, too, regularly experienced workplace changes without their consent or consultations. Veronica, a Latina transgressor who works at a Denver-area jail, accepted that higher-ranked individuals made decisions that dramatically impacted her work, but felt resentful about how little they involved her. She felt that social services providers would be well advised to recognize that she also struggled in an environment where very few factors were within her control:

> Of course decisions are made from higher up and brought down, but from the deputies' point of view things are shoved down their throats, too. No one's ever told, "This is what's gonna happen," it just happens. Like one day I walked into work and everything's getting moved and I'm like, "Oh my God, let me grab my stuff!" So I grabbed everything, and I have a big ol' stack of things I'm carrying all around the jail, and I'm like, "You guys could've warned us, you could've at least e-mailed." Instead, it's "Get over there and move, this is where you're moving."

Alliance professionals of all orientations felt frustrated by colleagues whom they regarded as insufficiently invested in street-involved women's futures, or who abused their authority. César, an idealist Latino prostitution diversion court counselor, criticized his colleagues who lack empathy and understanding:

> It's very hard to work with people that are jaded and working with this population because they have their preconceived notions and they don't want to change. It's unfortunate because a lot of these people are stake-holders, and that's where my frustration comes. I want to tell them, "Sorry, you are very jaded and you are a stakeholder." They don't have a sense of empathy. They have a sense of, "Where can we get more bang for our buck without spending as much?"—as if it's their personal money.

Ellie, a Latina diversion court worker with a transgressor orientation, likewise spoke of her encounters with probation officers who, while well intentioned, may overemphasize the enforcement aspects of their work in a way that abuses their authority:

> You can see that they care about these women but they are also very wrapped up in how much power they have. It almost disgusts me how much they play into their power, like, "Oh no, if you want them to do more UAs [urinalysis drug screenings] I will get on them to do that right now." Like, "I *am* the probation officer, I *am* the beginning and end of their world right now." They let phrases like that slip sometimes and you can just see that they are really loving the power they have over these women and how they can micromanage them.

Everyday police encounters also take place in this fraught context, where officers engage in the sometimes dangerous daily business of street-level law enforcement while remaining cognizant of their need to justify their actions to higher-ranked authorities who wield power over them.

Everyday Police Encounters

Street-involved women interact with police patrol officers in a context shaped by jurisdictional priorities, professional procedure, and the mood of all parties involved in fast-moving encounters. As we have seen, women construct many aspects of their sex trading in direct response to policing and actively avoid crossing jurisdictional boundaries from

Denver County to neighboring Jefferson County due to the higher like-lihood that they will face a harsher sentence if arrested in the latter. The women's encounters with police vary according to city priorities and associated policing procedures, and accordingly one jurisdictional approach to prostitution invariably influences the way prostitution takes place in another. Janine, a Latina probation officer with an enforcer orientation who oversees a caseload of women with prostitution con-victions, described the approach taken by her jurisdiction, a city that borders Denver County:

> We don't take the women to jail, we just issue them a ticket and then they can come back [to court]. A ticket is a summons, which means that you're gonna appear on the [court] date just by receiving the ticket from the officer. Then as long as you come to all your court dates, you don't go to jail. The officer does have the discretion to take them to jail and make them post a bond, and as long as they go to all the court dates they get that money back, but jail only happens if there's an extreme safety danger, like "please take me to jail because my pimp is gonna do something" kind of a thing.

Police patrol officers, detectives, and other Denver County criminal jus-tice professionals did not share Janine's positive assessment of her city's approach, which they generally regarded as encouraging the prolifera-tion of prostitution-related activity due to the limited threat of arrest it posed. This created additional pressures on officers, many of whom already felt overloaded with neighborhood-specific pressures to respond to particular types of citizen complaints in their police district. Steve, a White detective with an enforcer orientation, described how he and his colleagues struggle with the need to deal with the consequences of other jurisdictions' approaches to policing prostitution in addition to their many other responsibilities, the vast majority of which are driven by citizen complaints:

> There are jurisdictions, that will go unnamed, that surround the Metro area and don't do any prostitution enforcement. So we try to balance it, because they create a massive problem for us. Looking at the spectrum of work vice does, I'd say it's prioritized evenly between liquor and prostitu-

tion, because that's what [police] commanders have to deal with—the commander of District Six downtown, his complaints all revolve around bars and drunken activity. So, of course, he wants bars addressed. But somebody who's a commander that has East Colfax may say, "I have a problem with prostitution occurring on East Colfax." So, the way we've always put it is that "this is a job." Right, wrong, or indifferent, if someday they legalize it, then we won't enforce it anymore.

Police responses to citizen complaints and associated enforcement measures transpire within what Kurt, a White vice detective with a transgressor orientation, characterized as the "myriad of operations" that vice undertakes. Kurt described considerable daily variation in anti-prostitution policing:

> On a typical day we will get together and set up an operation to go on Colfax. We'll identify someone as the undercover and we'll go out and we'll try to contact a girl working on the street doing prostitution. So we could do that one day, the next day we could target Johns. The next day we could target Internet-based prostitution, or we could do like a massage-parlor-type operation.

Old school cougars, as well as other women with extensive street experience, frequently advised me not to wander the neighborhood on particular days of the week for precisely this reason. Conventional wisdom among a number of these experienced women held that Thursday is what they called "vice day," when undercover officers engaged in a concerted effort to offer women money for sex and then arrest them when they agreed.

Undercover police officers, like their uniformed peers, must pay close attention to behavioral cues they observe among women on the street to determine whether they have grounds to make an arrest. These observations require that they employ individual discretion, procedural norms, and, of course, their knowledge of prostitution-related municipal and state statutes in order to arrest a woman on a particular charge. Alejandro, a Latino patrol officer with an enforcer orientation, noted that he walks a fine line between discretion and procedure in street policing as he uses his observational skills to determine if a woman's behavior provides justification for arrest:

> We'll observe them maybe walking on the opposite side of the street so they can have that eye contact with oncoming traffic, or they're looking back, waving at the cars. Obviously you can see when a John pulls around the corner and she'll round the corner and walk up to the car and talk to him. If she doesn't know him, that's not what somebody on the street will usually do—that's indicative of prostitution activity. We see her load into a car, then we'll stop and interview them and see what the situation is there.

As Alejandro points out, police procedure is just one aspect of the street-level interactions in which officers must quickly ascertain whether they have sufficient evidence to make an arrest. Procedure derives from law but may also be unwritten and shared verbally among colleagues during the training and socialization of new officers, rather than codified in paper form due to the numerous contingencies that shape the situations in which arrest occurs. These contingencies may include the type of behavior a woman is engaging in, where she performs it, or the terms of the sex act she agrees to perform, all of which determine the prostitution-related statutes an officer may use to arrest her. Kevin, a White detective with an enforcer orientation, argued that the variety of prostitution-related charges available to prosecute women made gathering sufficient evidence considerably easier:

> Let's say you're driving around and doing surveillance and you see a male pick up a female. You tail them and they park in a block somewhere, you give them a few minutes and they're engaging in a sex act. Now that could just be [a charge of] indecent conduct or lewd activities in public, but then you can separate them and interview them, and figure out where it goes from there—that's where you get the rest, to figure out if there are other charges. With undercovers, people think we're really slick and stuff, but it's simply just that agreement for sex in exchange for anything of value. Ninety-nine-point-nine percent of the time it's money, but for our purposes [to make an arrest], we just need her agreement.

Kevin lists several possible charges a woman, and possibly her client, could receive if a police officer observes her engaging in various stages of a street-based sexual exchange with a man. Yet the arresting officer must be able to provide sufficient evidence as grounds for making the arrest to higher-ranking criminal justice professionals, such as workers in the City Attorney's Office and city or county court judges. This is particularly true for the Denver municipal statute "Furthering the Act of Prostitution," colloquially referred to by alliance professionals and women alike as "furthering." Women can be charged with this statute if a judge determines she has engaged in behavior designed "by word, gesture or action, to endeavor to further the practice of prostitution in any place" (Denver Municipal Statute 38–158–6). Peter, a career police officer with a bureaucratic orientation, observed that his colleagues must be careful in making furthering arrests since they rely so heavily on an officer's individual discretion that they can be easily dismissed at a higher level:

> It's very vague and I can tell you our City Attorney's Office does not like it. It's one of those things where just because I see someone walking on Colfax, I can't write them for that. If you're doing an enforcement action and you see a woman walking against traffic on Colfax, making eye contact with [men driving] vehicles, waving at them, stopping and contacting males, then she loads into a car, the first thing she says is, "Prove you're not a cop. Are you a cop or not a cop?" That, or if she gives directions about where to go, that would be furthering the act. So it's observing the multiple steps [of the exchange], like if a street officer sees her load into different vehicles and come back like ten minutes later, that might be enough to write a furthering.

Despite such considerable discretion and the number of prostitution-related offenses with which they may charge street-involved women, police officers, like many other criminal justice professionals, often described feeling trapped by legal and procedural limits they regard as inhibiting their abilities to make arrests that lead to convictions. Kurt and Peter both expressed the need for caution in making arrests to avoid accusations of entrapment or unprofessionalism by alliance professionals who work at higher levels of the criminal justice system:

KURT: You don't typically want to broach both sides when you're undercover. So I might tell her, "I have fifteen minutes, twenty bucks,
what do you think?" and she'll say, "Yeah, I can give you a blow
job. Twenty dollars." That's not entrapment, because each person is
broaching both sides, but you have to be careful about that.

PETER: As a male police officer, I can only do a pat-down for weapons
with the back of my hands, just pat the pockets, waistline, the back,
and the ankles. If we want to do a full search of a woman, we've got
to get a female police officer. So obviously we'd take her down [make
the arrest] and then we'd have to get a female police officer who's
working downtown to come do the pat-down. It's cumbersome.

Officers must carefully adhere to these legally and procedurally mandated
behaviors to avoid having the charge dismissed by the City Attorney's
Office or being challenged in court by an especially enthusiastic public
defender or, in rare cases, a privately hired attorney. They must do so in
the course of encounters that unfold very rapidly, all while considering
the possibility that a woman's prostitution activities may be coerced by a
third party who warrants their attention. Alan, a White idealist detective,
distinguished between a victim of trafficking and a victim of circumstance
in describing the difficulties he faces in making discretionary assessments
regarding a woman's motivations for engaging in prostitution:

Barring being forced or manipulated, everyone has conscious decisions
they make in life. So that is something that I look at: is this person making the conscious decision to do this, or are they being legitimately forced
to do this? By no stretch of the imagination do I think that every woman
involved in sex work is being trafficked. That's not true. That's not re-
motely true, but that doesn't mean that they haven't been victimized in
other ways, whether it's rape or assault or whatever. Most people aren't
going to choose to be in that line of work. They didn't grow up and say
they wanted to be there. When I make those encounters, I try to remind
myself that this is a matter of circumstance and it's unfortunate, but we
have to work through it.

Alan's awareness of the multiple exclusionary factors at work in the "matter of circumstance" through which a woman becomes street-involved

underscores how individual professional orientations inform the ways in which officers interact with the women. Peter drew on his lengthy career in law enforcement and bureaucratic orientation in acknowledging that officers' wide range of personalities and orientations inevitably shape their encounters with street-involved women:

> Most cops obviously were trained to treat people with respect until it's not given back, but I will tell you that most cops, just like most people, if the encounter is respectful and nice, that's how they're going to be. But that's not across the board. Some cops are just angry, or they got issues going on at home, or they have a distaste for the sex trade. But most people in vice, it's just business. When I worked vice, it was never a personal thing, it was never an angry thing, it was just, "Hey, you're under arrest—here's the situation."

Peter acknowledges that such encounters can potentially be impacted by an individual officer's mood, life situation, or attitude toward prostitution, which he contrasts with his own neutral approach. In so doing, he underscores some of the factors that inform discretionary practice in street-level encounters.

Steve, a White detective with an enforcer orientation, likewise reflected on how encounters can go bad very quickly, or how long-term involvement in criminalized activities via undercover police work can lead to professional misconduct. I interviewed Steve in his office the day after a Denver police officer with years on the force was arrested while off duty and soliciting a street-involved woman for sex in his civilian vehicle. Unaware of this arrest when I sat down at his desk, I was surprised to hear Steve say, "I'm sure you can imagine that morale's really low today." Since I did not know what he was talking about, he turned his computer monitor to show me a *Denver Post* story about the arrest, which was the talk of the station that day and serendipitously prompted a rather extensive discussion about what Steve glossed as "bad encounters":

> It's tough being a cop. When I first got here, I'd hear stories about guys doing that kind of thing and I'd be like, "Ah, that's a bunch of crap." You

want to support your own and you want to think that nobody in your field would do anything wrong, and then you realize that not everyone's the same. Look, I'm not going to sit here and say that I haven't been guilty of bad encounters. I treat everybody with the same level of respect, I don't care whether you're a hard-core murderer, but when it's not reciprocated, I can be just as much of a jerk. So you probably run into women that might be like, "That guy's a total jerk."

I reassured Steve that the few women who had mentioned him to me had not shared anything negative, which was true. However, his acknowledgment of my longstanding ethnographic relationships with many street-involved women helped to explain why it took considerable time to build sufficient rapport that allowed officers to speak openly with me. Simply put, I suspect that some of them feared that I would share details about police procedure with the women to help them avoid arrest, or that some of the women had spoken with me about them. I shared a particularly friendly bond with Alejandro, a Latino patrol officer with an enforcer orientation, who openly asked me if I had heard anything about him on the street, which I had not. We laughed as I told him that I had been waiting for an officer to ask me that question, and Alejandro added,

I just wonder sometimes, like if they think Black or Hispanic officers are aggressive because they have something to prove, like "I'm not going to be soft on this person just because they're from my community." A "whose side are you on?" kind of thing, like "You're making us all look bad by being out here."

Police officers face compound sources of stress as they go about their everyday activities and interactions with street-involved women. Some criminal justice professionals referenced the specific difficulties they felt accompanied sexualized situations that occur undercover. Kevin, a White enforcer who regularly organizes large-scale undercover operations, highlighted the inherent risks undercover officers face as they attempt to gather sufficient evidence to arrest a woman on a prostitution-related charge without committing legal or ethical violations themselves:

This revolves around sex, and being a male and being an officer who's appointed to deal with this industry you're in a room with a female who may be getting undressed, or you may be getting undressed. You have a lot of potential for physical contact there that doesn't need to happen, and you need to make sure that you are following all of your procedures and not getting yourself into a situation where you yourself are committing a law violation. There are a lot of times where you have to use crude language and you have to decide whether to take things to a certain level or not, and be careful about what that next level would be.

Decision making about "whether to take things to a certain level" is further complicated by the fact that young and inexperienced officers dominate in street-level policing, where their youthful energy and physical strength allow them to engage in chases and other demanding tasks that become less desirable or possible with age.[7]

Alan, a White idealist detective, described how his youthful enforcer orientation shifted with age, while readily acknowledging that his own personal pathway to an idealist orientation could have taken a different, more cynical course:

I was just a young street officer when I went through six months of vice training, then I picked up [a work assignment in the specialized unit dealing with] prostitution. I was just like, "This is fun undercover work!" I didn't think about any of the ramifications and the people I came in contact with—that doesn't mean I was disrespectful, I was just like "whatever." I'd have a night where I'd arrest like twenty-five people and be like, "Man, I'm really killin' it!" It's changed now to where I really don't care about that anymore. I'd rather direct somebody on a different path than just arrest them. Probably it's from getting older, too, but I look at the bigger societal issues now and go, "There's root causes for all this stuff that I didn't think about before." That's why a lot of cops become cynical—whether you're involved in gangs, drugs, or whatever, once you start looking at it like, "There's a reason why people are doing this" it's like, "I can't do anything about that stuff."

Taken together, police officers' accounts of their everyday encounters with street-involved women demonstrate the complex and multifaceted ways they experience their discretionary authority. Officers' propensity to regard their work with feelings of cynicism or even futility also stems from their keen awareness that no matter how hard they work to gather evidence or build an investigation, their efforts may be dismissed in court.

Criminal and Problem-Solving Courts

Following arrest, street-involved women become the subject of alliance professionals' discretion in criminal courts through case allocation, sentencing, and encounters with public defenders, judges, and, sometimes, juries. A judge, prosecutor, or public defender may alternatively decide that a woman is a good candidate for problem-solving court, usually in the form of prostitution diversion court, and accordingly recommend her for this much more intensive alternative to incarceration. Women can also receive probation, another form of court-mandated oversight in which an individual's professional discretion likewise determines the course of their future.

Steve, a White detective with an enforcer orientation, provides a concise description of how the criminal justice system as a whole allocates prostitution cases:

> The vast majority of our prostitution cases are city, they go to the City Attorney's Office. If it's an escort operation or an Internet-based prostitution operation, there may be state charges as well, and those would go through the District Attorney's Office through county courts. The majority is just city ordinance—the way the system's set up, the process is just easier, because the judges know everything, [and] maybe the women can get diversion.

Most prostitution-related offenses are misdemeanors and accordingly go before a judge in county court without a jury. In some instances where sex-trading activities take place in conjunction with felony offenses, such as pimping or organized drug- or sex-trafficking operations, a woman may testify in a jury trial in exchange for a reduced sentence or as a victim witness if she is not facing criminal charges against her. Alan, a White idealist detective, expressed frustration at the treatment he believed that women received when testifying against men who had forced them into prostitution or otherwise exploited their sex-trading activities:

> It's hard for us when we have a young lady who is manipulated or forced or coerced to do these acts of prostitution and you get them on the stand, and the jury is looking at them as a whore, as a street prostitute. Not as somebody who has had a broken home and has been sexually abused and then met this person who forced them or coerced them to do these acts. The jury looks at the pimp who's making them do this and they're like, "Well, that's just a guy trying to make a buck." Or they see the word "pimp" brought up as something cool, like they even have pimp Halloween costumes for kids now. The jurors are our peers, and I know that's how some of them look at that situation.

Alan contrasts what he regards as negative popular-cultural perceptions of women who trade sex with more positive cultural associations with pimping, a situation he attempts to resolve by ensuring the presence of expert witnesses at trial. Expert witnesses, who must receive the judge's approval, present evidence in support of a particular perspective on prostitution-related issues, but ultimately Alan recognizes that individual jury members come to trial with a lifetime of socialization that informs their perspectives on the sex industry. A similar dilemma arises with respect to women who may petition the court to remove prostitution-related arrests from their criminal record through a process known as "record sealing."

Aaron, a White public interest lawyer who works for a Denver legal aid services provider, explained that with such a request, which may or may not require a hearing, a judge must use her or his own discretion to assess the woman's request:

> What they're weighing is whether or not it's in the public interest to have it sealed, so they're weighing the benefit, the reason why the individual wants it sealed versus the public interests for safety. So you're getting positive versus negative, why they need it sealed so that they can get a job and move on, versus the public's need to know about possibly having a dangerous criminal out there.

Problem-solving courts often offer prostitution-related record sealing to those who successfully complete their program, which can be a significant incentive for women with an extensive history of prostitution-related arrests. The Denver-area prostitution diversion courts where I conducted interviews and participant observation prioritized admitting women whom diversion court staff regarded as particularly street involved, which they determined using a nationally used survey instrument, the Women's Risk Needs Assessment (WRNA),[8] in conjunction with their discretionary determination of each individual woman's readiness to end her involvement in street-based sex trading and illicit drug use.

As with so many other facets of the criminal justice system, multiple practical considerations constrain the discretionary process that determines a woman's ability to enter diversion court and live in the transitional housing facility specifically for the women participants. The program excludes women who have caregiving responsibilities for minor children due to its inability to house them, as well as women living with HIV/AIDS due to the court's belief that their status poses a public health threat through their sex-trading activities, a belief codified in the Colorado felony statute "Prostitution with Knowledge of AIDS." HIV-negative women without caregiving responsibilities come to the court in a variety of ways, neatly summarized by Diana, a White idealist attorney who works in a prostitution diversion court:

> From arrest, women are brought before the court from any number of different sources—a judge, prosecutor, public defender—once they know that she has a history of prostitution. The judge or the city attorney will notify probation, then one of the team will notify the woman and see if she is interested. The public defender, with attorney-client privilege, will meet with her and if they believe she is a good candidate she'll notify the city attorney, who has veto power. The next legal step in the case, if they've pled "not guilty," is a pretrial conference where the person's name comes to [diversion court] staffing and they are temporarily approved. The [diversion court staff] gives them the WRNA [assessment], then takes the results to staffing. Then, at the next court date, the public defender meets them to tell them about their options: the intensive two-year program or proceeding through the legal system. If they want to do the program, they

are then released to [the transitional housing facility], but they must first change their plea to guilty before they can enter the program.

The number of discretionary forces at work in the process of admitting a woman to diversion court is rather impressive, from point of arrest to the referral and screening processes she undergoes once identified as a potential candidate. Once approved as appropriate diversion court participants, women become subject to increased scrutiny and discretionary decision making regarding their movements, relationships, and decision making by the judicial team, including a therapist, a probation officer, a city attorney, and a coordinator who works at the transitional housing facility. A judge who oversees a Denver-area prostitution diversion court, which meets weekly to review e-mail correspondence regarding the women's daily activities, described a typical court session:

> When I interact with the women, I include the review of women's activities, congratulate them on their successes, and hold them accountable for their missteps in ways that have been agreed upon by the whole team. The only exception is if something occurred that was so concerning that the city attorney or probation decided a citation needed to be issued for violation of probation. Some examples of sanctions could include a written assignment, community service, restrictions on curfew, or restrictions on where someone can go. If there is a special event they had permission to attend, for example, we might have to say "no" because of a hot UA [urinalysis test positive for controlled substances]. It's important for them to know that this court won't hold them to strict accountability such that on a first misstep they'll be sent to jail. So long as they maintain a desire to succeed in our program, our job is to work with them.

Such restrictive conditions, combined with the long-term nature of a problem-solving court, prompt some public defenders to discourage women from pursuing the option of diversion court. Calvin, a White diversion court evaluator, described resistance to problem-solving courts among both public defenders and privately hired attorneys, whose legal training as advocates often encourages them to advise clients against longer-term criminal justice system involvement:

It's interesting to see the learning curve with the attorneys, particularly the defense attorneys. They're taught that they need to vigorously advocate for the defendant, but a lot of the time, drug court is rigorous: you can spend two years being tested for drugs, or you can go to jail for four months. It's a lot easier to go to jail for four months, so sometimes defense attorneys look at the short term, not in the best interests of their client, because in the short term they could spend more time in jail. They really need to take the long view, like getting help for mental health problems, drug abuse—those are really the long-term interests. In the short term diversion court is a greater threat to liberty, but the long-term benefits are potentially huge.

Although diversion court involves a uniquely high level of scrutiny over an extended period of time, women who receive probation for a prostitution-related offense must also regularly report to alliance professionals as a condition of staying out of jail. Janine, a Latina probation officer with an enforcer orientation who manages a specialized caseload of women with prostitution convictions, detailed the discretionary process she undertakes with women arrested on prostitution-related charges and assigned to her by the city court for correctional supervision:

So anyone charged and sent to probation for pre-sentence investigation, I meet with them for an intense interview process, research their criminal history, talk about their social ties, any mental health issues, substance abuse issues, employment, how long they've been in the sex industry. I'll make a recommendation to the court whether or not they're appropriate for probation or what my sentencing recommendations are. Some women, at the same time, have other cases in other jurisdictions and I make recommendations to allow supervision in both jurisdictions at the same time.

Women also face restrictions on their movements as part of the terms of their probation, often in the form of an "area restriction," which forbids women from visiting particular neighborhoods on penalty of arrest. Designed partially as a way to keep women out of areas where they may trade sex for money or illicit drugs, area restrictions were further described by Doris, an African American probation officer with a bureaucratic orientation, as essential to holding women accountable, a key aspect of the alliance ethos:

> We do have area restrictions as part of our terms of probation, and you will be jailed on an area restriction, meaning that you've already been placed on probation, you were given notice that you're not supposed to be in the area. So we will jail you. It's a low bond, five hundred dollars cash surety, but that's important because you're already on probation, you know that you shouldn't be in that area. So an area restriction is holding you accountable at that point.

It is self-evident that street-involved women and their probation officers might have considerable disagreements regarding what women need, including a fundamental difference of opinion regarding illicit drug use and sex trading. A woman placed on an area restriction might very reasonably complain that her loved ones, including her children, live in the neighborhood the court has forbidden her from visiting, and could likewise disagree with a probation officer's determination that she needs addictions treatment. Janine describes the considerations that inform her decision making as she formulates a case plan for a woman under her supervision as part of her specialized caseload:

> What's going on in their life? Are they pregnant? Basically they have to open up their life to me and I look at it and see what are the problem areas and then I assess, "what are we going to work on first?" and "are there fears of leaving the industry?" That's hard because they're not gonna be up-front and honest. It's a hard job because you work so hard to get a placement for them, get them out of jail, coordinate transportation, and then they choose to leave in thirty minutes and you're like, "Really?" We really do try to work with these women, we don't want to put them in jail. I went to a training where they said it takes almost seven contacts with law enforcement or probation before something happens for a woman to make the choice to change.

Janine expresses frustration with women who make choices that do not correspond with her understanding of what is in their best interests. In so doing, she draws on the language of the domestic violence movement in stating that it takes multiple attempts before a woman can leave prostitution, even using the number of times commonly circulated among battered women's advocates since the 1970s. This is particularly interesting given the gendered power dynamics at work between women and those tasked with their oversight, which many alliance professionals mentioned as a factor in their discretionary decision making. For instance, the presiding judge at a Denver-area diversion court described feeling that he was the only person adequately committed to the court, making him "reluctant to turn this over to another judge" despite his concerns about the gender dynamic at work in the courtroom:

> I actually asked, at the start of the program, if the participants might feel more comfortable with a female judge. Participants were adamant that they were pleased with my participation and did not want me to leave. On one side, they have been controlled by men their whole lives—they've had abusive fathers, many have been raped by their fathers, uncles, brothers, other males such as a pimp, Johns in general, and even, unfortunately, male police officers. It seems to me that having the ultimate authority in this court being a male is wrong, such that the women might feel, "Here is another male telling me what I can't do."

Ellie, a Latina diversion court worker with a transgressor orientation, echoed his concern, noting, "In the end, the judge has the final say with everything. So the only man in the room gets to decide."

Diego, a Latino court-mandated therapist with an enforcer orientation, noted that gender and ethno-racial identity do play a role in his interactions with street-involved women, albeit in a way that could push them to rethink perceptions he deems problematic:

> The girls I work with, majority are African American. They are glad I am not African American. They are glad I am not an African American female because the trust is just not going to be there. They have a very hard time trusting me because I am a man. One put it, "You are always going to be higher than us." That's cognitive distortion. They say, "You are always going to be over us because you are older, you are in law enforcement, and you are a man."

Characterizing women's recognition of male privilege as "cognitive distortion," Diego reframes the power imbalance between himself and the women he counsels through diversion court. Yet this reframing potentially overlooks the reality that a significant difference does in fact exist between him and the women in terms of occupation, ethno-racial identity, class, gender, age, and freedom from correctional control, among other factors.

Roxanne, a Latina corrections officer with a transgressor orientation, took a different view of gendered dynamics among alliance professionals in situating women as uniquely suited to what she described as "this authoritarian position":

> I think being a woman is important in this job because we have to know how to balance things whereas if someone came in and had the personality where they can't handle sass, then you come into this authoritarian position and trigger god-knows-what in these women. It's kind of like you're a parent trying to deal with crazy kids.

The operations of discretion are hard at work, and in troubling ways, as alliance professionals like Diego and Roxanne characterize adult women as "crazy kids" whose "cognitive distortion" requires altering before they can be free from correctional control.

Concluding Thoughts

Alliance professionals and street-involved women employ a dynamic combination of personal judgment and procedural norms, otherwise known as discretion, to guide their encounters with one another. Discretionary forces and processes operate in both alliance professionals' and street-involved women's lives at the level of prostitution-related policy formulation, intra-alliance relationships, everyday encounters between police and street-involved women, and criminal and problem-solving courts. In these contexts, it is those alliance professionals who interact most closely and regularly with street- involved women, including police officers who work vice or patrol, whose descriptions of the struggles street-involved women face in their everyday lives most closely mirror the women's own self-representations.

Alliance professionals who most regularly encounter the women readily acknowledge that the law is a blunt instrument ill equipped to address either the complexity of the issues at work in women's lives or the nuances of the transactional sexual exchange. Such professionals often expressed this view as a result of their experiences engaging in police work driven by citizen complaints as well as neighborhood, police district, and city-wide priorities that reflect the political will of much more financially and culturally powerful forces rather than the realities they see in their work. Ambivalence regarding the utility of criminalizing prostitution and addiction is commonplace among those alliance professionals who have the greatest experiential knowledge about street-involved women's lives.

It is unsurprising that in this challenging context social services providers and criminal justice professionals report a generalized sense of mistrust regarding punitive-therapeutic coordination efforts designed to eradicate prostitution. These efforts, which rely on acceptance of the alliance ethos, ultimately demand that professionals elide or ignore the glaring reality that a criminal record—even for a misdemeanor prostitution-related offense—functions to retrench the exclusion from housing, legal employment, and other basic needs that so often serve as antecedents to women's street involvement.

Criminal Thinking

It takes me a little while to locate the room in the Denver-area county courthouse that weekly holds prostitution diversion court, partly because I am still taken aback by the lengthy list of the day's cases scrolling on electronic display monitors. Each case begins with the momentous, "The People of the State of Colorado versus . . . ," followed by an individual last name. I think about the vice detective who told me that he sometimes emphasizes the seriousness of a particular case by rhetorically asking a person he is interrogating while in custody, "Do you understand what that means, that the entire state of Colorado is pissed at you?" After years of listening to women on the streets or in the transitional housing facility tell me about their experiences with the criminal justice system, I am both full of anticipation and intimidated that I have received permission to observe in a closed courtroom.

Despite all my hard work in establishing relationships with alliance professionals, I am unprepared for my emotional reaction when I enter the diversion courtroom and realize that I know all but two of the women seated on the benches. I sit in the far left corner of the last bench, waving in a friendly but not overly familiar way to women who acknowledge me. Even though we are all sitting in a courtroom specifically for women with a history of prostitution involvement, the social norms at work in this alliance-dominated setting are very different from those at work in the street or services-provision contexts where we have previously interacted. I realize that some women might not even remember me, given the number of strangers with whom they regularly interact, and the compromised memory that can accompany struggles with substance abuse. Rather than risk the potential for a woman to feel ashamed by reminding her, "We met when you were workin' the block," I smile politely at everyone and wait for them to initiate a conversation.

Within a few minutes, one of the two women whom I do not remember previously meeting comes and sits very close to me on the back bench, introducing herself as Roxanne before adding, "I don't know how to ask this nicely, so I'm just gonna say it: who the hell are you?" I burst out laughing, as do the other women, all of whom live together in the diversion court's transitional housing program. We relax into more familiar and loose body postures as we make small talk before the judicial team enters the room; as we stand up to show respect for the judge, Roxanne winks and opens her denim jacket to show me the school-size carton of strawberry milk she has hidden inside. "That's criminal thinking," she whispers, satirizing the term many alliance professionals use to refer to what the alliance ethos regards as inherently flawed decision-making processes that lead particular individuals to use illicit drugs or engage in illegal activities.

"Be seated," instructs the judge, and Annette, the first diversion court participant, approaches the stand, where the judge begins to recount her activities for the week, offering praise for her continued sobriety and a caution to behave more collegially with other women in the transitional housing facility. Her failure to do so, in the judge's opinion, does not warrant an extension of the curfew she requested in order to spend time with her children, who live on the other side of town with relatives. He asks her if she would like to speak, and Roxanne whispers, "You're about to see a show today, just wait." Annette puts her hands on her hips and asks the judge a single question that prompts several of the women sitting on the benches to utter "Amen!" and "Mmhm!" as if in church.

"Your Honor," she asks, "may I ask if you have ever lived in a house with fifteen other females?" The judge, who looks amused, responds that he has two adult daughters and a wife. Undeterred, Annette continues, "Well, then maybe you can understand my dilemma. There are certain women in this program who seem determined to sabotage my recovery by spreading gossip and lies." Annette and the judge continue in this fashion for several minutes, with the judge admonishing her to remember that "everyone deals with these issues, whether it's in the workplace or at home, and part of recovery means learning how to handle them as an adult." Annette looks visibly frustrated when the judge refuses to grant her curfew-extension request and asks her if she has anything more to say. "Your Honor," Annette says in what sounds like a mock-deferential tone, "I understand that I have to respect your decision. That's all I gotta say right now." As the next woman approaches the bench, Roxanne takes a clandestine sip from the strawberry milk carton hidden in her jacket and nods at me. "Criminal thinking," she repeats.

The diversion court judge's weekly interactions with women in the program differ significantly in character from criminal court proceedings, which I also regularly attended with women who wanted company as they waited for their case to be heard. In one such instance I spent several hours in a Denver-area county court with Lexi, who works under the radar and who, as so often happened through unexpected opportunities to engage in participant observation with the women, showed her sophisticated knowledge of the criminal justice system's powerful reliance on discretion and other independent processes. The first case involved a man arrested on a drunk driving charge, a monolingual Spanish speaker who said very little to his court-appointed Spanish-language interpreter. It took several minutes for the public defender, whom he had never met, to find his file, much to the judge's chagrin. "Look how scared he is," Lexi observed, as the man appeared to physically quiver in his jail uniform, his hands cuffed behind his back. "He's afraid that if he says anything it'll just make things worse." Within minutes he was on his way back to jail for several months.

The next case called involved an expensively suited young White man arrested on charges of driving under the influence of marijuana, which he had purchased legally. His similarly expensively suited and privately hired attorney called the arresting deputy as a witness and aggressively questioned him about the weather conditions on the night of the arrest. Over the course of the next thirty minutes, the deputy and the privately hired attorney debated matters ranging from police procedure to Colorado winter road conditions. At one point, the privately hired attorney asked the deputy, much to the judge's annoyance, "So if I produce weather reports that contradict your statement, you will continue to insist that the weather was clear?" Although the defendant received a substantial fine, he and his attorney left the courtroom together.

Lexi, who also met her public defender just minutes before her case, received a continuance, which delayed her hearing until a later date. "You see how it goes?" Lexi asked as soon as we left the courtroom. "These people just do whatever the fuck they want if you don't have a real attorney. I got lucky today."

Conclusion

At two in the morning, my cell phone vibrates loudly. I sleep with it next to me in case a woman calls the transitional housing facility's hotline number, which diverts directly to my phone, in need of a referral or just a sympathetic listener. Squinting at the bright screen in the darkness of my bedroom, I see a text message from Leelee that reads, "u must be mad at me." Another message arrives before I can respond, and I sigh with disappointment in myself as I read, "You forgot my birthday." Leelee was my closest confidante throughout this project, during the course of which our friendship survived the vicissitudes of her year in the transitional housing program, followed by her continued residence there as a peer mentor and her subsequent move to a Section 8 subsidized housing apartment nearby. I text an apology to her and ask if I can take her out for lunch, and she responds with a series of enthusiastic emoticons.

Leelee has an intermittent relationship with the transitional housing facility, which she feels overworked her in ways that led to a relapse when she took on a peer mentor role after finishing its twelve-month program. Staff hesitated to call the police when Leelee abruptly left the facility after stealing from it, unnerved by the possibility of adding to her already extensive criminal record. Leelee returned to the facility after four anxious days during which staff feared that Leelee's ex-girlfriend, who had a history of violently assaulting her, might have harmed her, or worse. After an extensive conversation with her, staff dismissed Leelee from her peer mentor role despite her protests that she felt pressured, out of gratitude for the services she had received, not to complain to staff about how overworked she felt. "And so I went back to what I know," she explained, meaning East Colfax Avenue.

The facility remains a big part of Leelee's life despite the fact that she no longer spends time there; the owner of Leelee's apartment complex is one of the major donors to the transitional housing facility, and most of the people Leelee relies on when she needs help with a problem are connected to it in some way. She is well aware of being one of the program's "success stories" because she is in stable housing, not using illicit drugs, and, until she recently gave up due to pervasive discrimination against people with multiple criminal convictions, actively looking for legal work. She now supports herself primarily through state disability benefits she receives as a result of a mental health diagnosis. Looking around the dilapidated complex, I realize that her living situation is the best many of the women can hope for when leaving the street *if* they are able to win a coveted place in the Colorado Housing Lottery for Section 8 federally subsidized housing, mobilize an extensive support network of employed persons they can call on in case of financial or other emergencies, and obtain low-wage service sector work or government benefits that will allow them to eke out a basic existence.

Leelee greets me with a big hug and points to the car she bought with money lent by a relative in another state. While it ran fine for the first few weeks that she owned it, the engine now has a serious problem that will cost several thousand dollars to fix, and the tires are completely deflated, angrily slashed open in the middle of the night by a woman she asked to leave her apartment for smoking methamphetamine. "Man," she says, "most days I feel just like them tires!" I nod silently, listening as she goes on to describe her enduring problems, many of which reflect the lack of financial and social supports that made prostitution the best option earlier in her life. She points out a man wandering around in the parking lot and tells me that he offered to fix her car but then engaged in a series of demeaning sexual gestures and comments that made her avoid him. The building's maintenance man, with whom she had a brief friendship, also regularly offers her money for sex.

There are some days with Leelee when I feel that we share a deep bond after six years of knowing each other, and then there are other days when I feel implicated in an unjust system that neither of us had much part in creating. Leelee's socioeconomic struggles understandably lead her to question why she decided to stop prostituting and using illicit drugs, as the alternatives available to her offer little more than poverty-level state benefits and the occasional generosity of people from her church or the transitional housing facility. I recall how different she was when we conducted street outreach or interviewed women together in motel rooms on East Colfax Avenue, where I, facility staff, and the women we interviewed all acknowledged her as an expert on street involvement. The social world outside of services provision and research, unfortunately, regards those life experiences as anything but expertise.

At lunch, Leelee orders far more food than we can eat as she tells me about these ongoing struggles, and I listen silently because I am exhausted after spending the morning meeting with potential transitional housing facility clients in prison. Yet my silence, punctuated by the occasional affirmation and praise for her fortitude in the face of adversity, is also part of an admittedly flawed moral calculus in which I attempt to repay the insurmountable debt I feel that I owe her for the insights she provided me with over the years. I feel deeply sad about how mutually exploitative our relationship appears when viewed through the grimy lens of a transactional exchange, but it is sometimes difficult to avoid doing so, particularly as we pack the large amounts of leftover food into Styrofoam boxes and Leelee exclaims, "We gotta go, my 2:30's coming!" She laughs as she says out loud what I am already thinking: "I'm makin' y'all sound like tricks."

When we return to the apartment complex there is an extraordinarily well-scrubbed young White couple standing outside her apartment door, looking around uneasily at their surroundings. Leelee explains that she knows them from her church, and I hug her goodbye quickly as she jumps out of my truck with her bags of food. I feel overwhelmed by emotions that I do not fully understand, despite my best efforts to do so using the social work skills I acquired throughout the course of this project. As I watch Leelee warmly greet the couple from church, I think about how her old tricks probably offered her far more than any of us new ones, and allowed her to set the terms of the exchange in much more honest and transparent ways.

Contradictions between the Alliance Ethos and Women's Street Realities

This book has argued that the criminal justice system's financial and ideological dominance over the alliance and its ethos results in a punitive approach that fails to consider the gendered socioeconomic realities that make sex trading the best available option for women like Leelee.

The preceding chapters detailed street-involved women's and alliance professionals' respective difficulties in navigating the fragmented results of the alliance ethos' implementation. The most significant of these—unrealistic services-provision parameters and criminal conviction–related discrimination—at least partially result from the contradictions inherent to this punitive-therapeutic partnership. Examining these contradictions helps to explain why so few women can meet the alliance ethos' narrowly defined expectations for success and why programs designed to assist them generally fail to be anything more than a temporary respite from the street.

Unrealistic Parameters for Services Provision

Leelee gave up searching for a legal job five years after leaving the street; for her, engaging in the hard work of addiction recovery offered precious little in the way of workforce participation options. Nonetheless, Leelee has met some aspects of the alliance ethos' criteria for success by finding stable housing and a legal means of self-support via her disability benefits. This alone distinguishes her from "failures" who relapse or hastily exit from addictions treatment or other therapeutic programs that abide by requirements incompatible with many street-involved women's life realities. Entrenched U.S. cultural values regarding self-reliance and financial independence inform both alliance and street contexts, where women frequently describe their hustles using the language of freedom, independence, and individual exceptionalism. Such a cultural climate encourages women to believe that addictions or other therapeutic treatment can help them to obtain the social status associated with financial independence and freedom from correctional control.

Incarcerated women who apply to the transitional housing facility routinely ask me some variation of the question, "What's your program's success rate?" When I respond with, "Every woman has her own unique definition of success," many women look unconvinced and pointedly ask me some variation of the question, "How many women relapse and drop out of your program?" Women ask me this because they know from their previous life experiences, as well as their exposure to the alliance ethos and its focus on individual accountability, that they face the disproportionate burden of making significant changes to their life circumstances. They also live in a dominant culture that privileges individual over collective success and discourages them from envisioning their struggles as anything but the product of their own choices. Given the considerable constraints that inform these choices, individual women like Leelee often eventually find it impossible to overcome barriers to obtaining legal work, long-term sobriety, stable housing, and other things that they would like to have.

The resource-poor, stressful, and sometimes chaotic environment in which services provision typically takes place forces alliance professionals to very rapidly assess street-involved women's readiness to change or otherwise comply with the alliance ethos. It is not uncommon for public defenders, therapeutic services providers, and other alliance professionals to have caseloads that number in the hundreds, a reality that demands quick decision making as a necessary precondition of remaining employed. Simply put, many of these alliance professionals are so overworked and pressed for time that they cannot devote the kind of personal attention that would be necessary to fully understand and respond to the totality of women's needs. Front-line alliance professionals who work most directly with street-involved women frequently feel exhausted and overwhelmed by their jobs, and know that available resources cannot adequately address anything but the most immediate issues at stake.

Such time and resource scarcity, coupled with the need to demonstrate efficacy to supervisors, requires alliance professionals to balance their knowledge about limited available services with the recognition that their decisions may result in the difference between a woman having a safe place to stay and becoming homeless or incarcerated. For instance, it is not at all uncommon for a woman's public defender to call a services provider on Sunday night requesting documentation to provide to a judge on Monday morning. When considering this request, the public defender may impress on the provider that without it, the woman will spend a significant amount of time in jail or prison. The provider often has just a few minutes to decide whether she can accept the client into her program on the basis of the public defender's description of her in conjunction with any previous encounters the provider may have had with the woman. These exchanges between criminal justice and social services professionals can be highly emotionalized and often involve deliberately manipulative tactics. As one criminal justice system professional told me when I informed her that the transitional housing facility had no space available to house her client, "Susan, I know you care about this woman and don't want to see her back in prison. I thought we had a relationship, but I guess I was wrong." Such working conditions, especially when combined with low pay, are not conducive to critical self-reflection, adequate time to discuss a woman's options, or even the retention of highly qualified and committed staff.

Conviction-Related Discrimination

Pervasive discrimination continues against individuals with criminal convictions despite the stunning reality that one in thirty-five U.S. adults is under some form of correctional control (Bureau of Justice Statistics, 2014). All street-involved women struggle with significant socioeconomic deprivation, evidenced by their near-universal eligibility for Medicaid, food stamps, and Section 8 subsidized housing, and their entrenchment in low-wage service sector work as their only legal income-generation alternative to sex trading. Once arrested, subject to various forms of correctional oversight, and legally obligated to inform prospective employers of their criminal record, women's socioeconomic opportunities become even further restricted in ways that entrench them in illicit income-generation activities. The loss of belongings, disrupted social ties, and other events that may transpire during a woman's incarceration—including new social ties formed in jail or prison—may encourage her return to criminalized income-generation activities following her release, perhaps even on an intensified scale.

Street-involved women also must contend with an acute shortage of affordable or Section 8 subsidized rental housing, which allows property owners the choice to exclude prospective tenants with criminal conviction records. Women with a history of criminal justice system involvement consequently end up living in neighborhoods where illicit drugs, as well as offers to engage in transactional sex, are far more readily available than legal work that pays a living wage. The alliance ethos regards all members of society as equally able to access housing, employment, and other basic necessities, and accordingly claims a neutral approach that obscures the significant similarities in street-involved women's gender, class, and ethno-racial characteristics. This approach mischaracterizes the socioeconomic inequalities at work in segregated neighborhoods as little more than the difference between individual women's decision making and the rule of law, and accordingly belies the overrepresentation of African American women, Latinas, and intergenerationally poor White women in street prostitution relative to other sex industry venues where women are less likely to face arrest, assault, robbery, and other forms of violence.

Women experience further fragmentation of their abilities to meet basic needs through the increased likelihood that they will face arrest in neighborhoods dominated by the criminalized economy and the extralegal problem-solving measures that often accompany it. Police patrol officers frequent East Colfax Avenue, where the women spend most of their time, in direct response to citizen complaints, 911 calls, and the neighborhood's general reputation as a "known prostitution area." In street-level policing as well as other forms of criminal justice oversight, the alliance ethos symbolically and structurally subjects the women to intensified forms of the power and control dynamic that their ethos regards as responsible for their sex trading and illicit drug use. Hence, in direct contrast to the women's own descriptions of their social and neighborhood ties as their main sources of support, the sociolegal intervention mandated by the alliance ethos positions both street-involved women and the neighborhoods in which they live as pathological, sick, and fundamentally in need of alliance intervention.

As part of this pathologization, alliance professionals often discourage or forbid women under their purview from engaging in intimate relationships while participating in drug or other therapeutic treatment. The justification for this restriction lies in the alliance ethos' understanding of alliance professionals as agents of intervention best positioned to assist women in their efforts to leave street-based sex trading, a process that this ethos regards as demanding a woman's highly individualized commitment to making significant changes to her life. This commitment requires that women focus the vast majority of their time and energies on themselves, irrespective of their caregiving and other responsibilities, as a necessary precondition of addiction recovery and permanently leaving prostitution. Alliance professionals' regular categorization of women's family members or intimate partners as "unhealthy" or "unsafe," due to their addictions and criminal justice system involvement, effectively discourages women from maintaining connections to their own communities. These practices take place in conjunction with the loss of many privacy rights guaranteed to other citizens, most notably through the collection and dissemination of information about the women in public criminal conviction records, or in alliance-specific case file data on women's physical and mental health status.

A Punitive-Therapeutic Paradox

Legislators and policymakers remain beholden to a general public with little real knowledge about the dynamics that inform everyday interactions between alliance professionals and street-involved women. The alliance's financial and political underpinnings emerged from an ideological stance that fundamentally views women's street involvement as a costly problem of law and order. So while the alliance may espouse the view that punitive measures alone cannot address the complex forces at work in street-involved women's lives, the neat replacement of the term "criminal" with "victim" offers street-involved women an interpretation of their lives that focuses on trauma. Proponents of this approach perceive its victim narrative as new and improved, but the reality is that the alliance continues to fail in the same ways as its exclusively punitive predecessor because it replicates the former's desire to stop shuffling street-involved women through the criminal justice system without addressing the reasons why they are there in the first place.

Positioning street-involved women as victims results in the construction of the "worthy victim" who, as a condition of services provision, is willing to evince endorsement of the alliance ethos and ways of being in the world that alliance professionals define as "healthy." Alliance professionals and street-involved women both experience constraints on their individual discretionary authority in the everyday contexts of policing, criminal and problem-solving courts, and probation or other forms of court-mandated oversight. Yet alliance professionals' discretion, particularly with respect to identifying individual street-involved women as particularly deserving of services, plays a powerful role in determining how alliance encounters will unfold—including whether or not a woman will receive services.

Alliance professionals ultimately have the power to decide on the veracity of women's disclosures, and some professionals are so oblivious to the operations of the powers they wield that when a woman feels unsafe in their encounters and accordingly withholds information, she is faulted for her perceived unwillingness to accept treatment deemed necessary. Differences in alliance professionals' assessments, definitions, and categorizations can create adversarial instead of potentially cooperative relationships, both among alliance professionals and between alliance professionals and street-involved women. Social services and criminal justice professionals both risk the possibility of their peers' scorn or disappointment, and concomitant potential for career derailment, if they advocate for a client who then relapses or otherwise fails to meet expectations. The potentially negative consequences of such advocacy disproportionately reward alliance professionals who reinforce the status quo, rendering the alliance little more than a repackaging of existing criminal justice approaches in which a predominantly class-privileged, White, and male group of individuals dominates the higher-status and better-paid alliance roles while women, working-class people, and people of color carry out their bidding.

Alliance professionals' adherence to the ethos that undergirds their work prevents them from enacting real and systemic change, which must take place at the level of law, policy, and prevailing attitudes toward street prostitution and addiction. This is particularly significant given the widespread popularity enjoyed by network television and other media forms that purport to document the lives of criminal justice system professionals and those they police or monitor. Legislators and policymakers remain accountable to a public saturated by such media as well as the influences of various moral-ideological forces that shape prevailing views on street prostitution and illicit drug use. Despite ample empirical research that demonstrates the failure of the prevailing alliance approach to remedy these pressing social issues, evidence-based recommendations have yet to make inroads into meaningful policy or legal change. Instead, the status quo is a vacuum in which the alliance ethos continues to echo *ad infinitum* with little evidence to suggest its success at anything but the continued cycling of street-involved women through the criminal justice system.

To the woman detained on prostitution-related charges, it makes little difference whether the officer who made the arrest did so under the guise of help, rehabilitation, or punishment. The results, ultimately, are generally the same in terms of jail time, a criminal record, or, if the woman is offered the opportunity to participate in diversion court, mandatory drug testing and extensive periods spent under court-mandated supervision. In considering meaningful alternatives to the continued incarceration of women engaged in survival behaviors, we must be clear about the limits of the criminal justice system's abilities to enact social change, whether in individual lives or in society more generally. The criminal justice system very effectively locks individuals in cages and, on their release, threatens them with a loss of liberty if they do not comply with specific requirements. It cannot succeed, and never has succeeded, in addressing deeply entrenched social problems that stem from poverty and multiple forms of gendered and racialized socioeconomic exclusion.

Sustainable Alternatives

Transactional sex remains a fundamentally gendered economic issue, regardless of the monetary amounts or other valued items exchanged, whether or how well the provider and client know each other, and where the parties involved carry out the encounter. Irrespective of whether or not legislators, policymakers, alliance professionals, or women engaged in these exchanges regard them as legitimate work, the fact remains that a need for money, sometimes in extremely constrained circumstances, motivates most women's decisions to engage in transactional sex. Many street-involved women combine money earned from sex trading with other criminalized income-generation strategies, most commonly the resale of marketable items such as prescription or illicit drugs, food stamps, and shoplifted clothing or electronics. The money street-involved women earn from these ventures goes almost immediately to neighborhood purveyors of controlled substances, and motel owners, as well as to the children and intimate partners the women support financially. Meanwhile, taxpayers fund a costly revolving-door criminal justice system that temporarily removes women from the street through incarceration without providing them on their release with any meaningful alternatives in terms of housing, legal work, addictions treatment, and other necessities. This situation is unsustainable for all parties involved due to its exorbitant socioeconomic costs.

Street-involved women's engagement in a variety of criminalized activities subjects them to arrest, incarceration, and court monitoring with a frequency that is unparalleled in other sex industry venues. As we have seen, street-involved women do not easily fit into ongoing cultural polemics about prostitution because they employ their sexual labor as a means to navigate their everyday struggles with addictions, homelessness, and compromised mental and physical health. Theirs is not an occupation that fits neatly within the language of choice or labor, and hence some sex workers' rights groups disassociate themselves from what they regard as the worst sex industry stereotypes embodied in street-based sex trading, including the prevalence of violence, addiction, and desperation in various forms.

Nonetheless, the prevailing political climate that informs public thinking about street-based sex trading also raises questions regarding how powerful legal and social institutions should respond to prostitution as an enduring issue. These exchanges take place in a street context that differs significantly from other sex industry forms in terms of the amounts of money exchanged, realities of addiction and homelessness, and a woman's likelihood of facing arrest. Yet no matter what form it takes and irrespective of moral-ideological stances that surround it, prostitution remains a solution to a fundamentally gendered economic problem for which women should not be arrested, prosecuted, and burdened with a permanent criminal record.

A powerful set of prevailing political and ideological forces endorse prostitution's continued criminalization, and hence it is most practical to offer two separate strata of meaningful alternatives. The first envisions possibilities following the decriminalization of prostitution, and the second offers more humane alternatives within the parameters of continued alliance predominance. Both sets of recommendations apply specifically to street-based sex trading yet also echo decades of sex workers' rights activists' calls to decriminalize prostitution and destigmatize sexual labor by regarding it as a form of legitimate work. As women in sex work concisely stated at the 1989 San Francisco World Whore's Summit, legal and social institutions need to work far harder to "outlaw poverty, not prostitutes."

Sustainable Alternatives under Decriminalization

Decriminalizing prostitution involves the removal of legislation that relates to the exchange of sex for money or something of value between consenting adults. As in Brazil and New Zealand, two countries implementing internationally lauded approaches to decriminalizing prostitution between consenting adults, legislation prohibiting third parties from exploiting women's sexual labor should remain in effect. Decriminalization ideally fosters a cooperative, rather than adversarial, environment among street-involved women, criminal justice professionals, and social services providers, such that women can more readily seek out assistance without fear of prostitution-related arrests or judgmental treatment. The women can also screen clients more effectively during transactional sexual encounters when they no longer fear arrest.

Decriminalization is a harm-reduction strategy based on the acknowledgment that prostitution will continue to exist regardless of policing and public opinion and that women involved in it should not be further marginalized and stigmatized. Decriminalization eradicates the scarlet letter of prostitution convictions that compound the exclusionary socioeconomic forces already prevalent in street-involved women's lives. Yet decriminalizing prostitution alone will not change the criminalization of illicit drug use or the disproportionate enforcement of drug laws against poor or working-class people and people of color. Hence any discussion of decriminalizing street prostitution must also address the need to likewise remove legislation that punishes addiction in ways that make real and meaningful individual change difficult, if not impossible, due to criminal, particularly felony, convictions' enduring discriminatory effects.

People use drugs and alcohol for many reasons, and the same is true of street-involved women who struggle with addiction. Prevailing approaches to drug treatment, when it is available at all to street-involved women, typically depict addiction as the product of a lack of self-control, an unwillingness to address unresolved psychological or emotional issues, or, at worst, an inherently flawed self. This is an all-too-familiar refrain for women who have in many cases struggled throughout their lives with poverty and oppressive forces related to classism, sexism, and racism that work in tandem as exclusionary agents. Women involved in street-based sex trading are just one small segment of those who use, or struggle with addiction to, illicit drugs and, as we have seen, drug use and prostitution play different roles in women's lives depending on how women engage in them.

Decriminalizing prostitution would help to facilitate peer-led and harm-reduction services provision options for street-involved women in ways that meet their complex needs. Alliance approaches currently mandate addictions and other therapeutic treatment for street-involved women under their purview in ways that actively condemn or ignore the creative strategies women use to help them avoid arrest and plan for financial and other exigencies that inevitably arise from theft, assault, and health issues that accompany addiction and chronic homelessness. At present women primarily teach each other these skills in correctional facilities, particularly jails, where women have a temporary respite from the daily search for money, illicit drugs, and housing while evading police. Decriminalization would allow for knowledge sharing that takes place on more widespread and equitable terms so that all street-involved women could learn to implement measures to reduce harm in what are indisputably difficult conditions. Peer-to-peer support centered on harm reduction remains the best (and internationally proven) approach to nonjudgmental services and skill building in the most practical aspects of day-to-day life working the street.

Decriminalization alone will not result in the cultural change necessary to shift or eradicate the considerable social endorsement for criminalization. Removing the legislation related to the exchange of sex for money between consenting adults will not eradicate stigma, just as the legislation itself does not create the considerable opprobrium that surrounds transactional sex. It is essential that decriminalization occur in conjunction with the allocation of stable and long-term funding for comprehensive services provision on terms that account for the complexities of street-involved women's lives. As we have seen, the alliance employs the concept of trauma as a means to justify intervention, surveillance, and other control mechanisms in the women's lives; yet, simultaneously, the women regard housing, food, child custody, and other immediate issues as understandably more pressing.

This sharp disconnect, which stems in part from alliance dominance over existing programs for street-involved women, functions to create at least some of the difficulties alliance professionals face in demonstrating "success" among the women. Unfortunately, sometimes program structure can unintentionally reinforce moral or ideological beliefs held by staff, rather than prioritizing the women's own perspectives on their needs. While street-involved women's needs are inevitably as diverse and varied as the women themselves, patterns do emerge in the ways in which alliance professionals construct the goal-oriented case plans that they develop for individual women. Sometimes these include changing behaviors or income-generation practices that staff members regard as unseemly. Rather than forcing a woman to evince a desire to pursue a particular path aligned with the alliance ethos, truly comprehensive services provision would recognize that not all women want to eschew prostitution, illicit drug use, or other behaviors staff members may deem objectionable.

All women, whether street-involved or otherwise, have a right to feel safe and cared for when seeking services. Street-involved women who approach transitional housing facilities or other intensive programs targeted toward them may find that program structure requires them to perform gratitude, demonstrate evidence of "reform," or evince other ways of being that add to the emotional labor of addictions recovery. Staff should actively consult with current and former street-involved women in designing and implementing programs as a means to ensure that "client-centered" is a practice rather than just a buzzword. Decriminalization will enable these practices by removing women's prostitution and illicit drug use activities from the criminal justice system's purview and placing them squarely within a framework that prioritizes women's needs.

Sustainable Alternatives under Continued Alliance Predominance

Potential alternatives to continued alliance predominance should be considered a form of harm reduction within an inherently punitive system that in many instances functions to further punish women in already very onerous circumstances. The primary means by which this harm reduction can be achieved involves reframing street-based prostitution as an economic activity undertaken in severely constrained socioeconomic circumstances. Ancillary recommendations include the provision of psychosocial support for alliance professionals to facilitate their commitment to the goal of therapeutic work, and equalizing funding available to social services providers and criminal justice professionals.

Alliance professionals do not exist in a vacuum separate from the deep-rooted social inequalities that pervade their work; in fact, their own life experiences and perspectives heavily inform how they approach their jobs despite their adherence to the alliance ethos. So while their individual work orientations vary, the fact that the alliance exists at all indicates that possibilities exist for perspectival shifts regarding street prostitution. This book has rightfully and extensively critiqued prevailing alliance approaches that position street-involved women as victims of trauma in need of alliance intervention. The alliance emerged as a result of extensive battles fought by advocates who wanted the criminal justice system's treatment of street-involved women to account for at least some of the circumstances that inform their decision making.

In the not-so-distant past, criminal justice professionals in particular widely regarded street-involved women in denigrated terms: as criminals, addicts, incorrigible, and profit driven. The alliance's widespread reframing of the women as victims continues to criminally prosecute them while simultaneously making room for a limited amount of previously unavailable social services, few of which operate with adequate funding. An evidence-based practical approach that accounts for the diversity of women's experiences and skills would reenvision street prostitution as a gendered economic problem, and accordingly reallocate the considerable municipal, state, and federal resources currently expended on such criminal justice oversight to services that meet women's needs in a sustained and meaningful way. Achieving this goal will require ideological bridge building between alliance professionals and street-involved women similar to what has already been accomplished with respect to mental illness in many alliance settings, especially police departments, where most officers receive training on appropriate ways of interacting with a person who presents as possibly having a severe mental illness. Prevailing contemporary understandings of addiction as a mental illness increase the likelihood that funding to support similar trainings on women's street involvement could derive from similar sources.

Rather than focusing on victimization discourse, the alliance should re-frame street prostitution as a "crime of necessity" that involves addiction, homelessness, and compromised mental and physical health. Ascribing victim status to street-involved women explicitly denies the complex reali-ties of their lives, which alliance professionals must attempt to understand if any real and meaningful change is to occur. Yet training alone will be insufficient and largely unenforceable given the significant discretionary authority alliance professionals exercise, often in situations that unfold very rapidly and in job-specific work cultures that prioritize particular ways of interacting with the women. Hence prostitution diversion court should be an option provided to every woman with a record of arrests or criminal convictions for offenses committed in neighborhoods where street-based sex trading commonly takes place. At present, women may only participate in diversion court if selected to do so by criminal jus-tice professionals, which excludes women who do not have prostitution-related arrest or conviction records, as well those who do not self-present in ways that make them appealing candidates for diversion.

However, social and institutional support must not be confined ex-clusively to street-involved women. If alliance professionals sometimes seem indifferent to the women's struggles, this is at least in part due to the tremendous overall indifference of the system that dictates the con-ditions of their work and asserts control over the women's lives. Mean-ingful, occupation-specific ways of addressing the emotional challenges inherent in front-line alliance professionals' jobs must be developed in order to assist them in effectively carrying out their work. Each alliance occupation presents its own challenges with respect to such support, in-cluding possible stigma attached to accessing it. For instance, workplace norms encourage police officers to value stoicism and emotional con-trol while social workers prioritize altruism and empathy. The system at present demands an enormous amount from professionals at all levels and offers precious little in the form of support beyond vague statements about the need to "leave work at work." While different impetuses un-derlie this pressure to suppress or deny the psychological impact their jobs impose on them, the result is identical in terms of prioritizing work at the expense of self-care.

Alliance professionals at all levels must acknowledge that front-line workers who engage most directly with street-involved women regularly witness or hear about violent or life-changing events in the women's lives, including overdose, assault, incarceration, child custody loss, or even death. Self-care is very difficult for alliance professionals to implement in work situations that take a heavy toll on their health, emotional state, and ability to care for their loved ones and themselves. No amount of professional training adequately prepares a person for these events, and continuing to express high levels of emotional investment in each woman results in a situation that photojournalist Wendy Perkins, who conducted the first photo-ethnography with Denver street-involved women, characterizes as "drowning in their own empathy."

The status quo could also be improved by equalizing funding available to social services providers and criminal justice professionals. The criminal justice system is a well-funded apparatus that receives the federal, state, and municipal resources necessary to sustain mass incarceration. Some criminal justice professionals who participated in this project expressed a desire for more specialized training to improve their abilities to work with street-involved women, yet none described concerns regarding job security. In sharp contrast, every single one of the social services providers I interviewed or interacted with spoke at length about their own financial insecurity as well as the lack of resources available to provide support to women struggling with addictions, homelessness, and compromised mental and physical health.

Under the prevailing approach, a street-involved woman will be far more likely to spend time in a correctional facility following her arrest than to spend time in an environment that offers her supportive resources. If she is lucky enough to encounter a specialized facility or services provider for women leaving the sex industry, it will often be staffed by underpaid, overtaxed, and frequently inexperienced young social workers. The best of these workers, due to personal and professional pressures of their own, will eventually leave for better paid, more secure, and benefited positions, many of which they readily find within the criminal justice system. This revolving door of burnout is particularly evident at nonprofits although it is generalizable to social services as a whole. Over six years I have watched numerous well-intentioned, energetic, and extremely capable social services professionals quit their jobs for more lucrative positions because they could not survive on nonprofit wages coupled with the high stress levels endemic to the work. As with advocates at domestic violence shelters, clinical social workers and support staff often find themselves in a position where they are asked to help clients find the very things that their jobs do not provide, such as a living wage, health insurance, and a happy, well-balanced life (Wies, 2008).

Street-involved women are well aware that, in the absence of a living wage and other benefits, such positions tend to attract women who have had their own experiences with addictions or abuse, and who may have altruistic motives that stem from their religious faith or political beliefs. As one woman put it as we sat together in the Denver correctional facility where she was incarcerated, "Susan, we know you wouldn't be up in here with us if you didn't have you no mess." Incarcerated women, as well as those still working the street, are unsurprised when services providers appear untrained, or even inept, precisely because of the very limited material rewards and respect that such jobs provide. Such low expectations extend to criminal justice professionals, as numerous legal aid workers and public defenders have explained to me during conversations in correctional facility lobbies. Many street-involved women fully believe that their cases are the training ground for inexperienced public defenders who are working their way up to the professional maturity paying clients require. Repeatedly hearing multiple variations of "when are you going to become a real lawyer?" from the neediest clients makes even the most committed advocate question her or his decision to work long hours for relatively low pay and limited respect relative to their peers in more lucrative areas of legal practice.

Such a situation hardly results in optimal services provision. Making federal, state, and municipal funding available for services tailored to street-involved women would lessen the considerable burden on costly and overcrowded correctional facilities. Yet a central problem remains with respect to how the alliance, and the broader cultural system that supports it, deals with individuals whose choices are socially constructed as problematic. Criminal justice approaches enjoy traction with the voting public because they appear to generate immediate results in the form of arrest, whereas social services rarely produce such expedient or readily quantifiable outcomes. Women's street involvement is a systemic problem that requires systemic solutions, but who or what will provide the financial and social resources necessary for the sustained support women need to make real and meaningful changes to their lives? How will this systemic change happen without a massive restructuring of dominant U.S. cultural values that prioritize material goods and other physical indicators of success over social well-being for all?

Centuries of stigma adhere to prostitution, and women who trade sex for money or other needed things have historically and cross-culturally been political lightning rods for a wide array of ideological, political, religious, and other social anxieties. The fundamentally gendered inequalities that underlie street prostitution constitute enduring social issues that warrant further critical examination into the ways in which the criminal justice system, and society at large, approach this important social issue. The nuances of street-involved women's lives require pragmatic, evidence-based legislative and policy approaches that reflect these complex realities; without these, the system will continue to fail the very women it aims to assist.

NOTES

INTRODUCTION

1 We identify Denver as the field site and ourselves as researchers but otherwise use pseudonyms (and general job titles) for all individuals in order to maintain confidentiality.

2 We use the term "street-involved woman" because it is more person centered than "sex worker" or similar terms that have little or no meaning for the women who participated in this project. Women who engage in transactional sexual activities to navigate their struggles with homelessness, addiction, and related problems rarely self-identify with the terms "sex work" or "sex worker." While no consensus definition exists among researchers who use the descriptive phrase "street-involved," a search of any scholarly database using this term will retrieve articles about North American people struggling with homelessness, addiction, and criminal justice system involvement. "Street-involved" summarizes the combination of these forces without focusing on one (such as prostitution) to the exclusion of others in ways that do not reflect understandings of these issues among those who experience them most intensely. Likewise, we use "street-based sex trading" or a variety of closely related synonyms to refer to the exchanges of sex for money or illicit drugs that take place in cars, motels, or semi-secluded public spaces near the area where women live and solicit clients.

3 Denver is a relatively ethno-racially homogenous city, with the vast majority of individuals self-identifying as White, Latino or Latina, or African American.

4 First initiated in Los Angeles and New York, "safe harbor" programs that advocate therapeutic treatment rather than criminal prosecution for minor girls involved in sex trading quickly became prototypes for other U.S. cities while adult women continued to face prosecution. An extensive legal and social sciences literature documents these age-related legal binaries with respect to the issue of consent in distinguishing between prostitution and sex trafficking; see for instance, Adelson, 2008; Adler, 2003; Brown, 2007; Menaker and Franklin, 2013; Mitchell, Finkelhor, and Wolak, 2010; Halter, 2010; Heilemann and Santhiveeran, 2011.

5 In her life history study of a woman with extensive street prostitution experience, Jody Raphael notes that "although women of color participate in larger numbers than would be warranted by their percentages in the general population, their stories and viewpoints have been largely absent from the literature" (2004, p. 7). The systematic impacts of structural racism and sexism contribute to the

overrepresentation of women of color, particularly African American women, in street-based, rather than safer and more lucrative forms of, sex trading. Hence even studies of street-based prostitution that do not feature race or ethnicity as explicit categories of analysis are likely to derive their results from interviews or survey data collected primarily with women of color. For instance, a Minneapolis study on age at entry into street-based sex trading reported that 80 percent of 117 respondents self-identified as African American, with an additional 6 percent reporting American Indian, Alaskan Native, or Latina ancestry (Martin, Hearst, and Widome, 2010, p. 1260). Women of color, particularly African American women, also predominate in court-mandated diversion programming, where they likewise report engaging in transactional sex at younger ages than their White counterparts (Clarke, et al. 2012).

6　Male researchers have carried out most of this ethnographic work with male interlocutors, which reflects a gendered culture wherein "girls and women have a very tenacious foothold in alternative street cultures, gangs, and highly gendered drug market roles" (Chesney-Lind and Irwin, 2008, p. 18). See also, for instance, Anderson, 1999; Bourgois, 1995; Liebow, 2003 [1967]; Venkatesh, 2009; Wilson, 2012 [1987].

7　Our work on violence against women appears in *Feminist Criminology*, *African Studies Review*, *Affilia: Journal of Women and Social Work*, *Sexuality Research and Social Policy*, *Women's Studies International Forum*, *Journal of International Women's Studies*, and *Conflict-Related Sexual Violence: International Law, Local Responses*, a volume we coedited for Kumarian Press/Stylus Books.

8　Women sign a form during the intake process at the transitional housing facility that grants staff members permission to use this material for research purposes. I was careful to protect women's confidentiality in compiling the database, and reporting results, to remove identifying information with respect to names and birth dates. Following standard ethnographic practice, I also used my free time at the transitional housing facility to take detailed fieldnotes on my password-protected laptop; I used pseudonyms for all the women in these fieldnotes as well as in analysis presented here. East Colfax Avenue does not have a pseudonym due to its notoriety throughout Denver and the U.S. West more generally.

9　The project's fifth year coincided with Tonia's year of residence at the University of Wyoming, which fortuitously allowed us to work together for lengthy uninterrupted periods analyzing the project results. We first engaged in open coding, during which we reviewed the one hundred verbatim transcripts of interviews, all of which the women gave Susan permission to record, and identified thirty-five distinct themes (with hundreds of subthemes) that occurred in more than half of the interviews. These included, as reflected in the structure of this book, themes of occupational risks, harm reduction and help seeking, and discretion, but also comprised narratives of entrepreneurship, experiences with clients, codes of conduct and penalties for violating these, and social support systems, among others. Susan, working closely with her students, engaged in inductive coding of these thirty-five themes in order to isolate material for effective and respondent-driven translation into the findings presented in this book. Susan followed a similar process with the alliance professionals during the project's sixth year, when research leave provided her with the time to triangulate her field notes with verbatim transcripts (and, for those who prohibited recording, notes) from her interviews with alliance professionals.

CHAPTER 1. WORKIN' IT, ADVOCATING, AND GETTING THINGS DONE

1 Many feminist researchers have addressed how, in the context of the socio-spatial estrangement faced by women like Janeiece and Noelle, the opportunities available to women and girls are often limited to their sexual capital. Sociologist Laurie Schaffner, in her study of minor girls in the juvenile justice system, describes the "oversexualization of this population of girls in trouble, facing racism and poverty in brutal ways. . . . [Y]oung women are viewed primarily as sex objects by many male adults in their worlds, view their own place in the world as mostly providing sexual titillation for males, and see sex as their best—or only—resource for problem solving" (2006, p. 99). Criminologist Jennifer Wesely also addresses these issues with emphasis on the relationship between such sexualization and punitive responses to girls' and women's involvement in the sex industry and street life. Wesely characterizes this social phenomenon as a continuum in which "one end represents sexualization that occurs as part of girls' day-to-day gender socialization and identity development. . . . The other end of the continuum represents sexual abuses and violence against women and girls, which are severe manifestations of sexualization. In between these two ends lies everything else that sexualizes girls in contemporary society" (2015, p. 3).

2 There is an extensive North American literature that explores street-based prostitution, problematic substance use, and violence as mutually reinforcing agents of harm. See, for instance: Rhodes, 2002; Bourgois, Prince, and Moss, 2004; Cusick, 2006; Cusick and Hickman, 2005; Singer, 2006; Miller and Neaigus, 2002; Romero-Daza, 2003; Craib, et al. 2003; Inciardi and Surratt, 2000; Erickson, et al. 2000.

3 In their work on the juvenile justice system, feminist criminologists Meda Chesney-Lind and Katherine Irwin note that "once on the streets, girls quickly discover both the dangers involved in street life and the narrow range of survival options available to them as girls. They also discover that they are in possession of a form of 'sexual capital' they can access, while boys tend to engage . . . in a wider variety of survival strategies" (2008, p. 84).

4 As noted previously, very few social scientists working in U.S. sex industry venues have explicitly engaged with race as a central analytical category; instead, most published works include discussions of race in the sex industry as an ancillary variable. Important exceptions to this general rule include Mireille Miller-Young's work on African American women in pornography, and Siobhan Brooks's ethnography on race and exotic dance (Brooks, 2010; Miller-Young, 2014).

5 Feminist critiques regarding the limitations of academic publishing are many and varied and we do not pretend to add anything to this already well-trodden terrain. For a particularly thoughtful reflection on these dilemmas, see Fine and Torre (2006), in which the authors note of their participatory action research in a women's correctional facility, "[W]e write this piece committed to participation and committing ironic betrayal. . . . We write here, explicitly without our collaborators' names, although with their review, permission, and blessing, because we speak some truths they dare not say" (Fine and Torre, 2006, p. 255).

6 There is no central database that lists all of the transitional housing facilities for women who wish to leave prostitution. An extensive Internet search conducted by Jennifer Hankel located such facilities in Baltimore (Samaritan Women), Lexington, Kentucky, Chicago, and Las Vegas (Refuge for Women), Phoenix (Sun Dance Lodge and Catholic Social Services), San Francisco (SafeHouse San Francisco), Florida (Created Women), Louisiana (Hope House), Los Angeles (Destiny House Restoration Center, administered by the group Hookers for Jesus), Denver (Esther House and Street's Hope), San Diego (Generate Hope), Las Vegas (the Dream Center Human Trafficking Program), Kansas (the Homestead), and Alabama (the Well House). Some of these organizations were founded and are staffed by women who left prostitution or other sex industry venues, while others were founded by individuals and church groups without sex industry experience.

7 This situation is extreme enough to prohibit the use of the term "sex work" because of the government stance that it constitutes "the use of language to justify modern-day slavery, to dignify the perpetrators and the industries who enslave" (U.S. Department of State, 2006). Unfortunately, funding available for services provision to (or, indeed, research on) women in the sex industry tends to focus on issues related to health or criminal justice, with the potential to further pathologize the women by focusing on disease transmission or arrest and incarceration. Careful researchers can subvert these restrictions by reporting on how, for instance, criminalization enables abusive labor conditions by effectively isolating women from police assistance and other protections (Kotiswaran, 2014; O'Doherty, 2011); the situation is considerably more restricted for services providers.

8 This metropolitan-area population includes residents of Adams, Arapahoe, Boulder, Broomfield, Denver, Douglas, and Jefferson counties.

9 Denver's six police districts publicly report statistics on instances of, and arrests for, crimes against persons, property, society, and all other instances of police calls, the largest numbers of which came from Colfax Avenue neighborhoods. Crimes against persons include instances in which the victims are individuals, whereas crimes against property are those involving theft or criminalized activities related to objects from which the perpetrator hopes to derive some benefit, and crimes against society are "vice" activities such as gambling, prostitution, and activities related to illicit drugs. The most recent available data indicates that the West Colfax neighborhood had a total of 8,498 reported instances from January through October 2014 comprising 1,360 crimes against persons, 4,371 crimes

against property, 825 crimes against society, and 1,942 other reports. The East Colfax neighborhood had 7,344 reports, including 1,239 crimes against persons, 3,457 against property, 881 against society, and 1,767 others. The neighborhood bordered by Colfax, Speer, and Broadway, known as the Golden Triangle for its large number of museums and historic sites, featured third in police reports, with 1,393 crimes against persons, 6,735 against property, 405 against society, and 2,008 others (Denver Police Department, 2015).

10 For a complete list of all Colorado and federal legal statutes related to prostitution extant at the time of the research, see Morris, et al. 2012 (appendix B, pp. 97–103).

CHAPTER 2. OCCUPATIONAL RISKS

1 For North American research that exemplifies this perspective, see Shannon, et al. 2008; Shannon, et al. 2005; Rhodes, et al. 2012.

2 Male privilege creates the street-based sexual economy and, in this resource-scarce environment, it is unsurprising that some men attempt to control and profit from women's sexual labor, which comprise a fourth component of risks related to gendered socioeconomic relations. Street-involved women I met throughout the course of this project almost never used the term "pimp," although they did talk at length about exploitative economic relationships wherein both partners struggled with addiction and homelessness. The majority of women associated the term "pimp" with a protective figure who assisted women in their transactional sexual exchanges, and women quickly noted that such men did not exist in their neighborhood. As detailed in Dewey and Epler, 2015, street-involved women in Denver tend to characterize neighborhood men as too addicted, desperate, and abusive to engage in the kind of mutually beneficial business relationship they believe true pimps provide to street-involved women.

3 Elsewhere we describe this as a process of "mystification," defined as legal and social processes either designed to obscure or resulting in a full or partial obscuring of particular practices. This is akin to, but not exactly like, what Marx (1992 [1867]) articulated as capital's mystificatory ability to reify workers' alienation from their labor (Dewey and St. Germain, 2014, p. 216). The street environment, with its drug informants, undercover police, and various other forms of intrigue related to substance abuse, addiction, and homelessness, lends itself to interpersonal mystification, in which what one person says and understands to be true about a given situation may be completely different from another person's assessment of, or knowledge about, it.

4 For a complete list of all Colorado and federal legal statutes related to prostitution extant at the time of the research, see Morris, et al. 2012 (appendix B, pp. 97–103).

5 Researchers disagree on the reasons why violence is so prevalent in most U.S. contexts where street-based prostitution take place, with some arguing that prostitution is itself inherently abusive (see Raphael 2004) and others contending that the criminalization of addiction, prostitution, and poverty more generally fosters violence against street-involved women (see Dewey, Zheng, and Orchard, 2016).

6 Anthropologist Didier Fassin and Richard Rechtman (2009) provide an excellent historical analysis of trauma's cultural construction from its nineteenth-century beginnings to its present status as what the authors term "an unassailable moral category." Trauma discourse has attracted its share of controversy, as evidenced by heated debates ongoing at the time of writing regarding the demand for "trigger warnings" in college campus settings, which likewise demonstrate trauma's widespread cultural salience.

7 Police officers, as well as other criminal justice professionals, do have therapeutic resources available to them through their jobs, but several officers explained to me that there can be a stigma attached to seeking such services in a field that places a high value on personality traits culturally valued as masculine, such as stoicism and control over one's emotions. One vice detective spoke about the therapeutic value he found in attending police-only social gatherings known as "choir practice." My career police officer father, who is perhaps more cynical due to the fact that he spent a good portion of the 1980s working undercover in a New York State narcotics unit, reframed this therapeutic value for me rather substantially when he dismissively explained the vice detective's therapeutic activities as, "Oh, 'choir practice' just means drinkin'!" For more on policing-related stress and associated coping mechanisms, see Amendola, et al. 2011; Freeman Clevenger, et al. 2015; Gershon, et al. 2009.

8 "Johns TV" is a program on public television, paid for with fines levied against men arrested during prostitution stings, that features the men's names and photographs with the intention of shaming and discouraging them from attempting to purchase sex in the future as part of End Demand initiatives.

9 Numerous studies of services provision or outreach to women in crisis contexts highlight the emotional toll that nonprofit or volunteer staff face while providing the essential services refused to street-involved women by the state. See, for instance, Wies, 2008; Cox, 2015; Knight, 2015; Kolb, 2014.

CHAPTER 3. HARM REDUCTION AND HELP SEEKING

1 Street outreach from the transitional housing facility, as with other organizations that work directly with individuals engaged in stigmatized and criminalized activities, ideally involves individuals like Leelee who are well known in the neighborhood targeted for outreach as a result of their current or previous residence there. While street outreach can involve many individuals, people often split into pairs to minimize the potential for women working the street to feel surrounded by strangers.

2 As discussed at length in chapter 1, harm reduction refers to efforts to reduce the negative consequences of particular activities, including illicit drug use and stigmatized sexual behaviors, while eschewing moral judgment. Many advocates of harm reduction characterize its practice as "meeting people where they are at" because of the way it eschews the moral-punitive judgment of abstinence-oriented approaches. Help seeking comprises the decision-making processes and associ-

ated actions women engage in as they negotiate their struggles with addiction, homelessness or precarious housing, and associated difficulties. For more on the ways in which harm reduction maximizes the potential for women in sex work to seek assistance on their own terms, see Cusick, 2006 and Rekart, 2005.

3 Throughout the world, women engaged in criminalized forms of transactional sexual exchange frequently report delaying or abstaining from seeking necessary healthcare services due to stigmatizing treatment or fear of incurring punitive sanctions or even criminal charges if they test positive for HIV (Overs and Loff, 2013). Harm-reduction advocates and human rights organizations almost universally support prostitution's decriminalization because it increases the likelihood that sex workers can access healthcare (Rekart, 2005; UNAIDS, 2012).

4 Many feminist researchers note the frequency with which many street-involved women have faced various forms of violence throughout their lives in conjunction with their criminal justice system involvement. Feminist criminologist Meda Chesney-Lind, for instance, describes prostitution and running away, the two categories for which girls face arrest more often than boys, as "criminalized victimization" because of the way in which gendered and sexualized vulnerabilities push girls into these activities (Chesney-Lind, 2002; Chesney-Lind and Irwin, 2008).

5 Psychologist Lenore Walker's work played an instrumental role in shaping contemporary understandings of intimate partner violence. In addition to introducing the concept of battered women's syndrome, Walker originated the cycle-of-violence model, which describes the common pattern in which an abuser commits an act of violence against his partner, followed by his exhibition of exemplary behavior in a "honeymoon period," and an eventual build-up of tension that leads to another violent episode (Walker, 1979).

6 In her ethnography of pregnant women struggling with addiction while living in San Francisco daily rent hotels, Kelly Ray Knight (2015) provides an outstanding discussion of the profound discordances that exist between the ways in which street-involved women and services providers regard different types of time. Healthcare providers often characterized drug-addicted pregnant women as "ticking time bombs," referring to the time until their delivery and, like their social services provider peers, required multiple appointments in order to monitor and assist women through their pregnancies. The women themselves attempted to balance these appointments with the much more pressing need to attend to the daily business of survival by earning enough money to stave off eviction, dopesickness, and other highly undesirable outcomes (Knight, 2015).

CHAPTER 4. DISCRETION

1 U.S. addiction-recovery narratives follow what anthropologist E. Summerson Carr, in her work with an addiction-recovery center's female clients, describes as "linear plotlines that proceed from a denoted dirty past to an anticipated clean future" (Carr, 2010, p. 12). Carr characterizes recovery narratives as predicated on

the listening audience's assessment of the speaker's sincerity. Therapeutic ideologies that underlie U.S. addiction-recovery narratives, Carr argues, are "thought to dramatically transform [the speaker] . . . [and hence] therapists posited that words could only heal the client-speaker to the extent that they revealed her" (Carr, 2006, p. 634).

2 Sociologist Laurie Schaffner observed similar tendencies in her work, such that court-involved "girls related relatively freely their sexual experience as victims. Many court-involved girls sense that they may gain sympathy by sharing accounts of their victimization. Although the girls were comfortable presenting themselves as sexual objects, they seemed less comfortable sharing their experiences of sexual agency" (Schaffner, 2006, p. 15).

3 For more on the Crime Prevention and Control Commission's activities, see Denver Department of Public Safety, 2014. For more on the development and impact of task forces to address the issue of sex trafficking see Dewey, 2014b.

4 The judge is referring to the 2003 film *Monster* (directed by Patty Jenkins), which tells the story of Aileen Wuornos, whom the state of Florida executed in 2002 for the murders of six different men who assaulted her on separate occasions in the course of their street-based sexual exchanges. Charlize Theron won an Academy Award for Best Actress for her widely viewed portrayal of Wuornos, whom street-involved women mentioned to me on several occasions during my research. In one particularly poignant instance, a woman told me that Wuornos had claimed self-defense in the murders by stating, "Every one of those men wanted to hurt me," and then explained that she did not have fingers to count how many men she would have to murder in order to exact revenge for abuses they had committed against her.

5 The dual criminalization of sex trading and illicit drug use, combined with criminal convictions for one or both of these activities, make it difficult for street-involved women to pursue other income-generation opportunities, even when they wish to do so, as part of a process Cusick and Hickman (2005) call "trapping."

6 Now condemned by the U.S. Department of Justice's Office of Juvenile Justice and Delinquency Prevention in response to significant evidence of their ineffective and even counterproductive results, "Scared Straight" programs began in the 1970s as an effort to deter young people from committing crimes by spending a day listening to incarcerated persons aggressively confront them about the realities of prison life (U.S. Department of Justice Office of Juvenile Justice and Delinquency Prevention, 2011).

7 Police patrol officers I encountered in the East Colfax neighborhood generally appeared to be in their twenties or thirties, although older and presumably more experienced officers were present during nights when the streets were very crowded or many arrests occurred. Anthropologist and sociologist Didier Fassin's ethnographic work in France has likewise documented this phenomenon in which the youngest and most inexperienced police patrol officers receive assign-

ments in neighborhoods their departments regard as particularly troubled and undesirable (Fassin, 2013).

8 The WRNA (Women's Risk Needs Assessment) is just one of numerous survey instruments used in correctional facilities to quantitatively determine the suitability of individuals for particular types of treatment. For more on these survey tools, see U.S. Department of Health and Human Services Substance Abuse and Mental Health Services Administration, 2005.

WORKS CITED

Adelson, Wendi J. 2008. Child Prostitute or Victim of Trafficking? *University of St. Thomas Law Journal* 6: 96–129.

Adler, Libby. 2003. New Perspectives on Labor and Gender: An Essay on the Production of Youth Prostitution. *Maine Law Review* 55: 191–209.

Amendola, Karen, David Weisburd, Edwin Hamilton, Greg Jones, Meghan Slipka, Jon Shane, Christopher Ortiz, and Eliab Tarkghen. 2011. *The Impact of Shift Length in Policing on Performance, Health, Quality of Life, Sleep, Fatigue, and Extra-Duty Employment.* Washington, DC: National Institute of Justice.

Anderson, Elijah. 1999. *Code of the Street: Decency, Violence, and the Moral Life of the Inner City.* New York: Norton.

Baker, Lynda, Rochelle Dalla, and Celia Williamson. 2010. Exiting Prostitution: An Integrated Model. *Violence Against Women* 16, no. 5: 579–600.

Beck, Ulrich. 2007. *World at Risk.* Cambridge, UK: Polity Press.

Begun, Audrey, and Gretchen Hammond. 2012. CATCH Court: A Novel Approach to "Treatment as Alternative to Incarceration" for Women Engaged in Prostitution and Substance Abuse. *Journal of Social Work Practice in the Addictions* 12, no. 3: 328–31.

Biehl, João. 2013. *Vita: Life in a Zone of Social Abandonment.* Berkeley: University of California Press.

Bourgois, Philippe. 1995. *In Search of Respect: Selling Crack in El Barrio.* Cambridge: Cambridge University Press.

Bourgois, Philippe, Bridget Prince, and Andrew Moss. 2004. The Everyday Violence of Hepatitis C among Young Women Who Inject Drugs in San Francisco. *Human Organization* 63, no. 3: 253–64.

Brooks, Siobhan. 2010. *Unequal Desires: Race and Erotic Capital in the Stripping Industry.* Albany: SUNY Press.

Brown, Geneva O. 2007. Little Girl Lost: Las Vegas Metro Police Vice Division and the Use of Material Witness Holds against Teenaged Prostitutes. *Catholic University Law Review* 57: 471.

Bumiller, Kristin. 2008. *In an Abusive State: How Neoliberalism Appropriated the Feminist Movement against Sexual Violence.* Durham, NC: Duke University Press.

Bureau of Justice Statistics. 2014. Correctional Populations in the United States, 2013. http://www.bjs.gov.

Burnette, Mandi, Renee Schneider, Christine Timko, and Mark Ilgen. 2009. Impact of Substance-Use Disorder Treatment on Women Involved in Prostitution: Substance

Use, Mental Health, and Prostitution One Year after Treatment. *Journal of Studies on Alcohol and Drugs* 70, no. 1: 32–40.

Butler, Anne. 1986. *Daughters of Joy, Sisters of Misery: Prostitutes in the American West, 1865–90.* Champaign: University of Illinois Press.

Caputo, Gail. 2008. *Out in the Storm: Drug-addicted Women Living as Shoplifters and Sex Workers.* Boston: Northeastern University Press.

Carr, E. Summerson. 2010. *Scripting Addiction: The Politics of Therapeutic Talk and American Sobriety.* Princeton, NJ: Princeton University Press.

———. 2006. "Secrets Keep You Sick": Metalinguistic Labor in a Drug Treatment Program for Homeless Women. *Language in Society* 35, no. 5: 631–53.

Chesney-Lind, Meda. 2002. Criminalizing Victimization: The Unintended Consequences of Pro-Arrest Policies for Girls and Women. *Criminology and Public Policy* 2: 81–91.

Chesney-Lind, Meda, and Katherine Irwin. 2008. *Beyond Bad Girls: Gender, Violence, and Hype.* New York: Routledge.

Cimino, Andrea. 2012. A Predictive Theory of Intentions to Exit Street-Level Prostitution. *Violence against Women* 18, no. 10: 1235–52.

Clarke, Ross, Elizabeth Clarke, Dominque Roe-Sepowitz, and Richard Fey. 2012. Age of Entry into Prostitution: Relationship to Drug Use, Race, Suicide, Education Level, Childhood Abuse, and Family Experience. *Journal of Human Behavior in the Social Environment* 22: 270–89.

Cox, Aimee Meredith. 2015. *Shapeshifters: Black Girls and the Choreography of Citizenship.* Durham, NC: Duke University Press.

Craib, Kevin, Patricia Spittal, Evan Wood, Nancy Laliberte, Robert Hogg, Kathy Li, Katherine Heath, Mark Tyndall, Michael O'Shaugnessy, and Martin Schechter. 2003. Risk Factors for Elevated HIV Incidence among Aboriginal Injection Drug Users in Vancouver. *Canadian Medical Association Journal* 168, no. 1: 19–24.

Cusick, Linda. 2006. Widening the Harm Reduction Agenda: From Drug Use to Sex Work. *International Journal of Drug Policy* 17: 3–11.

Cusick, Linda, and Matthew Hickman. 2005. "Trapping" in Drug Use and Sex Work Careers. *Drugs: Education, Prevention, and Policy* 12: 369–79.

Dalla, Rochelle. 2006. "You Can't Hustle All Your Life": An Exploratory Investigation of the Exit Process among Street-Level Prostituted Women. *Psychology of Women Quarterly* 30: 276–90.

Denver Department of Public Safety. 2014. Service Optimization. https://www.denvergov.org.

Denver Police Department. 2015. 2015 Crime Statistics and Maps. http://www.denvergov.org.

Dewey, Susan. 2014a. Recovery Narratives, War Stories, and Nostalgia: Street-Based Sex Workers' Discursive Negotiations of the Exclusionary Regime. *Anthropological Quarterly* 87, no. 4: 1137–64.

———. 2014b. Understanding Force and Coercion: Perspectives from Law Enforcement, Social Service Providers, and Sex Workers. In: *Human Trafficking: Recon-*

sidering the Problem (Rhacel Parreñas and Kimberly Kay Hoang, eds.). New York: Open Society Foundations (via International Debate Education Association), 102–15.

Dewey, Susan, and Rhett Epler. 2015. "Ain't No Real Pimps out There No More": Characterizations of Men Who Facilitate Women's Sex Work Activities in Denver, Colorado. *Wagadu: Journal of Transnational Women's and Gender Studies*. Special Issue: Race, Resistance, Reason 13. http://journals.cortland.edu.

Dewey, Susan, and Tonia St. Germain. 2015. Sex Workers/Sex Offender: Exclusionary Criminal Justice Practices in New Orleans. *Feminist Criminology* 10, no. 3: 211–34.

———. 2014. "It Depends on the Cop": Street-based Sex Workers' Perspectives on Police Patrol Officers. *Sexuality Research and Social Policy* 11, no. 3: 256–70.

Dewey, Susan, Tiantian Zheng, and Treena Orchard. 2016. *Sex Workers and Criminalization in North America and China: Ethical and Legal Issues in Exclusionary Regimes*. New York: Springer.

Dodge, Mary, Donna Starr-Gimeno, and Thomas Williams. 2005. Puttin' on the Sting: Women Police Officers' Perspectives on Reverse Prostitution Assignments. *International Journal of Police Science and Management* 7, no. 2: 71–85.

Erickson, Patricia, Jennifer Butters, Patti McGillicuddy, and Ase Hallgren. 2000. Crack and Prostitution: Gender, Myths, and Experiences. *Journal of Drug Issues* 30, no. 4: 767–88.

Fassin, Didier. 2013. *Enforcing Order: An Ethnography of Urban Policing*. Cambridge, UK: Polity.

Fassin, Didier, and Richard Rechtman. 2009. *Empire of Trauma: An Inquiry into the Condition of Victimhood*. Princeton, NJ: Princeton University Press.

Fine, Michelle, and María Elena Torre. 2006. Intimate Details: Participatory Action Research in Prison. *Action Research* 4, no. 3: 253–369.

Freeman Clevenger, Sharon, Laurence Miller, Bret Moore, and Arthur Freeman, eds. 2015. *Behind the Badge: A Psychological Treatment Handbook for Law Enforcement Officers*. New York: Routledge.

Gershon, Robyn, Briana Barocas, Allison Canton, Xianbin Li, and David Vlahov. 2009. Mental, Physical, and Behavioral Outcomes Associated with Perceived Work Stress in Police Officers. *Criminal Justice and Behavior* 36, no. 3: 274–89.

Hackett, Colleen. 2013. Transformative Visions: Governing through Alternative Practices and Therapeutic Interventions at a Women's Reentry Center. *Feminist Criminology* 8, no. 3: 221–42.

Hagan, John, and Bill McCarthy. 1997. *Mean Streets: Youth Crime and Homelessness*. Cambridge: Cambridge University Press.

Halter, Stephanie. 2010. Factors That Influence Police Conceptualizations of Girls Involved in Prostitution in Six U.S. Cities: Child Sexual Exploitation Victims or Delinquents? *Child Maltreatment* 15, no. 2: 152–60.

Heilemann, Tammy, and Janaki Santhiveeran. 2011. How Do Female Adolescents Cope and Survive the Hardships of Prostitution? A Content Analysis of Existing Literature. *Journal of Ethnic & Cultural Diversity in Social Work* 20, no. 1: 57–76.

Inciardi, James, and Hilary Surratt. 2000. Drug Use, Street Crime, and Sex Trading among Cocaine-Dependent Women: Implications for Public Health and Criminal Justice Policy. *Journal of Psychoactive Drugs* 33: 378–89.

Jasinski, Jana, Jennifer Wesely, James Wright, and Elizabeth Mustaine. 2010. *Hard Lives, Mean Streets: Violence in the Lives of Homeless Women*. Chicago: Northeastern University Press.

Kerouac, Jack. 1957. *On the Road*. New York: Penguin.

Knight, Kelly Ray. 2015. *Addicted.pregnant.poor*. Durham, NC: Duke University Press.

Kolb, Kenneth. 2014. *Moral Wages: The Emotional Dilemmas of Victim Advocacy and Counseling*. Berkeley: University of California Press.

Kotiswaran, Prabha. 2014. Beyond the Allures of Criminalization: Rethinking the Regulation of Sex Work in India. *Criminology and Criminal Justice* 14, no. 5: 565–79.

Kurtz, Steven, Hilary Surratt, Marion Kiley, and James Inciardi. 2005. Barriers to Health and Social Services for Street-based Sex Workers. *Journal of Health Care for the Poor and Underserved* 16, no. 2: 345–61.

Kushel, Margot, Jennifer Evans, Sharon Perry, Marjorie Robertson, and Andrew Ross. 2003. No Door to Lock: Victimization among Homeless and Marginally Housed Persons. *Archives of Internal Medicine* 163, no. 20: 2492–99.

Liebow, Eliot. 2003 [1967]. *Tally's Corner: A Study of Negro Streetcorner Men*. New York: Rowman & Littlefield.

Lipsky, Michael. 2010 [1980]. *Street-Level Bureaucracy: Dilemmas of the Individual in Public Services*. New York: Russell Sage Foundation.

MacKell, Jan. 2009. *Red Light Women of the Rocky Mountains*. Albuquerque: University of New Mexico Press.

———. 2007. *Brothels, Bordellos, and Bad Girls: Prostitution in Colorado, 1860–1930*. Albuquerque: University of New Mexico Press.

Maguire, Mary, and Thomas Nolan. 2011. Faux Hos: Woman Police Attitudes about Decoy Sex Work. *Police Practice and Research* 12, no. 3: 209–22.

Martin, Lauren, Mary Hearst, and Rachel Widome. 2010. Meaningful Differences: Comparison of Adult Women Who First Traded Sex as a Juvenile versus as an Adult. *Violence against Women* 16, no. 11: 1252–69.

Marx, Karl. 1992 [1867]. *Capital: A Critique of Political Economy*. New York: Penguin Classics.

Massey, Douglas, and Nancy Denton. 1993. *American Apartheid: Segregation and the Making of the Underclass*. Cambridge, MA: Harvard University Press.

McCorkel, Jill. 2013. *Breaking Women: Gender, Race, and the New Politics of Imprisonment*. New York: NYU Press.

Menaker, Tasha, and Cortney Franklin. 2013. Commercially Sexually Exploited Girls and Participant Perceptions of Blameworthiness: Examining the Effects of Victimization History and Race Disclosure. *Journal of Interpersonal Violence* 28, no. 10: 2024–51.

Metro Denver Economic Development Corporation. 2015. Population. http://www.metrodenver.org.

Metro Denver Homelessness Initiative. 2014. 2014 State of Homelessness Report: Seven-County Denver Metropolitan Region. http://mdhi.org.

Miller, Maureen, and Alan Neaigus. 2002. An Economy of Risk: Resource Acquisition Strategies of Inner-City Women Who Use Drugs. *International Journal of Drug Policy* 13: 409–18.

Miller-Young, Mireille. 2014. *A Taste for Brown Sugar: Black Women in Pornography.* Durham, NC: Duke University Press.

"Miss Colfax." 2014. http://www.colfaxavenue.com.

Mitchell, Kimberly, David Finkelhor, and Janis Wolak. 2010. Conceptualizing Juvenile Prostitution as Child Maltreatment: Findings from the National Juvenile Prostitution Study. *Child Maltreatment* 15, no. 1: 18–36.

Morris, Meagan, Brittney Dahl, Lindsey Breslin, K. Berger, Amanda Finger, and AnnJanette Alejano-Steele. 2012. *Prostitution and Denver's Criminal Justice System: Who Pays?* Denver: Laboratory to Combat Human Trafficking. http://www.combat-humantrafficking.org.

Murakawa, Naomi. 2014. *The First Civil Right: How Liberals Built Prison America.* Oxford: Oxford University Press.

Murray, Michael. 2002. City Profile: Denver. *Cities* 19, no. 4: 283–94.

O'Doherty, Tamara. 2011. Victimization in Off-Street Sex Industry Work. *Violence against Women* 17, no. 7: 944–63.

Oselin, Sharon. 2014. *Leaving Prostitution: Getting Out and Staying Out of Sex Work.* New York: NYU Press.

Overs, Cheryl, and Bebe Loff. 2013. The Tide Cannot Be Turned without Us: Sex Workers and the Global Response to HIV. *Journal of the International AIDS Society* 16: 1–6.

Pollack, Shoshana. 2010. Labeling Clients "Risky": Social Work and the Neo-liberal Welfare State. *British Journal of Social Work* 40: 1263–78.

———. 2007. "I'm Just Not Good in Relationships": Victimization Discourses and the Gendered Regulation of Criminalized Women. *Feminist Criminology* 2: 158–74.

Pupavac, Vanessa. 2005. Human Security and Rise of Global Therapeutic Governance. *Conflict, Security, and Development* 5, no. 2: 161–81.

Raphael, Jody. 2004. *Listening to Olivia: Violence, Poverty, and Prostitution.* Boston: Northeastern University Press.

Rekart, Michael. 2005. Sex-work Harm Reduction. *Lancet* 366, no. 9503: 2123–34.

Rhodes, Tim. 2002. The "Risk Environment": A Framework for Understanding and Reducing Drug-related Harm. *International Journal of Drug Policy* 20: 193–201.

Rhodes, Tim, Karla Wagner, Steffanie Strathdee, Kate Shannon, Peter Davidson, and Philippe Bourgois. 2012. Structural Violence and Structural Vulnerability within the Risk Environment: Theoretical and Methodological Perspectives for a Social Epidemiology of HIV Risk among Injection Drug Users and Sex Workers. In: *Rethinking Social Epidemiology: Towards a Science of Change* (Patricia O'Campo and James Dunn, eds.). New York: Springer, 205–30.

Richie, Beth. 2001. Challenges Incarcerated Women Face as They Return to Their Communities: Findings from Life History Interviews. *Crime & Delinquency* 47: 368–89.

Roe-Sepowitz, Dominique, Kristine Hickle, Martha Loubert, and Tom Egan. 2011. Adult Prostitution Recidivism: Risk Factors and Impact of a Diversion Program. *Journal of Offender Rehabilitation* 50, no. 5: 272–85.

Romero-Daza, Nancy. 2003. "Nobody Gives a Damn If I Live or Die": Violence, Drugs, and Street-level Prostitution in Inner-City Hartford, Connecticut. *Medical Anthropology* 22: 233–59.

Romero-Daza, Nancy, Margaret Weeks, and Merrill Singer. 2005. Conceptualizing the Impact of Indirect Violence on HIV Risk among Women Involved in Street Prostitution. *Aggression and Violent Behavior* 10: 153–70.

Sanchez, Lisa. 2004. The Global E-rotic Subject, the Ban, and the Prostitute-Free Zone: Sex Work and the Theory of Differential Exclusion. *Environment and Planning D: Society and Space* 22: 861–83.

Schaffner, Laurie. 2006. *Girls in Trouble with the Law*. New Brunswick, NJ: Rutgers University Press.

Scott, John. 2011. Governing Prostitution: Differentiating the Bad from the Bad. *Current Issues in Criminal Justice* 23, no. 1: 53–72.

Sered, Susan, and Maureen Norton-Hawk. 2011. Whose Higher Power? Criminalized Women Confront the "Twelve Steps." *Feminist Criminology* 6: 308–32.

Shannon, Kate, Vicki Bright, Janice Duddy, and Mark Tyndall. 2005. Access and Utilization of HIV Treatment and Services among Women Sex Workers in Vancouver's Downtown Eastside. *Journal of Urban Health* 82, no. 3: 488–97.

Shannon, Kate, Thomas Kerr, Shari Allinott, Jill Chettiar, Jean Shoveller, and Mark Tyndall. 2008. Social and Structural Violence and Power Relations in Mitigating HIV Risk of Drug-using Women in Survival Sex Work. *Social Science and Medicine* 66, no. 4: 911–21.

Shdaimah, Corey, and Shelly Wiechelt. 2012. Converging on Empathy: Perspectives on Baltimore City's Specialized Prostitution Diversion Program. *Women and Criminal Justice* 22, no. 2: 156–73.

Singer, Merrill. 2006. A Dose of Drugs, a Touch of Violence, a Case of AIDS, Part 2: Further Conceptualizing the SAVA Syndemic. *Free Inquiry in Creative Sociology* 34, no. 1: 39–51.

Thukral, Juhu, and Melissa Ditmore. 2003. *Revolving Door: An Analysis of Street-based Prostitution in New York City*. New York: Sex Workers Project at the Urban Justice Center.

UNAIDS (Joint United Nations Programme on HIV/AIDS). 2012. *UNAIDS Guidance Note on HIV and Sex Work*. Geneva: UNAIDS. http://www.unaids.org.

U.S. Census Bureau. 2012. State and County Quickfacts: Denver. Washington, DC: U.S. Census Bureau. http://quickfacts.census.gov.

U.S. Congress. 2000. The Victims of Trafficking and Violence Prevention Act.

U.S. Department of Health and Human Services Substance Abuse and Mental Health Services Administration. 2014. *A Treatment Improvement Protocol: Trauma-*

Informed Care in Behavioral Health Services. Rockville, MD: U.S. Department of Health and Human Services Substance Abuse and Mental Health Services Administration Center for Substance Abuse Treatment.

———. 2005. *Substance Abuse Treatment for Adults in the Criminal Justice System: Treatment Improvement Protocol (TIP) Series, No. 44.* Rockville, MD: U.S. Department of Health and Human Services Substance Abuse and Mental Health Services Administration Center for Substance Abuse Treatment.

U.S. Department of Justice. 2012. Arrest in the United States, 1990–2010. http://www.bjs.gov.

U.S. Department of Justice Office of Juvenile Justice and Delinquency Prevention. 2011. Justice Department Discourages the Use of "Scared Straight" Programs. *OJJDP News at a Glance*, March/April. https://www.ncjrs.gov.

U.S. Department of State. 2006. A Statement on Human Trafficking–Related Language. http://2001-2009.state.gov.

Venkatesh, Sudhir. 2009. *Off the Books: The Underground Economy of the Urban Poor.* Cambridge, MA: Harvard University Press.

Wahab, Stéphanie, and Meg Panichelli. 2013. Ethical and Human Rights Issues in Coercive Interventions with Sex Workers. *Affilia: Journal of Women and Social Work* 28, no. 4: 344–49.

Walker, Lenore. 1979. *The Battered Woman.* New York: Harper & Row.

Wesely, Jennifer. 2015. *Being Female: The Continuum of Sexualization.* Boulder, CO: Rienner.

Wies, Jennifer. 2008. Professionalizing Human Services: A Case of Domestic Violence Shelter Advocates. *Human Organization* 67, no. 2: 221–33.

Wilson, Ara. 2004. *The Intimate Economies of Bangkok: Tomboys, Tycoons, and Avon Ladies in the Global City.* Berkeley: University of California Press.

Wilson, William Julius. 2012 [1987]. *The Truly Disadvantaged: The Inner City, the Underclass, and Public Policy*, 2nd ed. Chicago: University of Chicago Press.

Wyckoff, William. 1992. Denver's Aging Commercial Strip. *Geographical Review* 82, no. 3: 282–94.

INDEX

abolitionists, 43–44. *See also* End Demand

abuse: alliance professionals motivated by their own experiences with, 240; as ancillary to street involvement, 195; belief as inherent to sex trading, 44, 194; consequences for those who, 170; impetus to emphasize formative impact of, 17; instances of, 120–21, 188, 200; mandated self-disclosure of, 171, 173, 188–89; of power, 108, 117, 122, 182, 202; popular and academic perceptions of street-involved women as victims of abuse, 6, 86, 114, 212; street-involvement as reifying stereotypes about, 45. *See also* trauma; violence

adoption, 8, 115, 126. *See also* children

Adam, 123. *See also* bureaucrats

addiction: as intrinsic to street-involvement for most women: 2–3, 8; costs of, 40; impact on sex trading orientation, 46–47; recovery from, 30, 42, 221, 226, 229, 236, 249–50; treatment for, 7, 12, 18, 22, 49, 53, 56, 73, 80–82, 114–15, 119, 122, 142, 173, 176, 192, 198–99, 234. *See also* alcohol; Alcoholics Anonymous; drugs; Narcotics Anonymous; substance abuse; therapeutic governance

adrenaline, 23, 56, 75, 77, 123, 179, 182

African American: alliance professionals, 10–11, 60–61, 81, 115, 119, 120, 122, 216; barriers to accessing addictions treatment, 115; child custody arrangements, 92; Denver population demograph-

ics, 89; neighborhood residents as predominantly, 40, 128, 151; over-representation in correctional facilities and most highly policed and violent sex industry venues, 16, 44, 87–88, 110, 229; potential to reify stereotypes about, 45, 88; segregation and ghet-toization, 20, 113–14; street involved women avoiding African American alliance professionals, 10, 217–18. *See also* Anne; Ashanti; bonded women; Deedee; Doris; Fred; Jayda; Joyce; Keanna; Kenya; K'neisha; Kyra; Macey; Marie; Mary; Ms. Ella; NeNe; old school cougars; Pearlie; race; racism; Shirley; Shondra; Traci; Wanda

age: alliance professionals and, 25, 47, 57–58, 108, 210, 239, 250–251; quantitative data on street-involved women's, 86–87, 88–90; socialization into cultural norms of street prostitution by family members or caregivers, 20, 48–49, 104–5; street-involved women and, 1, 15, 22, 49, 82, 109, 113–14, 212, 218, 244; younger women's lack of street acumen, 47, 98. *See also* bonded women; caregivers; old school cougars

Alan, 58, 119–20, 197, 207–8, 210, 211–12. *See also* idealists

alcohol: alliance professionals' struggles with, 57; street-involved women's use, 147, 194; use, 23, 234; use excluding women from services, 147–48, 161–62

Alcoholics Anonymous, 19, 186

ABOUT THE AUTHORS

Susan Dewey is a feminist anthropologist and Associate Professor of Gender & Women's Studies at the University of Wyoming, where she leads the Wyoming Pathways from Prison action research project. She is the author of nine books and numerous scholarly articles on sex work, violence against women, and feminized labor.

Tonia St. Germain, JD, is retired Director of Women's and Gender Studies, Eastern Oregon University. She holds a law degree from Antioch School of Law and a BA from Wheaton College.